BOOKS BY RALPH KEYES

We, the Lonely People: Searching for Community
Is There Life after High School?
The Height of Your Life
Chancing It: Why We Take Risks

CHANCING IT

CHANCING IT

WHY WE TAKE RISKS

Ralph Keyes

LITTLE, BROWN AND COMPANY
Boston — Toronto

⧣ 1109007l
DLC

2-26-46 5x

FIRST EDITION

The author is grateful for permission to quote "Bravado" from
The Poetry of Robert Frost edited by Edward Connery Lathem.
Copyright 1957, © 1969 by Holt, Rinehart and Winston. Copyright © 1975 by Lesley Frost Ballantine. Reprinted by permission of Holt, Rinehart and Winston, Publishers.

LIBRARY OF CONGRESS CATALOGING IN PUBLICATION DATA

Keyes, Ralph.
  Chancing it.

  Bibliography: p.
  1. Risk-taking (Psychology) 2. Decision-making.
3. Fear. I. Title.
BF637.R57K49 1984   155.2'32   84-19378
ISBN 0-316-49132-2

BP

Designed by Patricia Girvin Dunbar

Published simultaneously in Canada
by Little, Brown & Company (Canada) Limited

PRINTED IN THE UNITED STATES OF AMERICA

For my father,
who has always stood by me

ACKNOWLEDGMENTS

Although the writer's name alone is on the cover, many others contribute to the completion of a book. Among those who have contributed to this one are: Joe Adcock, Steve Aicholtz, Alonso Alegria, Larry and Mary Ballen, Philip Bartow, Superintendent Thomas Baynard and the Tredyffrin (PA) Township Police Department, Libby Blackman, Paula Bond, Marjorie Boyersdorfer, Bryce Britton, Diane Brown, Craig Carnelia, Gerry Cohen, Loretta Colla, David Coulson, Debbie Courter, Phil Courter, Nino and Betsy DeProphetis, Katy Dobbs, Dan Drooz, Jeff Evans, Tom, Beth, Elizabeth, and Justin Fitzsimmons, Arthur Frakt, Bob Frankel, Richard Goldberg, Phil Goldberg, Sue Goldman, Bill and Lynn Gonzales, Aberdeen Goodwin, Jane Gordon, Meyer Gordon, Reba Gordon, George Grider, Rick and Dottie Gross, Neil and Nancy Grunberg, John and Andrea Herrmann, Barbara Holland, Jack Horn, Jeff Jones, Landon Y. and Sarah Jones, Kevin Kennedy, Charlotte Keyes, Gene Keyes, Nicky Keyes, Scott Keyes, Gloria Klaiman, Julia Klein, Pat Krauska, Julia Lawlor, Judy Lin, Andy and Cathy Linck, Richard and Kathy Louv, Janet Maas, Marilyn Machlowitz, Tom Maeder, John Malarkey, Ruth Malone, Kathleen McCarthy, G. Ellen and Wayne Michaud, Rosalie Minkin, Jill Minkin, Scott Morris, Chris Mulford, Hank Noordam, Mim Noordam, Charles O'Leary, Richard Peacock, Rosalie Peirsol, Janna Rankin, Julia Robinson, Claude Robinson, Jeff Roseman, Arthur Sabatini, Helen Satterthwaite, Winnie Schoefer, Michael Schwarz, Margie Shoe-

ix

maker, Pearl Sickles, Grover Silcox, Maureen Silliman, Byron and Barbara Skinner, Robert Ellis Smith, Bill and Anne Stillwell, Dolores Strickland, E. Fuller Torrey, Rod Townley, Marcello Truzzi, Jan and Marlene Van Meter, Robin Warshaw, Holley Webster, Leonard Weeks, Debbie Weinstein, John K. Wood, Arnie Yasinski, and Bernie Zilbergeld.

For unusual amounts of help with research, circulating questionnaires, or manuscript criticism I'd like to thank Peggy Anderson, Judith Appelbaum, Jim Bell, Bob Chieger, Gay Courter, Jack DeWitt, Beth Gross, Chip and Bobbie Harvey, Barbara Leff, Liz Logue, Jan Mason, Janis Moran, Wolfgang Nadler, Cathy Pullis, Margaret Robinson, and Cindy Yasinski.

The staffs of the Free Library of Philadelphia (Fred Rosenzweig especially), the Swarthmore Public Library (Janis Moran especially), the Widener University Library, the Swarthmore College Library (Michael Durkan especially) and the Hahnemann Hospital Library were unusually helpful with my research.

Particular thanks are due my cousin Joe Palermo for coming to my rescue with a word processor; my editor Bill Phillips who had to do more than his share of editing on this one, and did so superbly; my agent, Don Cutler; copy editor Peggy Freudenthal; and, as ever, my wife Muriel.

CONTENTS

Introduction   3

1. The Wire Walker   7
2. What's a Risk? Who's a Risk Taker?   20
3. Risk Hunger   31

LEVEL I RISK TAKING   53

4. Stirring the Pot   70
5. The Skydiver   92
6. Wuffo?   110
7. Mainlining Danger   128

LEVEL II RISK TAKING   151

8. The Underlying Risk   167
9. The Entrepreneur   184
10. On Your Own   197
11. Ultimate Risk   216
12. The Family Man   234

IN CONCLUSION . . .   249

13. The American Way of Risk   251
14. Genuine Risk   273
Notes   291

AUTHOR'S NOTE

Everyone written about in this book is 100 percent real. There are no fictional characters, or composites. At their own request the identity of some of those written about has been disguised. Except where noted in the text, such people are identified by a first name only.

CHANCING IT

INTRODUCTION

In his midthirties, with a new son, mortgage, and Maytag washer-dryer, the author's thoughts turned to risk. Would he be taking any more of them? Or would risk taking be going the way of his Elvis Presley collection and twenty-eight inch waist?

He wondered if others were interested in this subject as well: risks, what they are, who takes them, and why.

Many were. When the subject arose, one old friend of thirty-eight, a father of three, mentioned going to an amusement park by himself recently in search of a good scare. That failing, he'd started flying lessons.

A newly married woman of the same age said taking risks wasn't something she was "into." "I don't even cross the street when the sign says Don't Walk," she explained. The woman wondered if she had a problem.

The most typical response was that of a middle-aged secretary. "I'd like to read something about risk taking," she told me. "Maybe it would help me take some."

This book is about risk taking. It is not intended as yet another tract urging one and all to "take more risks!" Presumably most of us would like to. Except we don't know how. Nor is it clear what "risk" means. Getting married? Starting a business? Leaping from an airplane with a parachute? Without one? Getting out of bed in the morning?

The last is not facetious. Among a wide range of definitions I've seen, one woman said that "risk" to her meant just that. Yet

3

one of the odder files of information I collected during this project dealt with occasions when objects falling from the sky — meteors, or pieces of airplanes — landed near people asleep in their bedrooms. In general, falling objects kill over 1000 people a year. As Robert Frost observed of living with such hazards:

> *Have I not walked without an upward look*
> *Of caution under stars that very well*
> *Might not have missed me when they shot and fell?*
> *It was a risk I had to take — and took*

Obviously "risk" has many meanings. In fact, coming up with a useful definition of this term became a major challenge of this book. Most considerations of risk, and risk taking, are based on the premise that we all ought to be doing more of it — going for it, if you will — and of course we all know what that means.

The premise of this book is just the opposite. My premise is that while as most of us would like to be taking more risks, not the least of our problems is figuring out what "risk" means. Compounding that problem is the many ways this popular buzz word is now used. Doctors talk of "risk factors." Executives do "risk assessment." Insurers offer "risk management." M.B.A.'s compare "upside and downside risks." Athletes say you must risk your body; actors talk of risking your "self." And in California, a Los Angeles expert in "relational skills" now specializes in "risking linking," which she describes as "combining risk taking and connecting to people."

Such verbal confusion reflects a deeper ambivalence about risk taking itself. It's not at all clear whether as a society we consider risk taking to be good. "Risk taker," is a real Jekyll-and-Hyde of a term. Like "S.O.B.," it can express affection or contempt, depending on the set of the lip. The same teenager will be praised for taking chances on the football field, then scolded for doing the same thing behind the wheel of a car. Ronald Reagan gives a speech praising entrepreneurs for taking risks, and two days later blasts the Soviets for their "international risk taking."

Trying to put the best light on his arrest for patronizing a prostitute, a Democratic candidate for the 1982 Ohio gubernatorial nomination gamely suggested that owning up to it proved he

4

was willing to "take risks." (The voters either didn't agree or didn't approve. He lost, badly.)

Assuming that we all mean the same thing when we talk about "risk" lies at the heart of our problem in determining which risks are worth taking. Not being more clear about the meaning of this term forces us back onto clichés: "a real risk taker," "high risk, high gain," and the ubiquitous "go for it!" Such clichés can discourage risk taking altogether by making it sound so daunting, or encourage taking bad risks because we think we ought to be going for it.

When an Air Florida jet crashed into Washington's Potomac River during the winter of 1982 with a heavy loss of life, the cockpit tape revealed that the plane's co-pilot had been concerned about the wing icing that was to kill him but was unable to voice his concern except in nervous banter. The pilot stayed cool. Their last words before takeoff were:

PILOT: Slushy runway. Do you want me to do anything special for this, or just go for it?

CO-PILOT: Unless you got anything special you'd like to do.

They went for it.

So if we seem a bit puzzled about "risk," "taking risks," and whether that's to be commended, perhaps this is understandable.

In one sense I never got beyond the initial challenge of defining "risk" in writing this book, because what it's become is an exploration of "risk's" different meanings to a wide range of people in various contexts. Risks to the body are considered, to the pocketbook, the ego, and to the soul. So are questions about the relationship between risk taking, gender, and age. By looking at this subject from such a range of perspectives, I've tried to help reader and author alike put their tendencies to take some risks and avoid others in perspective. I've tried to suggest — as I came to believe — that factors of temperament influence our perception of "risk" to a far greater extent than we realize. (Recent discoveries about our brain chemistry are persuasive along this line.) In particular I came to feel that much of what we imagine to be courageous risk taking may actually reflect a need for stimulation that is best satisfied by living dangerously. And that less gaudy risks that are low in stimulation may in fact be the more daunting ones to take.

My approach overall is to suggest that the best way to take more risks is to first determine what "risk" means — to you. Only when we understand how we perceive risk personally can we proceed to determine which risks we'd actually like to take.

This is why defining "risk" is so much more than a semantic exercise. Repeatedly I've discovered that those who are apparently taking big risks turned out on closer examination to be risking little; little of value, that is. (Question: If you risk a life you don't value, have you taken a risk?) They themselves were often the first to admit this. By contrast, the very, very many who denied taking any risks routinely turned out to be daring indeed, in ways they seldom recognized.

There's not a hero in this book. Like all of us, everyone written about is taking some risks and avoiding others. Often the risks we avoid say more about who we are than those we take. And when we do take risks it's not always clear — even to ourselves — what it is we're risking, what's actually at stake.

My original plan for this book was to seek out a range of risk takers, find out what made them tick, then summarize and report the results.

The first problem was getting anyone to admit that they took risks.

THE WIRE WALKER

To my eyes, Philippe Petit looks like a risk taker.

At least I'd call walking across a wire strung between the towers of New York's World Trade Center risky.

The risks were not only the obvious ones of surviving crosswinds to walk seven times across a 138-foot cable strung 1350 feet above lower Manhattan. In order to get his cable strung in the first place, Petit had to maneuver a minefield of hazards.

He'd first seen a sketch of the proposed 110-story building in a magazine at a Paris dentist's office in 1968. Coughing to mask the crime, Petit ripped this picture out. Later he threw it in a box at home called PROJECTS. In the meantime, Petit engaged in a clandestine walk between the belfries of Notre Dame, and another anchored by two towers of the Sydney Bay Bridge in Australia.

As the World Trade Center towers neared completion in 1973, Petit's interest in them revived. To his eye these structures looked incomplete. They would remain so until connected by a wire-walker's cable. Yet Petit realized that the twin towers' owners were unlikely to see it that way. So the challenge became to smuggle half a ton of cable and related gear to the top of one tower, figure out a way to get the cable across the quarter-mile of space to the other, then tighten it sufficiently to support 150 pounds of Frenchman carrying a 55-pound balancing pole.

These were the obvious challenges. During months of planning, other dangers made themselves known. For example, the winds between the two towers are so turbulent that Petit was unable to find a helicopter pilot willing to fly him between them for a look. More ominous yet was the unanswered question engineers posed to the wire walker: Wouldn't natural sway in the structures to which his 21-ply, ⅞-inch cable was anchored be likely to snap it like cheap cotton thread? Finally — and to Petit this was the greatest danger of all — even if he were able to string his wire, there was the likelihood of his being nabbed before he got a chance to set foot on it. Then not only would Petit be unable to pull off what he called his "coup," but he would look like an imbecile in the process.

All of these hazards were woven as tightly as a cable's strands in Philippe Petit's mind as he and a small crew of confederates prepared his walk in earnest during the early months of 1974.

In order to minimize the physical risks, Petit pored over purloined blueprints of the World Trade Center. He and his crew made perhaps a hundred visits to examine the structure-in-progress. Sometimes they posed as tourists with cameras, at other times as workers wearing hardhats, or even displayed phony press credentials from a French architectural magazine. They also created a dummy Fisher Industrial Fence Co., complete with its logo on a truck, with which to deliver Petit's cables to the construction site.

The final days of preparation caught Petit up in a sleepless frenzy. Disguised as workmen, he and a helper were able to sneak the cable up in a freight elevator to the top of the south tower late one afternoon in early August. It was a week before Philippe Petit's twenty-fifth birthday. In the only available hiding space, these two huddled motionless beneath a tarp on a steel beam for five hours while a security guard made his rounds just a few feet away.

Posing as architects with briefcases, two other members of the crew had made it to the top of the north tower. Finally one of the two — Petit's oldest friend, Jean Louis Blondeau — pulled a crossbow from his briefcase. With this, Blondeau shot a weighted nylon thread across the dark void. He had one chance to succeed. A miss would mean spending an hour rewinding the thread, an hour they didn't have. With barely an inch to spare, the weight landed on the south tower's roof. The twin towers were now connected by one thin strand of nylon.

Along this strand a stronger cord was slowly pushed across on a ring. The next few hours of darkness were spent painfully inching the heavy, cumbersome cable across this cord, then tightening it with a combination of muscle power, winches, pulleys, and a heavy-duty ratchet.

Just before sunrise, the cable was relatively taut (to three tons of tension). It was wrapped around beams at either end, then clamped to them securely. Rudimentary guy lines were set in place to give the cable a bit of stability. At the last minute one guy line turned out to be uselessly upside down, which meant that the entire cable might sway wildly after Petit stepped on it. But as the wire walker contemplated this thought, the large metal wheel of a nearby elevator began groaning beside him, bringing the day's first workmen to the top. Gripping his 35-foot, 55-pound balancing pole in both hands, Petit gingerly set one black-slippered foot on the cable. It trembled like a loose guitar string. He rose, steadied his pole, reconsidered for one last second, then placed his second foot irretrievably into the void.

"Look! There's a tightrope walker!" shouted two of Petit's confederates from the street below as they pointed to his tiny silhouette in the sky.

To the raised eyes of a fascinated world, Philippe Petit's seven crossings of his cable — dancing, spinning, grinning, lying down in the middle — became a lasting metaphor for daring. If anyone in recent years has brought to life the wires we all might walk if only we dared, it's been Philippe Petit. Certainly he did for me. The willingness of one slight Frenchman to risk everything for a stroll among the birds made my own caution feel stark by comparison. Hearing of his feat made me dream that one day I might become more of a risk taker; more like Philippe Petit.

When we met several years after his most renowned walk, one of the first things I asked Petit was how he came to be such a risk taker. And one of the first things the wire walker told me was that in no way, shape, or form did he consider himself to be a taker of risks.

"I don't see wire walking as risk taking," he insisted in his

9

heavily accented English. "I have no room in my life for risk. You can't be both a risk taker and a wire walker. I take absolutely no risks. I never use the word 'risk.' I plan everything the most that I can. I put together with the utmost care that part of my life."

Petit gets especially incensed when the label "daredevil" is applied to him — or the French "casse cou" (literally a "break neck," or "neck breaker").

"I am absolutely the contrary of a daredevil," he said with a bit more volume.

Then once again for emphasis, "I take no risks."

At first I thought Petit was quibbling. But after talking with him at length over a year's time, watching him prepare to walk on cables and actually do so, I began to see what he meant. Philippe Petit is one of the most *prepared* people I've ever met. To Petit "risk" implies "chance". He prefers to leave nothing up to chance. If it were possible, Philippe Petit would rig every wire he walks on himself, attach all guy lines, and pour the molten steel for each of its 21 strands.

The day we met in his New York apartment, Petit was completing an intricate scale model of Lincoln Center. He'd been working on this balsa wood and Styrofoam model for hours at a stretch, Petit explained, often skipping meals to do so. In a few months he'd be walking on a cable at the Big Apple Circus there, and he wanted to make sure his rigging was dependable. Building a three-dimensional model of the grounds was the only way to make sure the wire and poles supporting his life were set up within an inch of where they were supposed to be.

As Petit told me this, he moved about his model with fast, intense, and rather jerky, if precise, movements. He is not a large man, 5'6" at most. But with his muscular frame, luminous blue eyes, and imposing manner, Philippe Petit takes up a lot of space.

Petit at last finished his gluing. After placing a book on top of his model to set the glue, he left his apartment to go out with me for lunch. In the hallway an ancient elevator waited for us half a foot over floor level. Petit hesitated before entering this small cubicle. As the elevator creaked, groaned, and jerked its way downward, he explained that cables are something he's familiar with, and the cables of elevators — old ones especially — are not ones on which he likes to stake his life. His preference is for stairs. Not only are stairs safer than elevators, said Petit, but they are more interesting as well. On stairs, he pointed out, you might find a dead rat. Or perhaps a new thought.

Such themes dominate Philippe Petit's outlook: a craving for new experience, and a need to control every aspect of his life. At times the two collide. Talking with authors of books can provoke such a collision. As I jotted a few notes while we awaited our soup in the French restaurant Petit had chosen, my companion kept looking beyond his wineglass to see what I was writing. His responses to my questions alternated between mumbled mono-syllables and pointed inquiries of his own about what I intended to write.

Much as I wanted to get to know this man, the price began to seem steep. Finally I set my pad aside and wondered aloud if we might not be better off finishing lunch and going our sepa-rate ways. While I couldn't guarantee that he'd like what I wrote about him, perhaps he could approach talking to me as a risk.

As he pondered this suggestion, Petit visibly relaxed. Finally he smiled a bit and said that okay, he'd take the risk of talking to me. And he did. From that moment on, Philippe Petit seemed to talk freely without grilling me about my intentions or attempt-ing to review my notes. He did ask that I carry a tape recorder to record his words precisely.

The next time we met was beneath a piece of the Trade Center cable strung 15 feet over a hardwood floor in a Manhattan gym where Petit was rehearsing for his Lincoln Center walk. Within seconds after bustling into this gym late one fall morning Petit had carefully lined up on a table a stop watch, a regular watch, and an inch-by-inch, second-by-second plan for the walk he was rehearsing with two musicians. Squeezed onto a small piece of paper in his fine hand, this schedule indicated precisely where on the wire he would be at any given moment in the musical accom-paniment, and what he would be doing.

"In exactly five minutes we will begin," Petit announced to the piano and trumpet players. He then introduced me to them, explaining with something of a smile that I was writing about him and risk taking, though he didn't know why because he took no risks.

Petit's thumb was wrapped in a thick, white gauze bandage. He said that this was because he'd recently cut himself by accident with a carpet knife. To protect his thumb Petit had improvised a laced, leather cap. After he pulled this cap over the bandaged thumb, Petit thrust it toward me and asked if I'd mind tying the laces.

Would I mind? Well, yes. Actually I would mind. A lot. Suppose I tied it badly? And suppose because I tied it badly he fell? And suppose because he fell he died because I tied his thumb cap badly? Did I want Philippe Petit's life in my clumsy fingers?

This is exactly the sort of attitude Phillipe Petit loathes. His real friends, he once explained to me, are the ones who help him do what he chooses to do regardless of their fears for his safety. False friends are ones who are so afraid he'll die doing what he wants to do that they'd rather he open a grocery. I tied the cap.

Philippe Petit has very mixed feelings about "safety" in general and his own in particular. During the rehearsal I watched, as in all of his rehearsals and every performance, there was no net between him and the ground. True, throughout one walk over Belvedere Lake in New York's Central Park, three lifeguards stood by in case the nonswimming aerialist should need their help. But Petit says that this was the sponsor's idea, not his. When asked if he'd accept a rescue should he fall in such a case, the wire walker looked startled. Of course he'd accept a rescue. Why shouldn't he? He has no interest in dying. He'd swim "sixty miles" to save his skin, said Petit. After that he might hide out for a few years from shame. Or commit suicide. But first he'd accept a rescue.

When it comes to safety measures such as seat belts, Petit said he seldom feels any need to buckle up because he considers himself a good driver. But if he's tired, or it's foggy, or the traffic is heavy — anytime he doesn't feel "one hundred percent in control" — he will wear his belt. On the other hand, if anyone tells him he *should* buckle up, Petit adamantly refuses. Only if such a suggestion is made by "an old man I'm having dinner with" might he humor his companion and do so. On principle Philippe Petit is opposed to any law designed to ensure his well-being and goes out of his way to violate such laws. The very idea of being so concerned with personal safety strikes him as absurd. Why not just encase babies in plastic at birth for their own lifetime protection? "I think risk is something that is good," he said, "because it is no good to protect your life too much."

After hours and hours of conversation, this was the first time Petit admitted that danger has any appeal to him. Part of the reason he's loath to admit this, he then said, is for fear of being lumped together with someone like Evel Knievel, for whom confronting danger seems the sum total of his work. Another reason that Philippe Petit plays down the danger of his work is to reassure himself. In a relaxed moment he will admit to being plagued by doubts before a major walk. Perhaps the cable's not taut enough. Maybe the winds are too strong. Or he's too tired to stay alert. But rather than admit to such concerns, Petit will turn them into jokes. "I don't share my doubts with anyone," explained the wire walker. "Maybe becuase I don't trust anyone enough."

Petit fell once: 30 feet to the ground while practicing for the Ringling Brothers and Barnum & Bailey circus, which he joined briefly after the World Trade walk. This was his first and (so far) last major miscue. It took months to recuperate from the broken ribs, collapsed lung, smashed hip, and ruptured pancreas that resulted. Yet Petit looks back on that experience with something like nostalgia. "One fall in the life of a wire walker is needed," he said. "One serious accident makes you consider everything."

Although he refers to his fall as a rite of passage, the real rite was getting back on the wire again. Within a year after falling, Petit did this at the Astrodome in Houston, where after only fifteen days of practice he pranced across a high wire for nearly half an hour to the tune of Ravel's "Bolero." The best thing this walk did, says Petit, was to restore his confidence that he wouldn't fall, and couldn't fall. Logically speaking he knows this is absurd. He fell once; he might fall again. But *feeling* that it could never happen again is the only thing that allows Petit to mount a wire in the first place.

His passion for preparation makes Petit take his time about actually mounting the wire. At the gym where I watched him rehearse, after Petit spent the better part of an hour repeatedly walking through his 13½-minute act on the ground beneath his cable, my attention and eyes began to wander. But when I looked around for him on the ground at one point, he was nowhere to be seen. Petit was on his cable now, walking swiftly from side to side, dancing slowly to the music, falling to one knee, juggling a ball, sauntering with pole on shoulders, lying on his back, pulling off his white slippers to tiptoe the length of the cable conspiratorially with an index finger "shhhhhing" his lips. He made it look so *easy;* little different walking on the wire than on the ground. Yet 15 feet beneath him was only polished hardwood.

For the dramatic finale, Petit was to remove a purple scarf from his waist, tie this over his eyes as a blindfold, then walk backward to the accompaniment of a lone trumpet. In the middle of the cable, still blindfolded, Petit sat down. Then he turned a backward somersault. During this maneuver, Petit seemed to falter. "Wait a minute!" he cried, ripping the scarf from his eyes. "I think I hurt my head!" After catching his breath, Petit completed three more somersaults and a victory strut across the wire.

When he finally came back to earth, Petit seemed flushed and a bit agitated. He was panting, and soaked from sweat. His hair looked more as though he'd been swimming than wire walking. Was everything okay up there, I asked? "No," replied Petit. "That was a big disaster." Then he smiled sardonically and added, "For you it was perfect!" In paying too much attention to his cut thumb, Petit explained, he'd lost track of where his head was and cracked it on the cable while rolling backward.

Philippe Petit discovered a taste for challenging heights early on. His fondest childhood memories are of building tree houses, swinging from ropes, and maneuvering primitive bridges of his own design. For Christmas in his sixth year Petit said his parents gave him what he asked for: a book about mountain climbing. By then he'd already begun teaching himself how to climb the steep rocks around the Parisian suburb of Nemours where his father had retired as a colonel in the French air force.

At fifteen Petit left home. For a time he thought of fighting bulls for a living and says he even practiced on some baby bulls in northern France. But wire-walking soon beckoned. Or more precisely, rope walking, which he began doing on his own on a line strung between two trees. Eventually Petit apprenticed himself to a master wire walker (whom he later consulted about the Trade Center walk). With this skill, added to the juggling and prestidigitation he'd learned before, the Frenchman has made his living ever since — primarily as a street performer. But his first love is high-wire walking.

Out of curiosity, the executive secretary of the Big Apple Circus once called an insurance agent to see if they'd sell a policy on a wire-walker's life; that of Philippe Petit in particular. After checking, this agent said, Why not? The premium wouldn't even be that high. Actuarially speaking, the odds are good that Petit will live to a ripe old age like his hero, the great French wire-walker Blondin, who died at seventy-seven, or even his rival Karl Wallenda, who was seventy-three when he went down. Insurance companies know that acrobats in general and wire-walkers in particular tend to be careful people. By being less cautious, the average citizen is more likely to die in an accident than is a Philippe Petit. So when he claims not to be a risk taker, Petit has an ally among the actuaries.

But there's even a more important, more subjective reason that Philippe Petit looks like less of a risk taker in his own eyes than in ours. To his audience, Petit's risk is the ultimate because we put ourselves on the wire with him and tremble. But to him there are scarier things than walking on high wires. Touching spiders, for example. Petit shudders at the very thought, saying he'd rather do 10,000 backward somersaults on the wire than touch a spider. He's also none too keen on snakes, or animals of any kind. Another fear is of water. Only in his thirties was Petit able to discipline himself to dive into water without panicking.

Something else that scares Philippe Petit is height. The wire-walker says that his fear of falling from on high is probably about average; certainly no less. "People think that height does nothing to me," he explained. "It's the contrary. Height does a lot of things for me. Height affects me tremendously."

But in that statement is the essence of his attitude toward fear. Fear is not something Petit denies feeling, even when walking wires. To the contrary, he regularly uses words such as "afraid," "terrified," even "petrified," to describe how he feels before getting on a high wire. At that moment Petit often has to beat down the urge to flee in panic so he can get on with his work. But fear doesn't just inhibit that work; fear is its essence. On one level Petit may refer to being afraid as a mere "technical detail," to be solved much like a rigging problem. On another level fear is a more worthy opponent than the void itself. Without fear there would be no challenge. Worse yet, there would be no ecstasy — because according to Petit, by the end of a walk this is exactly what fear has become.

As Petit describes the process, fear is at the beginning of the wire, joy at the end. One is born of the other. "I am cold with fear," he says of this duality, "and drunk with happiness." And: "I transmit that fear into excitement, into enthusiasm, into being drunk of heights." On the Trade Center cable, Petit found out that after he began walking, fear proved less of a problem than "trying to discipline my mind from the tremendous waves of happiness." He adds that most of that walk was done in such a blissful trance that only afterward did he realize how long he'd been up there (about 40 minutes).

A final purpose fear serves Petit is as a lifesaver. He says the closest he's come to disaster was during two walks just after his most famous one: first over Belvedere Lake, where he slipped off the wire, grabbed it with his hands, and had to pull himself back up; and then in Laon, France, when he walked in winds that were too strong because ABC-TV was there with cameras ready and waiting. In retrospect, Petit realizes, his Trade Center triumph had left him so impressed with himself that he lost the measure of self-doubt that underlies his passion for preparation.

Although he makes a point of scorning "highest this" or "longest that" when it comes to his profession, on his own biographical sheet Petit notes that the Trade Center walk "made him the highest wire walker in history." In describing his feats, mild breezes are likely to become "ferocious winds." A 200-yard walk will soon be doubled in memory.

Over the years she's known him, Executive Secretary Judith Friedlander of the Big Apple Circus (who managed, and dated Petit for a time) said she found that Philippe Petit routinely improvised his own statistics. "What number are we using now?" Friedlander said was a question she regularly put to him.

"What did he tell you?" she asked of what Petit hopes will one day be his longest walk ever, one kilometer across the Sydney Harbor. "That it's a mile? Three miles?" Friedlander then spread her hands and said in an exaggerated French accent, " 'Eet's three miles. It will take me seex months.' " And she laughed affectionately.

Friedlander, with whom Petit suggested I talk about him, said she thought that her friend's exaggeration of his own achievements merely reflects his insecurity. "Maybe to him what he does is not as extraordinary as it is to us," she suggested. "What he does is beautiful. In my lexicon, it stands on its own. To him it doesn't. It surprises me that he would want or need to do that. He is extraordinary to the degree that the dimensions are really irrelevant."

Petit agrees that his admitted tendency to embellish the truth has more to do with his need to impress himself than to dazzle us. He has no idea why he should feel such a need. It's as if by now he so takes for granted what the rest of us find phenomenal that he has to enhance his own appreciation of himself by exaggerating. Like the rest of us, Petit also may simply be far more conscious of the risks he's ducked than those he's taken.

Philippe Petit once told me that while he felt perfectly comfortable taking physical risks, "Some I find impossible to take are personal risks with people."

The idea of living with someone just appalls him. Getting married, of course, he's opposed to on anarchic principle. "I just don't believe in marriage," Petit said. "But I think it takes a lot of courage to decide to live with someone and it takes a lot of strength to believe that another life parallel to yours isn't going to shorten yours but might lengthen it. I think it's going to shorten mine and destroy mine; that's why I just cannot . . .

"When I talk about that with someone who says the contrary, I am confused. I think maybe they are right, maybe I'm a very narrow person who doesn't have the courage of risking to share my life, thinking it's going to be destroyed. . . . I am teased by the idea of living with someone, but if I would ever do it, it would be the most tremendous act of courage of my whole life — absolutely. It's the end of the world, this thing."

As opposed to living with someone, the idea of having children intrigues Petit. Just as his cable linked the World Trade Towers, a child would link him with time. But tempting as he finds it, Petit keeps brushing aside the idea of having children. The major goal of his life is autonomy. It is no accident that he's chosen a career that he pursues alone, above everyone else — sometimes above even the birds. Since this is the life he prefers, the prospect of having to give up any part of it to someone else, or even of having to hesitate for a second when about to do something dangerous out of consideration for another person, fills him with dread. This is how he looks upon the idea of fathering a child.

"Having children," said Petit, "it is something that I am very attracted to and it's my biggest fear. . . . This is something like death. It attracts me quite a lot, but it's something that is so immense that I just cannot give an answer. I keep running from the answer. . . .

"To continue on the side of deep philosophy . . . intimate fear is itself a very personal, deep self-question. Since I know myself quite well, I sometimes believe all of what my good friends tell me as an attack: 'You're full of shit; and you're this and that.' I say, 'Well, maybe,' and if it was, it will be a disaster to have lived a life of disaster and self-cheating . . . and that frightens me. The issue is, Was I right to live my life like this, or am I an easy person who only does what is easy for him, which is to live the way I do without accepting to answer these questions which frighten me? . . . Sometime I am going to die. When I am getting old, I will reflect a lot. And I will be so destroyed if the answer is, You spent a lifetime fooling yourself. That's something very hard for someone in the field of art and performing, where you all the time have to express yourself in a spectacle situation where you really don't question yourself. . . .

"I don't enjoy this kind of talk. I find it straining. I don't enjoy it. No, I find it good. . . . I am surprised that I'm telling you what I'm telling you. I'm even surprised that I think what I'm saying. . . . But I enjoy this; I like the seriousness of going deep into questions like this. But it is very tiring. . . ."

What are we to make of Philippe Petit?

The high-wire walker who denies taking risks?
The fear embracer who avoids touching spiders?
The debunker of records who exaggerates his own?
The fastidiously well prepared free spirit?
The courageous neck risker who's scared of having children?

In the case of Philippe Petit we can't resolve such contradictions. He doesn't even try.

Like all of us, when it comes to taking risks Petit is a mass of crosscurrents: daring in one area, timid in another; here a hero, there a coward. In his case the contradictions stand out more vividly because everything about the man does. When it comes to risk, Philippe Petit is just like everyone else, only more so.

WHAT'S A RISK?
WHO'S A RISK TAKER?

At the age of forty, after twelve successful years as an architect, Timothy Prentice left the firm he founded to become a sculptor. From the outside this looked like a gutsy move — leaving a secure position for which he was well trained and paid, to embark on an uncertain career with no assurance that he could make a living, let alone a success. "People sometimes lionize me for 'taking a risk,'" says the tall, sandy-bearded ex-architect. "'Oh, it must have taken great courage,' they say. But that's their trip. They're putting their own conception on me. I don't see it that way."

As Prentice points out, his financial risk was cushioned by savings, a working wife, and a settlement from his old firm. The worst thing he figured could happen financially was to have to reduce his standard of living. That prospect didn't particularly faze him. And while he did take a risk by leaving a successful career to start a new one, in another sense Prentice says he ducked a bigger risk in the process. As he explains, the more successful he became as an architect, the more his aspirations rose. Rising with his aspirations were self-doubts. The next challenge professionally was to make an original contribution; a building or even a plan that would win recognition for its originality. "That was the next level for me in architecture," he says. "I didn't know if I could reach it. So in a sense I avoided the risk of answering that question by becoming a sculptor."

"Risk" is a virtuous word to Timothy Prentice. But like the rest of us, he's not sure precisely what it means. On a panel discussing public buildings, he once suggested that risk more than good taste attracted the public to such structures. When panel members tried to zero in on what "risk" meant, they quickly grew tongue-tied. One corporate executive mumbled about "risk-reward ratios." Others merely mumbled. Prentice himself wasn't sure what he meant by "risk" beyond the example of Rockefeller Center with its unprecedented sunken skating rink, which could have been a flop but which has proved to be a magnet for urban bodies. The only thing he was sure of was that "risk" implied the possibility of *failure*.

This is why his very success as a sculptor didn't resolve the doubts in Prentice's mind about whether his new work involves genuine risk. Six years into his new career, Prentice's apartment was littered on the day I visited with the wire, tubing, and metal mesh bricks he uses to create gigantic mobiles and surreal animals. His massive, detailed pieces of kinetic sculpture have been favorably reviewed, featured on the "Today" show, and purchased for display in the lobbies of major corporate offices. There they sit, a silent reminder to their creator that he's probably not really a risk taker.

Before leaving Timothy Prentice's Upper West Side apartment, I mentioned that the next person I'd be speaking to was Philippe Petit. Prentice's eyes lit up at the very name. "Philippe Petit!" he exclaimed.

"Now, you talk about risk takers!"

The case of Timothy Prentice illustrates some basic themes of this chapter, this book, and the entire subject of risk. Like Prentice and Petit and so many of the people I talked to, most of us are far more conscious of the risks we're avoiding than those we're taking. This is why so few of us admit to being risk takers. And because we are so aware of the risks we avoid, it's easy to assume that others are taking bigger risks — especially if they're ones we're ducking. Except they may be ducking risks we're taking. So risk, in this sense, is in the eye of the beholder. Or more precisely, in the fears of the beholder.

WHAT'S A RISK?

When we think about what "risk" means, we generally think first about physical danger. This is how my dictionary defines "risk": "to expose to hazard or danger." Objectively speaking, this definition is as good as any. But problems arise when we try to apply such a concept of risk to specific situations and people. In the first place, how do you know what's hazardous or dangerous these days? Does that include saccharin? Cholesterol? One part dioxin per billion? Two? Rain that might contain acid? Moderate amounts of radiation? And what's moderate? Only experts seem qualified to tell us what's really risky, and they can't agree among themselves.

So even when we try to pin risk down objectively as being based on physical danger, it's hard and getting harder to determine what's actually dangerous.

A second, and more fundamental, problem of relying on an objective definition of "risk" is the logical assumption that follows, that once we know what threatens our health and well-being, we'll adjust our behavior accordingly. If this were true, few of us would smoke and most would buckle up. In fact, despite massive education campaigns about the lethal risks, nearly a third of American adults still smoke, but far fewer use seat belts.

Obviously our personal assessment of risk includes factors other than objective danger. When it comes to choosing risks we'll take or avoid, statistics, odds, and averages are for other people.

Let me give an illustration. Bubonic plague has recently made a comeback in the American Southwest. During the summer of 1983, twenty-four cases of the plague were confirmed in New Mexico, resulting in three deaths. Needless to say, this left residents of the affected areas jittery and sometimes panicky. Statistically speaking, the danger of dying from bubonic plague was virtually nil. As an epidemiologist advised fearful New Mexicans, "If people would shrug it off, stop smoking, and wear their seat belts, they'd be taking appropriate health measures."

Impeccable as such logic might have been, it took no account whatsoever of the ways human beings actually perceive risk. In polls he's conducted of American attitudes toward risk, psychologist Paul Slovic has consistently found that a rare disease such as botulism is perceived as only slightly less lethal than a common one such as asthma. In fact, asthma is 900 times more likely to kill you than botulism. And while the risk of being murdered is generally seen as equal to that of dying from a stroke, strokes actually cause 11 times more deaths than do murderers. "Apparently," Slovic and two colleagues concluded after noting such discrepancies, "lay people incorporate other considerations beside annual fatalities into their concept of risk."

More than any other factor, Slovic has found *dread* determines our perception of risk. When he's asked subjects not only which risks they think are most dangerous, but which ones they most dread, the psychologist has found nearly a perfect correlation. Nuclear power, for example, routinely tops both lists. When experts try to refute such perceptions by pointing out how few fatalities have ever been caused by nuclear power, they might as well be speaking Swahili. Among thirty possible hazards Slovic asks about in his polls (including crime, nuclear war, skiing, floods, fluoridation, and tornadoes), he has found that in every case the level of fear determines the level of risk felt from such hazards far more than actual danger — even when such danger is known.

This is why "risk" is so hard to define. What from the outside may appear to be a major risk doesn't necessarily involve real fear of danger to the person involved. Yet to that person a seemingly minor risk might be so terrifying that it can't be taken.

One woman I interviewed had been a professional actress for two years. Before that she'd taught in public school, following twelve years as a nun, from ages seventeen to twenty-nine. The day we met, Jocelyn was cleaning houses on the side to support her fledgling career on the stage. Here, it seemed, was a rich menu of risks to discuss: leaving a convent, quitting a tenured job to act, acting, auditioning. Yet none of these risks felt terribly dangerous to Jocelyn. When she left the convent, it was time to go; also adventurous. Once her teaching job grew boring it wasn't hard to leave. She enjoyed the challenge of auditioning for parts. And performing for her was pure pleasure (except for the time her devoutly Catholic mother almost came to see her in a semi-nude role). So none of the risks I'd come to talk about felt that risky to her. What does, I asked? "Roller coasters!" replied Jocelyn without hesitating. "That's what I'm most scared of. Amusement rides." She shivered. "I went on one once when I was a little girl. It was over in a minute. But the terror! I can still feel it. In every part of my body!"

Our sense of risk is based on our fears. To be useful, therefore, our concept of risk must be flexible enough to fit each person's sense of fear, and danger of possible loss. A "risk," as I'll use the term in this book, is "an act involving fear of possible loss."

This is how most of us actually think of risk. When we describe an activity as "risky," what we usually mean is that it's scary — to us. And because so few of us are doing what we actually fear, hardly any of us see ourselves as "risk takers." Yet when we see someone else doing something that would scare us, it's hard to imagine that it doesn't scare them. And since we all do weigh risks on the scale of our own fears, we then dub that person a "risk taker." By definition. Ours. Except they may not see it that way themselves. They have their own definition of "risk" — whatever scares them. By someone else's definition *we* might be taking the bigger risks.

Comedienne Adrianne Tolsch, at thirty-five the veteran of two failed marriages. told me of a middle-aged woman who tugged at her sleeve as she walked off the stage one night. "I admire your courage up there so much," said the woman. "How do you *do* it?"

"Are you married?" asked Tolsch. The woman nodded.

"How long?" The woman said thirty years.

"How do you *do* it?" asked Tolsch.

Among the endless flood of neck-breaker television shows was one hosted by actor Robert Conrad called "The Daredevils." Featured was a thirty-three-year-old accountant whose specialty was leaping from an airplane without opening a parachute and connecting up with the diving plane he'd just exited, or with a parachutist floating to the ground. During a subsequent interview the skydiver/accountant observed that risk is relative; that starting a business or changing careers was a risk just like skydiving. Conrad looked incredulous. "Do you think you can compare changing jobs with jumping out of an airplane?" he scoffed.

But in this case the subject was more perceptive than the interviewer. In saying job changing might be risky like skydiving, I'm sure he was speaking for himself, just as Conrad was speaking for himself in putting daredevilry above all other risks.

Voluntarily putting your life in danger would seem like the ultimate risk — especially to a physical coward. In a poll I conducted for this book, "physical risks" were called hardest to take by more than any other kind (37 percent said this). Yet in my experience, those who voluntarily risk their lives are protected in three ways: 1) most of them take scrupulous safety precautions; 2) the loss of their life does not feel to them like the ultimate loss; and, 3) most are sure this couldn't happen to them anyway.

Real fear of possible loss is central to actual risk. Objective danger counts for less than perceived danger. Too many so-called risks are ones the risk taker feels can't be lost no matter what the actual odds are. A pure risk taken with the full awareness of possible loss is rare. Most acts of apparent daring are usually motivated by a mishmash of ignorance, bravado, derring-do, carelessness, reduced stakes, peer pressure, and the desire to impress.

A simple test can assign weight to any apparent risk. That test is simply to add the word "what" to risk in evaluating any act claiming that title. "Risk what?" becomes the determining question. Anything real? Anything valued? Something the risk taker would mind losing? Something the risk taker is aware might be lost?

If you don't fear losing your life, is it a risk to play Russian roulette?

If commitment to a relationship is a low priority, is getting divorced risky?

If your financial base is secure, is it a risk to play the commodities market?

What it boils down to is this: if actual risk involves real fear of loss, few of us are daring to do what really scares us. Even the once-scary paths we do brave soon become passable and therefore no longer so risky. We take our courage for granted and brood over our cowardice. It's almost as if, "Anything I'm doing is by definition not a risk." (Or: "If I'm doing it, it couldn't really be risky.")

Risks, it seems, are what other people take.

WHO'S A RISK TAKER?

Early in this project I met a middle-aged couple from Virginia. "We're not risk takers," the wife said emphatically when talk turned to this subject. "I leave that to the skydivers and river rafters," agreed her husband. As the conversation continued, I learned that this woman had just been made the manager of a bank branch where she'd worked for years as a teller. Reporting to her was a corps of men eager for her failure. Her husband, who now sold appliances at a department store, was the sole survivor of his World War II bomber squadron. This couple had been married for three decades and had raised three children. On vacation when we met, they would soon be heading toward New Orleans, perhaps getting there, maybe not, as circumstances dictated. They didn't have reservations anywhere. I know skydivers and river rafters who wouldn't take *that* risk.

The self-appraisal of this couple was anything but atypical. On a questionnaire I devised with the help of psychologist Cathy Pullis, only 6 percent of the 512 people filling it out said they felt themselves to be "definitely a risk taker." "More of a risk taker," felt true to 32 percent; "more of a risk avoider," to 41 percent. Seven percent called themselves "definitely a risk avoider," and 10 percent marked "don't know."

Those taking this poll came from a wide variety of backgrounds. Ranging in age from seventeen to seventy-two, they were drawn from groups of clergymen, nuns, go-go dancers, doctors, lawyers, middle managers, Marines, policemen, college students, computer programmers, roofers, small-business owners, nurses, secretaries, social workers, drug dealers, anti-nuke activists, and Daughters of the American Revolution.

As the biggest risk she'd ever taken, one of the DAR members, a woman of sixty-nine, wrote, "I walked across Central Park at dusk in 1951." A twenty-six-year-old computer programmer mentioned drinking at questionable bars as his biggest risk, adding that he reduced his sense of risk by carrying a Smith & Wesson Model 28 (.357 Magnum) pistol. For her biggest risk, a twenty-five-year-old receptionist wrote, "Going into house full of flames to rescue my dog."

But such drama was the exception. Many cited risks at work as their biggest, or simply speaking out for an unpopular point of view (this was noted by a policeman). Four people said that buying a house was their biggest risk, including one market researcher who mentioned buying three houses in six months and having to float five loans to do so. Then there was a forty-one-year-old designer who reported as her biggest risk, "Interacting with a man whose wife had been murdered. Apparently I was a lookalike for his wife."

To the general question "What kinds of risks would you say are hardest for you to take," 37 percent said "physical risks (of life and limb)"; 22 percent, "emotional risks (in relationships)"; 20 percent, "financial risks (of losing money)"; and 1 percent, "intellectual risks (dealing with new ideas)." Asked if they thought they would join a wagon train headed west a century ago, 11 percent said "definitely," 34 percent "probably," 48 percent "probably not," and 6 percent "definitely not." Caution ruled here. Yet when given a hypothetical choice between driving *south* on the Pacific Coast Highway with a more spectacular view but greater danger of driving off the edge, or *north* with less risk but less view, only 26 percent said they'd take the safer route, while 72 percent preferred the more scenic one.

Extending the poles of daring and caution just slightly, only 9 percent of this group admitted to taping shut already-sealed envelopes regularly or even often, while 32 percent said they seldom do, and 67 percent said almost never. At a Chinese restaurant, 33 percent use chopsticks regularly or often, 18 percent seldom, and 46 percent almost never. Given a choice of six comparably priced restaurants in a strange city, 32 percent chose to have lunch at the Country Kitchen, 19 percent at Burger King, 16 percent at Doña Maria's Mexican, 13 percent at the Indonesian Isle, and 9 percent at Sam's Diner. The Holiday Inn Coffee Shop was preferred by 8 percent of those filling out the questionnaire.

This sampling of their responses gives a fair profile of the group surveyed: neither ultracautious nor particularly daring, but willing to take some chances under certain circumstances. In other words, about like most of us.

Throughout this book specific results from this survey will be used to cast light on different aspects of risk taking. I was particularly struck, for example, by the ways people would rank their risks when more than one was listed as "biggest," and how such risks compared with responses to other questions. A thirty-year-old divorcée said that leaving her husband was number one for her. "But close seconds are risking bodily injury or prison in 'anti-nuke' work." Next came "talking a kid with a gun into not shooting me but giving me the gun."

As his biggest risk, a thirty-one-year-old policeman and father wrote, "With a person pointing a gun at me, I reached down and drew my weapon from my holster and fired." (He didn't report the outcome.) But the biggest risk this man said he could imagine taking was "quitting my job as a policeman and starting my own business."

As her biggest risk, a thirty-eight-year-old mother of three listed two events. The *second* was "sneaking into a house full of drug addicts, armed with a gas gun to get my daughter out. I planned to point the gun at one of her friends and force them to call for the police if she wouldn't come with me when I asked. She wouldn't, so I did. The first officer on the scene was in plain clothes and I pointed the gun at him, thinking he was one of them. He identified himself and I told him it was only a gas gun as I slowly lowered it. I don't know how risky this was, since it all worked to my plan."

And her number-*one* most risky activity?

"The first time I ever sent an article to a magazine."

It seems that one's tendency to perceive risk in one area of life has little or nothing to do with one's tendency to perceive risk in another. In fact, as I discovered repeatedly, taking certain types of risks may even preclude taking others.

At one point I talked with a bachelor in his mid-thirties who had just returned from three months spent seeking out the most daring ski adventures he could find. These involved jumping off cliffs, being helicoptered into remote Canadian glaciers to ski back, and skiing straight down steep slopes at speeds exceeding 90 miles an hour. Bob said that since he'd returned, this experience had spilled over into other areas of his life. "Nothing scares me now," was the way he put it. Nothing, I asked? How about getting married?

"That's a risk I wouldn't take," Bob replied immediately.

Having kids?

"No way," he said.

It's almost as if we're all subject to a Law of Maximum Takeable Risks. By this I mean that there's a limited volume of risks any one of us can take, but that we can *only* take certain risks by avoiding others. We're deluded by dramatic and visible acts of daring into assuming that they're engaged in by nervy risk takers not afraid to gamble across the board. In fact we purchase boldness in some aspects of our life with caution in others. And the cautious parts of our lives are usually more evident to us than the bold ones.

This takes us right back to where we began in this chapter: the fact that so many apparent risk takers deny taking risks. The principal reason is that, like anyone, they see too clearly the risks they're avoiding as the price of those they take.

I've even come to wonder if the risks we *do* take — authentic though they may be — are ones standing in for more profound risks we're avoiding. In other words, that when we do take a chance, no matter where it ranks on other people's scale of fear and risk, on our own it's seldom at the top. Therefore, regardless of their actual danger or how they appear to others, even the risks we do take feel to us like lesser risks taken by avoiding bigger ones. In some cases we take lesser risks not only *by* avoiding bigger ones, but *to* avoid them.

A woman I met in the course of this project was thinking of building on her successful career as a novelist by writing a play. The prospect terrified her. Could she pull it off? Or would she look like a fool for even trying? The possibility of disaster looked great. So instead of starting her play, the novelist enrolled in Outward Bound. And she knew exactly why. Taking the lesser risks of kayaking white water and rappeling down cliffs on rope — scary as they were — were not as scary as attempting to master a new literary form. Outward Bound became her surrogate risk, a sort of stand-in for the more ominous hazards of trying to write a play.

In my own case, I soon became aware that the risk I'd most like to have taken as part of my research was to do stand-up comedy. The opportunity was there and offered to me. Even if I failed, the experience could be written up as a worthy experiment. But the risk of telling jokes before a live audience was never one I could take. Instead I went rock climbing. This was risky enough; something I'd never done and that frightened me. But struggling up and down sheer rock faces didn't feel nearly as dangerous as telling jokes from a stage and having no one laugh.

This is why I became at least as interested in risks avoided as those taken. In many ways, the risks we duck say something far more profound about who we are and how we feel than those we take. They speak to us of our deepest fears.

On the one hand, this feels like a discouraging conclusion. If genuine risk involves actual fear, no wonder we take so few. But this conclusion needn't be discouraging at all. It all depends on how you approach fear.

THREE

RISK HUNGER

We once went canoeing with friends on a mild river with a single stretch of rapids. On this stretch our companions, a married couple in their late thirties, capsized. Gail at first thought she was going under. Roger pulled and talked her into grabbing a tree branch, then onto a little island. He then returned for their canoe, which was bobbing in rushing, chest-high water above uncertain footing. Finally Roger coaxed his canoe, his wife, and himself onto dry land. All they lost was an old straw hat.

Afterward Roger and Gail's words said one thing ("What a *terrible* experience!"), but their demeanor said another. Both were flushed, excited, and giddy as teenagers. For the next hour this little catastrophe was all the two could talk about, reviewing the experience second by second as they held hands and celebrated themselves for surviving the ordeal. I'd never seen them closer.

There's an irony here. We do our best to make life safer, more secure and predictable. Yet we find most memorable those moments when all our efforts are for naught. Only then do we rediscover that our bodies have a taste for danger.

One reason we're so perplexed about risks and reluctant to take them is that we regard the fear of danger that accompanies risk as an affliction to be cured. With only a touch of irony, one pharmacological researcher has defined anxiety as "that emotion that five milligrams of Valium makes better." By taking such an approach, we lose track of how essential feeling afraid is to our survival, and especially to our ability to be daring.

You often hear the term "fearless risk taker." By the definition of this book, that's a contradiction in terms. Any genuine risk involves fear. Fearlessness is not only the antithesis of risk taking, but a highly dangerous state. "I do what I can to get away from those fellows who never get scared," the explorer Peter Freuchen once said. "They are very dangerous men. They get you into all kinds of trouble — those fellows who are scared of nothing. They die soon. I am always scared."

In terms of evolution, those primitive beings who were best able to both feel and respond to fear were probably the ones most likely to survive. Those who were too afraid, on the one hand, or too nonchalant, on the other, were more likely to be picked off by predators. Relative to the predators surrounding them, primitive human beings were frail, weak, and slow of foot. Recent evidence indicates that our earliest ancestors compared in size to today's schoolchildren.

In the absence of better physical gifts, the ability to confront fear and take chances has been basic to our biological success. Especially through migration, this willingness has made *Homo sapiens* the only species found in every part of the world. "Biologically speaking, you need risk taking," says epidemiologist Jeffrey Roseman. "Risk taking is a dimension along which selection takes place." The late biologist René Dubos went so far as to call the ability to take chances "a condition of biological success."

Being able to take risks and confront the fear of danger calls for nearly inhuman courage. Yet for most of human existence such fear was a typical part of the day. Even a summer thunderstorm can be terrifying without a weatherman to tell us when it will be over, and air conditioners to mask its fury. In time our bodies learned to cope with perceived danger — or rather, they were selected for this ability. Those who are best able to endure the night of fear and arrive at a peaceful dawn were the ones who could survive daily peril. Eventually their nervous systems not only learned how to endure fear but developed a taste for it. We are their heirs. In a very real sense we've outgrown our bodies. The fact that systems equipped to deal with danger so seldom have clear-cut, resolvable opportunities to do so is central to our confusion and frustration about taking risks. You might say we suffer from risk hunger.

"So far as evolution is concerned, it was practically yesterday when we stopped taking daily risks," points out research physician Sol Roy Rosenthal. Rosenthal believes that the body and mind not only respond well to regular doses of danger but may even need them. "Physical risk has been gradually eliminated from man's daily life," he suggests, "but the need for action and risk remains in man's genes, so to speak."

This is why the fear that accompanies risk is not necessarily regarded as an enemy by our bodies. Aside from its obvious value as a blinking light of caution, fear's value is expressed in two persisting forms: at a first level, where our nervous systems enjoy short-term stimulation when danger is confronted and transcended; and at a second level, where the long-term need to affiliate with others is a byproduct of feeling scared. (These levels of fear are translated into levels of risk, which will be discussed later in this chapter.) In a nutshell: fear provides both a tonic to our body and spirit and an incentive to forge human ties.

A TASTE FOR DANGER, I

Since confronting danger and tolerating fear does call for inhuman courage, our systems developed potent, immediate, and tangible rewards for managing fear and taking risks. Although we now experience feeling afraid as primarily negative, our forebears probably didn't. They couldn't; not if each day wasn't to be one of unrelieved agony. We forget that although fear begins as a negative sensation, once endured it can be something quite different: exhilaration, arousal, and a source of camaraderie when shared with others. This is why survivors of what appear to be awful experiences — floods, hurricanes, plane hijackings — so typically describe their ordeals in the most glowing terms and schedule reunions to relive them. Inadvertently they've rediscovered how well equipped we are not only to endure but to flourish in the face of intense fear.

Like Philippe Petit, many of those who confront serious danger later recall not only how afraid but how happy they felt. After witnessing several fatalities in his years as a mountain climber, David Roberts later observed that although some of the worst moments of his life had taken place on mountains, "nowhere else on earth, not even in the harbors of reciprocal love, have I felt pure happiness take hold of me and shake me like a puppy."

Describing the sensation of facing imminent attack during the Vietnam war, veteran James Webb wrote in his novel *Fields of Fire*, "They ran wildly toward Hodges and the others. Closer, closer they came, and Hodges felt a joy and anticipation so hard to contain that he found himself bobbing up and down inside the trench where he hid. . . .

"A rush that resembled passion crept from the insides of his guts and somehow drew the skin from every part of his body toward that center of his joy and fear, so tight that when he smiled it made his cheeks burn. . . ."

At such levels of intensity, the bodies we've inherited make little distinction between positive and negative arousal. During peaks of excitement our responses tend to merge. Tears of joy can't be distinguished from those of grief. Laughter can be a sign of happiness, or hysteria, or both. Yawning is a common response to exhaustion and terror. The face of orgasm resembles that of pain. (When he wanted to induce an orgasmic look on the face of fifteen-year-old Brooke Shields for the movie *Endless Love*, director Franco Zeffirelli squeezed her big toe until he got the expression he was looking for.)

It's an ongoing neurological mystery that both pain and pleasure can be aroused by stimulating the same area of mammalian brains. One school of psychological thought believes that the body makes no real distinction between strong feelings of any kind — anger, love, fear, excitement — until the mind picks up cues and tells the body which is which. Perhaps this is the way that our bodies evolved to cope with trauma, by not regarding it as traumatic. In time the arousal born of danger and fear came to be regarded as normal, even desirable.

The sexual rewards for braving danger are suggestive here. Even today feelings of sexual arousal can be hard to distinguish from those of fear: the throbbing heart, the panting, the subsequent sense of exhilaration and release. Indeed, one response to danger itself is to become sexually aroused. (Ask a veteran.) Many explanations have been suggested for this overlap. My own is that for our very survival, human nervous systems developed common rewards for desirable behavior. Ecstasy may just be nature's common reward for behavior she most wishes to encourage: making babies, and taking risks.

Only an actual masochist enjoys danger as such. Yet we all enjoy its by-products: alertness, intensity, and a sense of elation once danger has passed. With its faster pulse, shortness of breath, and copious perspiration, the body responds to moderate stress much as it does to physical exercise. This may be no coincidence. For most of our existence, exercise and danger were bundled in a common package as we pursued prey or escaped from predators. One reason jogging seems so appreciated by our bodies is that human beings have spent so much of their existence running to and from danger. Presumably our cardiovascular systems came to depend on such stimulation and don't appreciate being deprived of it.

As with exercise, short doses of tolerable stress are essential for keeping body and spirit tuned. During a lifetime devoted to studying this topic, Hans Selye concluded that by jolting the body into new patterns of response, a reasonable amount of stress was essential for any healthy organism. But it must be emphasized that this means occasional stress at tolerable levels. There is little good to be said for even occasional panic, constant phobias, or nagging anxiety.

When I mentioned to a mother of three in her mid-thirties that one thing I'd be writing about in this book was the tonic effects of fear, she responded, "If that's true I'm going to live to be a hundred and fifty." But what this woman meant (as she went on to make clear) was that she experienced constant low-level fear that was seldom resolved. To bodies conditioned for short bursts of cathartic stress, such anxiety can be deadly. Lasting stress without hope of resolution not only isn't healthy but may be implicated in diseases such as hardened arteries, ulcers, heart disease, and even cancer.

When it comes to stress, our bodies prefer a jagged line of peaks and valleys to a wavy, regular, and constant line. In response to such intermittent stress, the body releases a range of chemicals to help us deal with our perceived danger. Such chemicals include adrenaline, as we've long known (and now break down into adrenaline and "noradrenaline"), but also a wide range of brain chemicals including the endorphins, or "nature's morphine" — our natural opiates.*

Such opiates do double duty as mood regulators and pain-killers. There are strong indications, for example, that the anesthetic property of acupuncture is due to the soothing effect of opiates released by our nervous system in response to the prick of pins. The euphoria experienced by many women after giving birth may also be due to the release of endorphins (whose level is known to rise in the latter stages of pregnancy). Even the "runner's high" that marathoners describe is probably a result of the endorphins that have been found in abundance in the blood of distance runners following races.

The endorphins seem to play an especially valuable duet in conjunction with adrenaline. Even as the latter is firing up our nervous system to prepare it for danger, the former raise our pain threshold and promote a sense of detachment that allows us to be calm in the face of calamity. The adrenal response might be likened to a car engine being gunned to take off, the endorphin response to a cooling system that makes sure the engine doesn't overheat and explode under pressure.

We've all had experiences — a near auto accident, say, or a close call while skiing — in which at the peak of danger our fear was tempered, body relaxed, and mind calmly focused on the danger at hand as if it were happening to somebody else. Seconds later terror may have crashed upon us in waves producing uncontrollable trembling and utter confusion. But during moments of danger it's typical to stay cool.

Long before we knew about endorphins, we had clear reports of their effects at work. Late last century, a Swiss geologist

---

* Our knowledge of brain chemistry has progressed to the point that the term "endorphins" is a little simplistic since we now know that such a wide range of natural opiates are released in varying combinations to suit particular occasions. However, since the term "endorphins" has entered the language as synonymous with natural opiates in general, and for the sake of clarity, I use it that way in this book.

named Albert St. Gallen Heim summarized material that he had gathered from survivors of near-fatal falls in the Alps. Heim compared these reports with others from those who had been wounded during wars or had survived accidents at work, on railroads, and in the water. Whatever the cause of their brush with death, Heim found his subjects had predictable responses:

> There was no anxiety, no trace of despair, no pain; but rather a calm seriousness, profound acceptance and a dominant mental quickness and sense of surety. Mental activity became enormous, rising to a hundred-fold velocity or intensity. The relationship of events and their probable outcomes were overviewed with objective clarity. No confusion entered at all. Time became greatly expanded. The individual acted with lightning quickness in accord with accurate judgment of his situation. . . . Consciousness was painlessly extinguished, usually at the moment of impact. And the impact was, at the most, heard but never painfully felt.

Neurobiologist Candace Pert, who codiscovered endorphins, thinks our evolving brain grew dependent on them because of its need for undivided attention in the midst of constant danger. At times of emergency, those whose brains were most responsive to the opiates released were the ones best able to disregard irrelevant information and concentrate on the peril at hand. Those who couldn't, perished. Thus the ability to pay what Pert calls "selective attention" may have determined who survived emergencies, and lived to have descendants.

By helping us decide what information to concentrate on for survival, Candace Pert believes that endorphins continue to play a key role in our "filtering" of environmental information. The only problem is that the programming of our brains for such decision making was done millions of years ago when the information being processed was rather different from that which we're coping with today. As Pert's colleague Solomon Snyder points out, only in a situation of extreme physical and mental stress, such as combat, may contemporary humans exercise their full neurochemical capacity to cope with trauma.

In his World War II memoir *Goodbye Darkness*, ex-Marine William Manchester gave the following description of how it feels to have a mortar shell explode nearby and be lying motionless with a rifle poised ready to shoot a Japanese sniper or be shot by him:

> When my wits returned I felt, surprisingly, sharper. . . . A cathedral hush seemed to have enveloped the gorge. I could almost hear the friction of the earth turning on its axis. I had literally taken leave of my senses. There remained only a trace of normal anxiety, the roughage of mental diet that sharpens awareness. Everything I saw over my sights had a cameolike clarity, as keen and well-defined as a line by Van Eyck.

Nearly three decades after Manchester's episode, former revolutionary Jane Alpert recorded how she felt on a bus going to plant her first bomb:

> A kind of agitation coursed through my body, heightening all my faculties. I cushioned the purse on my lap, protecting it from the bus's sudden jolts. I noticed the large, calloused hands of a Puerto Rican woman opposite me, the dirty toenails of a sandaled teenager next to me. I was absolutely happy and, in spite of my racing pulse, felt very calm, as when the first rush of an acid trip subsides.

Finally, here is Stephen Crane's account in *The Red Badge of Courage* of Henry Fleming's feelings as he awaited his first battle during the Civil War:

> It seemed to the youth that he saw everything. Each blade of green grass was bold and clear. He thought that he was aware of every change in the thin, transparent vapor that floated idly in sheets. The brown or gray trunks of the trees showed each roughness of their surfaces. . . . His mind took a mechanical but firm impression, so that afterwards everything was pictured and explained to him, save why he himself was there.

There is a name given to our detailed recollections of such fearful moments. They are called "flashbulb memories," to suggest the role stress can play in illuminating vividly everything in sight during moments when we feel in danger. Recent evidence indicates that brain chemicals released by stress are instrumental in fixing even irrelevant details of anxious settings in our memory. This includes everything from what we were wearing the day we heard John Kennedy was killed (or John Lennon, or

Martin Luther King, Jr., or . . .) to the names of our high school classmates. While such total recall of moments when we felt afraid may no longer be necessary in a world of videotape and data banks, early human beings would certainly have been more likely to survive a dangerous setting again if they recalled it vividly from their first encounter. So "flashbulb memories" are probably yet another evolutionary artifact of bodies designed to cope with danger.

At a fortieth reunion of Pearl Harbor survivors I attended, it was striking how detailed were the memories most had of that languid Sunday morning when in an instant their world of peace became one of war. One retired firefighter from Oregon even remembered the name of the book he was reading beneath the shade of a tarp on the U.S.S. *Honolulu* (*Rain in the Doorway*), its author (Thorne Smith), and the color of its cover (green). Others recalled markings on the planes come to bomb them, and even the expression on the faces of their pilots.

Pearl Harbor veterans gather continually to relive that day. Across the country they have scores of chapters of the Pearl Harbor Survivors Association. Ostensibly this group is dedicated to its credo: "Remember Pearl Harbor, keep America alert." In fact, as its members freely admit, their reason for gathering is to relive an experience that bonded them as no other could. This is the great value of fear at the second level: the way it makes us need each other.

A TASTE FOR DANGER, II

As any veteran of combat knows, we instinctively huddle more closely when frightened. (In their quaint way, psychologists call this "fear affiliation.") A constant challenge to military discipline is getting soldiers under fire to spread out and present less of a target, when their every nerve ending is tugging them as close to each other as possible. This sharing of danger and fear is what veterans say forges the closest human ties many of them have ever known. They come to fight for ideals or adventure; they stay to fight for each other. As General Jimmy Doolittle observed during a thirty-sixth reunion of survivors of his World

War II raid on Tokyo, "I would say there are two interesting emotions that bring people together. One is love, and the other is sharing hazard."

Feeling afraid is what makes infants cling to their mothers. Even after they loosen their grip a bit and go off to explore the world, when anything frightening happens an infant will dash back to its mother's arms for reassurance. Only then will exploring be resumed. So fear has the paradoxical effect of encouraging a child to seek security, which in turn instills the confidence to go forth and risk being frightened once again. After continually observing such a process in the chimpanzees he's studied for years, psychologist Harry Harlow has concluded that here is yet another evolutionary value of fear. As Harlow has written with colleague Stephen Suomi, the ability to respond to fear is "one of the most potent forces in keeping rearing groups relatively intact, the social orders stable, and hence the species more apt to survive and prosper."

One reason that a sense of community has become such a rare commodity in contemporary life is simply that the decline of immediate hazards has reduced our need for each other. In his book *Landscapes of Fear*, geographer Yi-fu Tuan points out that while we may lament the loss of social intimacy in modern life, "we forget that fear was and is a common reason for weaving close human ties. Remove the threats of environment, whether they be by the forces of nature or human enemies, and the bonds of community tend to weaken."

This has been a gradual process, of course. Tuan considers eighteenth-century Europe a watershed in which life grew both more secure and increasingly anxious. As weather conditions and food-distribution systems improved, famine and starvation declined. The result, he concludes, was that "local calamities gave way to something better — in a rather desperate sense — namely, a generalized pattern of chronic distress. The improved availability of food in particular permitted a boom in population which exchanged famines for widespread under-nutrition in a setting of constant anxiety about feeding one's family."

In a broader sense, this seems to be the inevitable trend of progress and civilization: the exchange of immediate fear soon resolved for ongoing, unresolved, and unresolvable anxiety. Our heads may regard this as a fair exchange, but our bodies don't. As far as our bodies are concerned, being resolvably scared (within reason) is what keeps them tuned, alert, and in need of other bodies.

Both levels of responses to fear are equally adaptive: the intense immediate arousal, and the lasting bonding. When we need to confront imminent danger, it helps to find risk exhilarating. Yet in the long run, it's every bit as necessary to cope with danger and fear by creating ties to others and risk losing those ties. A model of balance might be that of Native American tribes that put equal emphasis on courage in the face of adversity (and designed rites to promote such courage) and communal ties so strong that banishment was considered the ultimate punishment.

One result of the relative security of modern life is that we seldom *have* to respond to immediate danger by taking risks at either level. Instead we're free to limit our risk taking to one level or the other (or in some cases neither): to go primarily for excitement or commitment. And our nervous systems fall in step.

LEVELS OF RISK

This distinction between approaches to risk is one I call Level I and Level II risk taking, corresponding to the two levels of fear.

Risks at the first level are what most often go by the name "risk taking": highly stimulating, exciting activities that are often dangerous and seldom last very long. In this category might be put thrill sports, performing in public, and going to war.

Level II risk taking is longer lasting, rarely dramatic, and usually unstimulating activity that involves more danger to the spirit than to the body. This category includes getting married, starting a family, and building a career.

Here is a chart to suggest some traits and interests that broadly distinguish those who are more likely to take Level I risks from those who are more likely to take Level II risks.

LEVEL I	LEVEL II

Traits

aggressive	conforming
extroverted	introverted
fidgety	patient
impatient	phlegmatic
individualistic	punctual
mobile	relaxed
restless	reliable
tense	sedentary

Values

action	attention to detail
change	calmness
excitement	community
freedom	dependability
intensity	even temperament
speed	predictability
variety	security

Key Fears

boredom	abandonment
commitment	chaos
routine	injury

Problem Areas

attention span	agoraphobia
drug use	making friends
insomnia	overweight
maintaining friendships	simple depression
manic-depression	staying awake
smoking	television dependency

Favorite Expressions

Had a ball!	Take it easy.
Let's get a move on.	What's the rush?
Time for a change.	I don't know . . .
I'm bored.	Steady as she goes.
Let's party!	Never say die.

Preferred Modes of Transport

motorcycle	feet
skateboard	bicycle
a turbo-charged car	any station wagon

Favorite Sports

basketball	baseball
canoeing, white water	canoeing, lake
football	cricket
hockey	croquet
rodeo	golf
skiing, downhill	marathons
sprints	skiing, cross country

Favorite Authors

Joseph Conrad	Ann Beattie
Ernest Hemingway	Joan Didion
Judith Krantz	Henry James
Jack London	James Michener
Homer	Marcel Proust

For Example . . .

Bella Abzug	Alan Alda
Muhammad Ali	Erma Bombeck
John Belushi	Chou En-lai
Lord Byron	Calvin Coolidge
Winston Churchill	Gary Cooper
Gandhi	Walter Cronkite
Mao Tse-tung	Hugh Downs
Nietzsche	Dwight D. Eisenhower
George Patton	Ralph Waldo Emerson
Pablo Picasso	Betty Friedan
Burt Reynolds	John Lennon
Theodore Roosevelt	Abraham Lincoln
Phyllis Schlafly	Walter Mondale
Ariel Sharon	Mister Rogers
Ted Turner	J. D. Salinger

Vocational Guidance

ambulance driver	accountant
commodities trader	actuary

43

cop	archaeologist
criminal	author
drug counselor	cabinetmaker
entertainer	civil servant
evangelist	clergy
journalist	computer programmer
lawyer, trial	dentist
paramedic	editor
politician	lawyer, corporate
process server	librarian
rock star	marriage counselor
sales, commission	mortician
soldier, combat	pharmacist
steeplejack	sales, salaried
stunt person	secretary
window washer	soldier, career

Obviously this is a simplified breakdown. No one is exclusively Level I or Level II in all circumstances. We might go for excitement in our choice of sports, for security in investments. Or the stimulation of a life fighting fires could make us appreciate uneventful weekends at home. Yet even though we all do combine elements of both levels of risk taking, most of us lean more in one direction or the other depending on our need for stimulation.

Contrasting levels of need for stimulation are among the most quickly evident in children. The active ones let their parents know what they're in for early as they struggle to crawl and walk no matter how many times they fall. This is the kid who later plays with electric plugs no matter how many times his hand gets slapped, or who continually dashes into the street despite a guarantee of punishment. Others, even siblings of such budding sensation seekers, may spend long months on hands and knees thinking it over before daring to make a crawl, and need to get their hand slapped only once to get the message about electric plugs. In such contrasts we see the genesis of lifelong attitudes toward stimulation and risk.

Ever since human beings began to observe and reflect on each other, one of their principal observations has been that some of us need more stimulation than others. Pavlov contrasted "strong" nervous systems, which require a lot of stimulation to get up to speed, with "weak" ones, which quickly grow overloaded. Coining his own terms, British psychiatrist Michael Balint has suggested that we all tend either to be "philobats," who cope with the trauma of separation from our mother's breast by seeking *more* separation in exciting forms; or "ocnophils," who spend a lifetime seeking to recreate the security of a mother's embrace. Biologically speaking, Hans Selye — the father of modern stress research — distinguished those he called "racehorses," who thrive on the stimulation of hectic, stress-filled lives, from "turtles," whose nervous systems plead for a more serene pace. Following in Selye's wake, research has been done comparing "stress-seeking" with "stress-avoiding" personalities, or, more recently, "Type A" and "Type B."

All such distinctions are based on a common assumption that our nervous systems respond differently to the same amount of stimulation. Just as a four-cylinder engine needs to rev faster to achieve the same power as a six-cylinder one, some of us must be more stimulated than others to reach the same level of arousal.

LEVEL I RISK TAKERS

During two decades of studying the trait he calls "sensation seeking," University of Delaware psychologist Marvin Zuckerman has found that a high need for stimulation characterizes not only thrill-sport participants but streakers, snowmobilers, sexual experimenters, cops, volunteer firemen, smokers (women especially), drug users, encounter groupers, breast-feeding mothers, delinquents, crime interveners, and those who prefer hot and spicy over bland and mushy food. He emphasizes that the forms this trait takes vary with factors such as age, marital status, income, and gender. Not surprisingly, those under thirty test far higher on sensation seeking than do those over. Single people as a group test higher than married ones, and men on the whole higher than women. Yet there are nuances. Female lawyers, for example, test higher on sensation seeking than male ones (presumably because as a sex-role violation their career itself is evidence of an adventurous disposition). The same is true of alcohol abusers.

Zuckerman's interest in this subject began in the late 1950s. At that time he noticed the same faces volunteering repeatedly for psychological experiments regardless of the nature of the experiment or how much was being paid. Zuckerman wondered if novelty and excitement were their real reason for volunteering, income and the experiment itself secondary.

To explore whether the need for excitement was a more basic drive for some human beings than for others, he began in 1961 to develop a test of the sensation-seeking trait. Since nothing like this existed, Zuckerman had to work largely from scratch. The psychologist reviewed mentally those he thought of as sensation seekers. One man came to mind who loved to party and ride motorcycles. An excitement-oriented woman he knew enjoyed both an active sexual life and spicy food. Zuckerman himself — moderately sensation seeking in his own estimation — liked to party, and took part in political demonstrations.

From such leads his Sensation Seeking Scale evolved. Today it is recognized by psychologists as one of our most reliable tests of a human trait. This test consists of 144 statements designed to distinguish high- from low-sensation seekers, based on their interest in a variety of arousing activities. These range from thrill sports ("I would like to try parachute jumping") to weather preferences ("I am invigorated by a brisk, cold day"), arousing art ("A good painting should shock or jolt the senses"), gambling ("I like to gamble for money"), carousing ("I like 'wild' uninhibited parties"), sexual variety ("Most adultery happens because of sheer boredom"), variety in friendship ("I get bored seeing the same old faces"), being boring ("The worst social sin is to be a bore"), and overall attitudes toward novelty ("I like to have new and exciting experiences and sensations even if they are a little frightening, unconventional or illegal").

The assumption is that responding positively to many such statements indicates a constant need for lots of stimulation, which can be satisfied in a variety of forms. While something like skydiving leaps to mind when we think of sensation seeking (and indeed a group of skydivers scored high on this test), Zuckerman points out that such an activity is limited to those who have the money, time, and wherewithal to take part. The rest of us satisfy a need for sensation by driving recklessly, picking fights, taking drugs, sleeping around, and generally carrying on.

A key trait distinguishing high- from low-sensation seekers is "boredom susceptibility." As this trait suggests, those with a strong need for outer stimulation may feel understimulated inside. This idea has gained broad credence in recent years. Hyperactive children, for example — tomorrow's sensation seekers — are now generally assumed to be compensating for a lack of inner arousal through manic behavior.

In a practical application of this insight, the military has found that understimulated types are the ones they prefer for dangerous missions. One means of selecting such recruits is to test their speed at reading words or symbols flashed briefly on a screen. The longer the reading time, the more "tuned down" the subject's nervous system is assumed to be and the greater his need for excitement. As a check, the personal life of these recruits is then examined. If they turn out to be drinkers, smokers, and social gadabouts who drive fast cars and wear flashy clothing, more's the better. This reinforces the assumption that they're stimulation-starved soldiers who would welcome the goose of some danger.

Only recently has it been discovered that high-sensation seekers seem to produce less of the mood-regulating opiates released by stress than do low-sensation seekers. This could help explain the frequently noted antidepressant quality of thrill seeking — the fact that those who engage in it can be so "up" after a thrilling activity, and down in its absence. Those whose brains are producing less than their share of endorphins may need constant arousal to release extra opiates into starved nervous systems. Seeking sensation — even in highly dangerous forms — can be an excellent means of achieving such arousal. Biochemically speaking, the fact that risks must be taken to do so is incidental.

After examining records of the Carnegie Hero Fund Commission and interviewing some of their award winners, psychologist Ervin Staub found that many had a history of participation in thrill sports. As a group he characterized them as displaying traits of "adventurousness," or more precisely, "stimulus seeking." After years of research on altruism of all kinds, Staub has found that it is temperament as much as conviction that distinguishes those who dare to help others in danger from those who don't. The most important trait of all is what the psychologist refers to as an "action tendency."

Others have reached similar conclusions. Among a wide range of psychological tests administered to a group of interveners in crimes-in-progress, the only one that consistently distinguished them from noninterveners was a test of their sensation-seeking tendencies. Even a group of twenty-seven Christians who at great peril to themselves helped rescue Jews during World War II were found when studied later to be united only by a love of daring. As psychologist Perry London reported of this group:

> Almost all the rescuers interviewed, regardless of where they came from and what they did to fall into our sample, seemed to possess a fondness for adventure. They had not only a desire to help, but also a desire to participate in what were inherently exciting activities. For example, we interviewed a man from the Netherlands who responded to a question about his recreational preferences by describing what had been his favorite adolescent hobby — racing motorcycles, especially over narrow boards on top of deep ditches. His work as a rescuer in the Dutch underground was a fairly tame job, but he and his friends had a sort of extracurricular hobby of putting sugar in the gas tanks of German army trucks. This was not part of any organized sabotage, just something they did for fun.

To say that heroes are motivated at least partly by adventurousness needn't belittle their heroism. Ideally the two can mesh nicely: a need for excitement and the desire to be of service. As a volunteer member of an ambulance corps in New Jersey once explained of his motives, "I find it exciting to help people in distress." But such evidence about daring altruists suggests that important differences in temperament may influence not only our willingness to be heroic, but our attitudes toward risk in general.

LEVEL II RISK TAKERS

In contrast to high-sensation seekers, low ones have been found to produce more than their share of the opiates that elevate mood. Presumably these chemicals help keep them on an even keel emotionally. For them to achieve the same level of arousal as their sensation-seeking cousins, they just have to sit tight. In fact, too much stimulation could quickly raise their level of brain chemicals past the saturation point.

If so, this probably explains why low-sensation seekers have typically been found to be what is called "reducers" of external stimuli. They are aroused enough inside as it is. This also could be why so many creative people who are so daring in their art seem such slaves to routine in their personal lives; Marcel Proust, hiding out in his cork-lined chamber, or Thomas Hardy, who was said to resemble a retired railway conductor. Perhaps those who in their imagination are already climbing mountains and conducting symphonies don't need to do so in fact, but do have a need to balance their inner excitement with outer tranquility.

What this suggests is that when it comes to seeking or avoiding stimulation by seeking or avoiding risk, our outer behavior is a perfect mirror of our inner systems. Tuned down inside, we try to tune up by our actions. Aroused within, we seek calm without. Balance is the common goal.

If Level II types do have more than their share of nature's opiates, their risk would be to put this wealth of endorphins in danger. Just as a Level I type may be looking for ways to pump more endorphins to head off depression, his cousin at the second level is trying to avoid giving any up so as not to be depressed.

There is evidence that the most effective way to reduce the endorphin levels of Level II types is to separate them from loved ones. Experiments at Ohio's Bowling Green University have found that when they are injected with an endorphin antidote, chicks and baby guinea pigs begin to squeal and cry in exactly the same way that they do when taken from their mother. By contrast, chicks and pups who are already crying because separated from their mother stop doing so altogether once injected with an endorphinlike opiate. So an excess of natural opiates may be central to strong dependency needs. The deprivation of such opiates could underlie feelings of panic upon separation from a loved one.

If so, as opposed to Level I types who look for peaks to scale to increase their endorphin flow, Level II types try to keep their attachments solid to make sure that their flow isn't decreased. To them there is risk in the extreme from the danger of losing such attachments and the endorphins they guarantee.

In his book *The Chemistry of Love*, psychiatrist Michael Liebowitz suggests that this could be the biochemical underpinning of what we call "separation anxiety." In other words, that the warm, secure feeling we get in the presence of a parent or other loved one may be due in part to the generous flow of opiates guaranteed by their presence. And that those who grow to depend on such feelings are the ones most likely to suffer extreme anxiety when the chemical flow that underlies them is interrupted. This is their risk. To such a person, the panicky, painful quality of such separation anxiety resembles narcotic withdrawal. It may literally be that.

To summarize: for more than 99 percent of human existence, danger, fear, and the need to confront fear were our daily companions. We were risk takers because we had to be. In response, our systems adapted at two levels: in the short term by releasing tonic brain chemicals; and in the long run by coming to depend on a constant flow of such chemicals that resulted from lasting human ties.

Both approaches involve risk: the first, short-term and physical; the second, long-term and psychic. Ideally the ability to take both types of risk is balanced within each of us. We all need a blend of excitement and security, adventure and community. But in recent centuries our ability to substitute anxiety for fear has reduced the need for either response to danger. As a result, both our nervous systems and our social bonds are creaky from disuse. We suffer from risk hunger.

Without always realizing why, we do seek risk — if only to keep our bodies tuned. (One theory about the origins of war is that once the excitement of hunting was replaced by the tedium of farming, we beat our plowshares into swords and began to attack each other out of sheer boredom.) Inevitably most of us look for risk more at one level than the other. Then our systems follow suit, becoming more adapted to Level I or Level II type risks. As a result, most of us are out of balance, far better suited to taking risks at one level than the other.

This is why our perception, assessment, and choice of risks to take or avoid has as much to do with temperament as pluck. The real risk is in going against one's need for more or less arousal. When we think of what it means to "take a big risk," we usually think first of something like a retiring civil servant leaving his family and going off to climb the Himalayas. For such a person, that probably would be a big risk. But equally risky, if not more so, would be a climber of the Himalayas committing him- or herself to something or someone ongoing; having a family, say, and becoming a civil servant.

It's futile and beside the point to try to judge which level of risk is riskier. As Marvin Zuckerman points out, those with high or low needs for stimulation have such different perceptions of danger and concepts of risk that it's difficult even to find a basis for comparison. But in this society especially, when we talk about "risk takers," Level I types are the ones we usually mean.

LEVEL I

RISK TAKING

The great object of life is sensation — to feel that we exist, even though in pain. It is this "craving void" which drives us to gaming — to battle, to travel — to intemperate, but keenly felt pursuits of any description, whose principal attraction is the agitation inseparable from the accomplishment.

— BYRON

Let's begin this section with a quiz. Match the description of an activity on the left (identifying details are omitted) with the activity itself on the right.

1. There was a buildup of tension as I contemplated the danger . . . , then a rush of excitement at the moment of [action], and finally a delicious sense of release.

    a. skydiving
    b. shoplifting
    c. streaking
    d. hang gliding
    e. combat

2. First the sense of daring, then the nervous anticipation . . . the last, fleeting moment of fear before you start . . . the pounding heart during . . . and the warm sense of accomplishment at your goal.

3. I ached with fear. . . . During . . . fear vanished and in its place came a feeling of cold resolution, cunning, and ruthlessness. When _____was over . . . a deep, rich sense of joy made my body tingle.

4. I was scared. . . . For the next four seconds, I blacked out from pure terror. . . . From that point on, it was smooth sailing . . . a sense of complete relaxation, a denouement after the long buildup of tension . . . not unlike the fulfillment one feels after a sexual climax.

5. It's like asking someone to go to bed with you. A feeling of being afraid, then a rush.

ANSWERS: 1-b; 2-c; 3-e; 4-a; 5-d.

As this quiz suggests, there are stages common to Level I risk taking of many kinds: tension beforehand, concentration during, and elation followed by profound relief once the actual danger has passed.

The best term we have for such feelings overall is "intensity." This is the way veterans of combat describe the bittersweet temptations of life under fire when each day stands out in vivid detail because it might be your last. Most of us (with luck) will never find out exactly what they mean. But we did survive high school. And "intense" is the word most often used to describe those three or four years. Some call these "the best years of your life." The assumption seems to be that any experience that memorable must have been happy. This is inaccurate — for most of us. High school for most of us was miserable: frightening, degrading, embarrassing. But it was *intense*, therefore memorable, and missed.

Dedicated as we are to the pursuit of happiness, Americans have trouble making sense of experiences that are both traumatic and tempting. When it comes to taking risks, our confusion mounts. As good Americans, we're supposed to take risks *and* we're supposed to be happy. Yet the two seldom go hand in hand. At the first level in particular, taking risks has little to do with positive outlooks, happy endings, or success of any kind except successful excitement. And excitement is far more likely to be found in experiences that promise danger and fear than happiness. If anything, happiness is a bit of a bore.

"Nothing is harder to bear than a series of good days," Goethe once observed. At some level we all know this. Who doesn't thrill to the promise of a siren? Or become aroused by a tornado warning? Everyone yearns for a little calamity, ideally not lethal, to rescue us from a day like any other. "Are we afraid quiet afternoons will be interrupted by gunfire?" asked Walker Percy in *The Second Coming.* "Or do we hope they will?

"Was there ever a truly uneventful time, years of long afternoons when nothing happened and people were glad of it?"

One of the principal traits distinguishing Level I from Level II types is that the former don't feel guilty about enjoying bad news. First-level risk takers are closer to our early forebears in making little distinction between positive and negative aspects of intense experience. It is not their level of fear but their attitude toward fear that distinguishes Level I and Level II risk takers. Marvin Zuckerman has found that the same type of arousal will be labeled "anxiety" by low-sensation seekers and "excitement" by high ones. Those who find sweaty palms, a racing heart, and tingling neck hairs exciting will seek out experiences that arouse such reactions. As Henry Fonda once reflected, the first time he stepped on a stage and felt his neck hairs rising, he knew that acting was for him.

This taste for fear shows up early. A woman who's now involved with scuba diving and aerobatics recalls of her childhood, "Fear and facing up to fear are among my most vivid memories. I used to do things on purpose — like climbing to the top of a tree I just fell out of, or terrorizing myself watching *Frankenstein.*" Adds race driver Dan Gerber, "As a child I loved violent weather. Clear, terrifying bolts of electricity snaking to the horizon, potentially devastating winds, and dam-bursting down-pours put me in ecstasy."

A mother tells me that at the age of three her youngest son stuck a butter knife into an electrical outlet and got a hair-raising shock for his efforts. If fear breeds avoidance, this boy should have developed a lifelong wariness of electrical outlets. Instead he kept coming back to the same outlet, knife at the ready. To him the danger of being shocked was obviously more exciting than inhibiting. Now grown, this is the son who plays rock music for a living and rafts white water for sport.

As a child, the late Lenny Bruce recalled loving "confusion": blizzards, electrical failures, stopped-up toilets flowing over into the hallway. To him, serving in World War II was rewarding because it felt the same way. But once the war ended, Bruce found peacetime service so tedious that he went AWOL. As the comedian later explained, "I was not as afraid of being killed in battle as I was of being bored. . . . While the war was on, the alternation of routine and confusion sustained my interest, but then it was over and I wanted out."

A low threshold of boredom is the main trait Level I types have in common. *Arousal* is the principal goal of their varied pursuits. This is why the rest of us can be so perplexed by the seemingly illogical, antisocial, and even self-destructive nature of so much Level I activity. As those engaged in it know too well, when the system needs a goose, concepts such as bad and good, constructive or destructive, positive versus negative are beside the point. The body doesn't care. To an understimulated body, one source of arousal is literally as good as another (pre-sumably because it opens the faucet of endorphins into a parched nervous system). If anything, at the first level, experiences we call "negative" may be preferred to those we call "positive," simply because they're more likely to be dangerous, therefore scary, and stimulating.

With our taste for self-improvement and happy endings, this is a bitter pill for Americans to swallow. We have a fundamental problem in coming to grips with the fact that so many of us prefer the powerful charge of illicit risks to the mild static of more acceptable varieties. Rather than face the fact that many of us engage in destructive behavior for the simple sake of excitement, we look instead for explanations based on masochism, self-destructiveness, or wishing for death. But even Theodore Reik, the bard of masochism, emphasized that actually hurting themselves is seldom the goal of those he called masochists; the excitement of *risking* pain — even if self-inflicted — was their real goal. At the first level, pain, or death, is not the goal but the stakes one bets against excitement. Along the way distinctions between safety and danger, or even life and death, can grow blurry.

Those who work with would-be suicides have found that dying per se is not necessarily their goal. Many are simply gambling their lives in hopes of improving them. They are not seeking death so much as rebirth. The end of their life is not their goal so much as their risk.

In a biographical note on his friend, the successful suicide Sylvia Plath, A. Alvarez suggested that the poet didn't really expect to die in the process. "She had always been a bit of a gambler," explained Alvarez,

> used to taking risks. The authority of her poetry was in part due to her brave persistence in following the thread of her inspiration right down to the minotaur's lair. And this psychic courage had its parallel in her physical arrogance and carelessness. Risks didn't frighten her: on the contrary, she found them stimulating. Freud has written: "Life loses in interest when the highest stakes in the game of living, life itself, may not be risked." Finally, Sylvia took that risk. She gambled for the last time, having worked out that the odds were in her favor, but perhaps, in her depression, not much caring whether she won or lost. Her calculations went wrong and she lost.

Among twenty-four survivors of wrist-slashing, one study found that most described the experience in terms little different from those of anyone braving danger: rising tension before the act, intense concentration during (so intense that few even felt any pain while cutting their wrists, and only realized they'd actually done so when they saw blood), followed by a feeling of relief so profound that afterward many reported being able to relax and sleep for the first time in days, or weeks. Some compared the relief to that following intercourse, the act to sex itself.

Autopsies done on the brains of successful suicides have found that many of them have far fewer "receptor" sites capable of responding to antidepressant medicines and presumably their own opiates as well. This reinforces the conviction of suicidologists that many of those who try to kill themselves are less interested in dying than in risking death to break out of a chronically bored state.

As a young man, Graham Greene played Russian roulette. Had he lost this gamble, his death would have been recorded as self-inflicted. But as the novelist has written, "This was not suicide, whatever a coroner's jury might have said: it was a gamble with five chances to one against an inquest."

Greene describes himself as suffering from lifelong chronic depression. Or as he calls it, "boredom sickness." In his early manhood this feeling became so acute that for respite he was prepared to fight as a mercenary on either side of any conflict "so long as I was repaid with excitement and a little risk."

Instead, Greene played Russian roulette. Here is how the novelist has described his first experience of that game:

> I put the muzzle of the revolver into my right ear and pulled the trigger. There was a minute click, and looking down at the chamber I could see that the charge had moved into the firing position. I was out by one. I remember the extraordinary sense of jubilation, as if carnival lights had been switched on in a dark, drab street. My heart knocked in its cage, and life contained an infinite number of possibilities. It was like a young man's first successful experience of sex.

Later, Greene found himself enjoying immensely the three blitzes he survived in London. Not only did feeling afraid lift the clouds of despair, but it made him downright randy as well. "Fear has an odd seduction," he wrote. "Fear and the sense of sex are linked in secret conspiracy."

This is yet another bonus of the arousal reward for taking Level I risks: their power to act as an aphrodisiac.

A reporter once described for psychologist Albert Ellis how surprised she was by her response to being threatened with physical mayhem by a burly operator of unauthorized methadone clinics she was investigating. Her response was to want to go to bed with him. Was this perverted? To the contrary, said Ellis. Feeling afraid often produces a sexual response. He himself could recall getting an erection when he was scared he wouldn't pass an algebra board in college.

When Albert Kinsey's colleague Glenn Ramsey took erotic histories from 291 adolescent boys, half of them reported having been stimulated to erection by nonsexual events. According to Ramsey, such events "usually involved elements of fear, excitement or other emotional situations." Among them were carnival rides, accidents or near accidents, watching war movies, watching soldiers march, riding in an airplane, being chased by the police, playing a musical solo, losing balance when on heights, reciting before class, taking tests, being late to school, playing in exciting games, watching big fires, fast car rides, electrical shocks, setting a field afire, looking over the edge of a building, and reading adventure stories.

As far back as Aristotle, it's been noted that sexual arousal can be one response to fear. As a French psychiatrist has pointed out, his countrymen use the term "*afoler*" interchangeably as "to cause anxiety" and "to excite sexually." Their phrase "*tu m'affolles*" can mean both "you are making me anxious" and "you arouse me to the point of orgasm." And lest we forget, the term "risk" itself evolved from the French "risque" and was spelled that way well into the nineteenth century.

The sexiness of fear is a point grasped far better by novelists, amusement-ride designers, and Level I risk takers of all kinds than by most psychologists, to whom fear and sexual arousal have generally been held incompatible. Before we make love, they usually say, we must stop being afraid. In an interesting refutation of their colleagues' wisdom, sexologists William Masters and Philip Sarrel once studied a group of eleven male victims of "rape" by women. Presumably this crime would be nearly impossible to consummate because fear in the men — most of whom were threatened with weapons — would make penile erection unlikely. In fact, all eleven victims not only were able to get erections and perform sexually, but some got repeated erections and performed rather well. Only later did impotence set in as a reaction. But while in a state of alarm, concluded Masters and Sarrel, contrary to accepted dogma, for some men "fear contributes to sexual excitation."

So how did it come to pass that psychologists have told us fear is the saltpeter of sex, not its Spanish Fly? And why do psychologists, as two of their number have noted, "almost never . . . acknowledge that it is fun to be frightened; that it's enjoyable to have a strong emotional response; that reactions to danger can be labeled in positive as well as negative ways; that excitement is an antidote to boredom"?

Marvin Zuckerman has an interesting response to this question. Most of his colleagues, suggests the psychologist, and analysts in particular, are low-sensation seekers. From their perspective, anyone who needs a high level of stimulation to stay aroused has a problem. They need to be "cured" of their need for sensation, because by seeking sensation in such hazardous forms, they've demonstrated clearly their self-destructive tendencies.

But as we've seen, seeking sensation has more to do with arousal, even sexual arousal, than it does with self-destruction. There are other rewards as well that Level I risk takers enjoy as a bonus for their derring-do. Since, other than arousal itself, such rewards all begin with the letter *C*, I call them the "C-virtues" for taking risks at the first level: control, concentration, calm, camaraderie, and character.

CONTROL

After racing a Ferrari 308GTS from coast to coast at outrageous speeds, writer P. J. O'Rourke reported, "There is no more profound feeling of control over one's destiny that I have ever experienced than to drive a Ferrari down a public road at 130 miles an hour."

If that doesn't make any sense to you, you're probably not much of a Level I risk taker. Among those who are, taking charge of their own lives is routinely put high on the list of rewards for seeking excitement. As the skydivers say, after you exit a plane but before you pull the ripcord, your life is in your own hands.

It's a psychological commonplace that the risks we feel we control are less frightening than those we don't. This is why, for example, so many more people are scared of flying than driving, even though the latter is demonstrably more dangerous. But with a steering wheel in our hands, we just feel in greater control of the situation than with an in-flight magazine. And psychologically speaking, a feeling of control is equivalent to actual control.

It's also well known that those who feel they have more control over their own lives are less likely to have accidents, commit suicide, or engage in extreme behavior of any kind. In a seeming paradox, these facts are related: taking extreme and even death-defying risks can actually reduce one's sense of being at risk because it increases a sense of control over one's own destiny.

Creating a little environment of hazard that feels controllable for many makes far more sense than sitting tight, waiting for the bombs to fall. One way of looking at an act such as climbing a mountain or crossing the Atlantic in a dinghy is as a personal response to the impersonal dangers of missiles overhead and dioxin at our feet. Fear is sought because (unlike anxiety) it feels as if it is subject to our will. In islands of created danger, the danger creator is king.

Such danger can be physical, but it doesn't have to be. In a study of those engaged in activities ranging from professional dancing to rock climbing, psychologist Mihaly Csikszentmihalyi found that their sense of control over a perilous situation was central to the satisfaction participants reported. One chess player explained that while playing in tournaments he felt "in complete control of my world." And rock climbers said that it wasn't the danger of their sport as such that tempted them but the feeling of mastery they gained through coping with its dangers. Second only to such feelings of control while climbing rocks were the rewards of concentration that the activity demanded.

CONCENTRATION

"When I start on a climb," one climber told Csikszentmihalyi, "it's as if my memory input had been cut off. All I can remember is the last thirty seconds, and all I can think ahead is the next five minutes. . . . With tremendous concentration the normal world is forgotten."

Even the nonlethal feelings of jeopardy felt by a dancer while performing or by a chess player in a tournament demanded a total concentration that the participants welcomed, noted the psychologist. Among all of those he studied, Csikszentmihalyi found that at the peak of their efforts, concentration could become so total that it resembled a state of religious transcendence. I've found the same thing. From comedians to motorcyclists, I've heard descriptions of trancelike feelings during moments of peril in which time seems to slow, detachment feels serene, and concentration is absolute. This implies that for many of us the urge to seek danger may differ little from the wish to be creative. Anyone in jeopardy may enjoy exactly the same feeling of complete absorption felt by an artist at work. We can't all paint a picture, but anyone can take a chance.

The ability to concentrate may sound like a meager reward for putting yourself in jeopardy. But in a world of ringing telephones, bills coming due, crying children, honking horns, changing traffic lights, watches, clocks, ten-second spots on the radio, and television's shifting images, anything that commands our complete attention brings relief.

As part of my research for this book, I joined a rock-climbing group on three separate occasions. This was not something I'd ever done before and with luck will never do again. The amount of tension and fear I felt while *concentrating* on squeezing my fingers into barely visible cracks of granite 50 feet off the ground or casting my feet about looking for quarter-inch ledges on which to stand is not my idea of a relaxing day in the out-of-doors. However: I can't remember when I've felt so able to concentrate, so relaxed, so calm all around as I did the day *after* each outing. Not just my mind but my entire body, my skin, even my fingernails felt relieved of tension in a way I've rarely experienced as an adult. Furthermore, the day following the last climb — 70 feet of sheer terror — was by far the most serene of the three. After finishing that climb I'd remarked to one of the instructors that I couldn't imagine scaling cliffs for fun. The day after, it wasn't hard to imagine at all.

CALM

There's something about raising your levels of fear and tension that ultimately releases them. Among the least appreciated and most valued rewards for seeking stress is the calm that follows. This is what rock climbers, performers, and skydivers all say. As the survivor of a first parachute jump once noted of his drive home from the airport, "I did not speed, or at least there was no desire to speed. Another change I noted was that when I put on the tape recorder, I did not want to hear it loud."

The military has even found that some paratroopers respond to the tension of jumping by relaxing so completely afterward that they fall asleep. In this sense the term "stress seeker" is something of a misnomer. One of the main reasons for seeking stress is to enjoy the subsequent tranquility.

Once fear is resolved, tension is peeled away. Everyone grows more attractive after danger passes. The pressure of fear literally twists faces out of shape from tension, then restores them to a smoother, more relaxed, and younger countenance in the calm afterglow.

You see each other differently during and after the sharing of danger — more accurately, I'd say. Few people can keep up appearances in the midst of calamity. I think that's one reason we avoid taking risks — for fear someone might catch a glimpse of us. Yet this is one of the great attractions of even contrived danger. While sharing such experiences with others, our fears, quirks, and hidden strengths surface. A sense of brotherhood follows — because everyone has seen everyone else naked, so to speak. The union we feel with others at such moments can be nearly religious.

CAMARADERIE

"Camaraderie" is the name most often given this feeling of union. Men especially find it one of the principal rewards for seeking danger with others. As Antoine de Saint-Exupéry wrote of the brotherhood of pilots in peace and war:

> Men travel side by side for years, each locked up in his own silence or exchanging those words which carry no freight — till danger comes. Then they stand shoulder to shoulder. They discover that they belong to the same family. They wax and bloom in the recognition of fellow beings. They look at one another and smile. . . .
>
> And these human relations must be created. One must go through an apprenticeship to learn the job. Games and risk are a help here. When we exchange manly handshakes, compete in races, join together to save one of us who is in trouble, cry aloud for help in the hour of danger — only then do we learn that we are not alone on the earth.

One of the great attractions of sports is the brotherhood it builds. It's ironic: the playing field is supposed to be a place where we revert to our more brutal selves; yet when retired athletes describe what they miss most from their sport, the camaraderie of the locker room invariably gets mentioned before the playing field itself.

A fundamental quality of the camaraderie forged by sharing risk is that it needn't have anything to do with *liking* the other members. As Philip Caputo said of the brotherhood of soldiers in Vietnam, "The communion between men is as profound as any between lovers. Actually, it is more so. It does not demand for its sustenance the reciprocity, the pledges of affection, the endless reassurances required by the love of men and women." (Caputo presumably had read his *All Quiet on the Western Front*, in which Erich Maria Remarque writes of two soldiers sitting by a fire between battles, "We don't talk much, but I believe we have a more complete communion with one another than even lovers have.")

Caputo went on to say that the reason he and so many others went to Vietnam in the first place was "one that has pushed young men into armies ever since armies were invented: I needed to prove something — my courage, my toughness, my manhood, call it whatever you like."

CHARACTER

As is often noted, since most soldiers are on the brink of manhood, war can be their rite of passage. This is one of the great appeals of death-defying challenges of all kinds. The need to take even lethal chances as a test of character is especially strong between child- and adulthood. Knowing this, nearly every society for most of time has provided its young with rites of passage. Such rites usually involve deliberate, often harrowing stress created by such means as scarring the adolescents' bodies, isolating them during first menstruation, or even sending them through a gauntlet of club-swinging adults.

As a relatively new and more "enlightened" culture, we offer our young little more than a driver's test with which to prove their right to be an adult. As a result, few of us grow up with any sense of having been tested. I once asked a group of American adults what for them felt most like a rite of passage out of adolescence. Getting a driver's license was mentioned most often. Having teeth braces removed came up more than once. One man found some recognition of his manhood in the solicitations he began to receive after age eighteen to buy cigarettes, razor blades, or subscriptions to men's magazines.

Women in particular found making love a rite. "If there's any doubt in your mind that you're no longer five years old," said a thirty-year-old mother about her first sex at nineteen, "that takes care of it." Another woman said that she ritualized this occasion further by treating herself afterward to a patty melt at Denny's restaurant. To this day, she said, the flavor of medium-rare hamburger topped with melted cheese on rye always mingles deliciously with first sex in her mind.

What was lacking in the examples mentioned was any clear sense that their mettle had been tested and good character confirmed. For this reason there was little satisfaction involved in "passing" those tests that seemed like rites. As a middle-aged minister finally said after searching his memory unsuccessfully for some rite of passage into manhood, "I don't think I ever had one. I'm still an adolescent."

So this is a final, and profound, reason for taking risks at the first level: as proof of one's character.

Character in this sense has little to do with goodness. It's closer to what's called "heart" on the street, or "moxie," or what Tom Wolfe calls "the right stuff." As Samuel Johnson put it, "Courage is a quality so necessary for maintaining virtue that it is always respected even when it is associated with vice."

The need to confirm our good character can be present at any age, particularly if we feel this didn't happen during adolescence. But during adolescence especially, the hunger for heroism rivals that for sex. Often the best and sometimes the only means to be heroic are antisocial or self-destructive. In the absence of worthy challenges, any kind will do.

Psychiatrist Thomas Szasz points to the self-testing that can be involved in even such flagrantly self-destructive activities as smoking cigarettes, popping pills, or drinking to excess. In Szasz's opinion, those engaged in such activity usually know quite well the harm they risk doing to themselves. But precisely because they are so potentially harmful, self-destructive risks play an important role to us as what he calls "sham adversaries." To test our mettle, those of us who abuse such substances will first consume, then try to master them ("hold your liquor," etc.). In this distorted and futile way, we challenge ourselves to continual tests of character gone awry.

Sham adversaries don't even have to be as destructive as alcohol or drugs. One's very weight can become such an adversary, providing the opportunity to engage in gallant struggles to lose it. For some women especially, dieting to excess feels like their only chance to be heroic. Even *anorexia nervosa* — the nonsensical self-starving engaged in mostly by teenaged girls — can make perfect sense to them as a demonstration that at a time when little else seems subject to their control, they can at least control the shape of their own bodies. This is known as a key reason for engaging in such radical dieting. And as a former anorexic once told me, something that the rest of us will never understand is how *exciting* the struggle can be to lose that much weight.

As in so many first-level risks, engaging sham adversaries may appear to be simple masochism but actually has more to do with some or all of the rewards we get for taking even outrageous risks. The explainable motivations for behavior that seems inexplicable set a context for the next four chapters on different forms of Level I risk taking. From the outside, most such activities appear self-destructive. They may include that element. But the typical Level I risk taker doesn't care much one way or the other about self-harm. Given the option, most would rather stay alive and whole. But if seeking excitement and the rewards for excitement (control, concentration, calm, camaraderie) call for risking their well-being, they will take that risk. At one time or another most of us will take apparently inexplicable risks — just to stir up some action. In the absence of natural challenges with which to bring boredom to its knees, we seek the best challenges we can find. We may even create some. I call this "Stirring the Pot."

STIRRING THE POT

W hen I think about what it means to stir the pot, Kay Collins*
comes to mind.

A shapely, good-natured redhead with a huge smile, Kay left
Iowa at twenty-five to sample the mysteries of southern California. Within a year after settling in Long Beach, she had left her
husband, taken up with a biker, and consumed an astonishing
menu of drugs. Eventually Kay settled in with the bartender at
the nightclub where she made her living as a topless dancer.

To outer appearances, Kay Collins had changed very little.
She still was an unassuming, fun-loving woman who looked like
she'd recently plowed the south forty. Kay just had this other
life. "I loved almost every part of it," Kay says of that life. "I
wouldn't trade that part of my life for anything. I feel like I grew
up during those five years in Long Beach."

Kay Collins describes herself as someone who doesn't plan too
far ahead. "As long as things are going good," she says, "I hang
around to see what will happen next. I get bored easily so I need
risks of some kind in my life. Maybe this is true of everybody,
but most of the risks I have taken have been out of desperation
for a change due to boredom. As soon as things get easy and
good, I tend to get bored and search out something new."

Kay puts leaving Iowa in that category. After eight years of
marriage, she and her husband Charley were bored with each

* A pseudonym.

other. At least she was bored with him. They'd married right out of high school. Four years later, while Charley was overseas for a year in the service, Kay began to realize how much she had missed by marrying so young. During that year she often would go to the drive-in. Her favorite movies were the ones with titles such as *Rebel Rousers, Wild Angels,* and *Hell's Angels on Wheels.* The way of life they portrayed looked very interesting. Certainly more interesting than her own.

Soon after arriving in Long Beach, Kay got a job as the book-keeper for a motorcycle parts shop. A lot of its customers looked like people she used to see on the drive-in screen back in Iowa. They wore heavy black boots, greasy jeans, and cutoff Levi's jackets. Kay would peek out at them from her little office in the rear. "All I could think about was all those biker movies I had seen in the drive-ins," she recalls, "and wonder if any of these people were really like those people."

Kay had left Charley by now. She began to spend a lot of time with the bike shop's owner, Cowboy Joe. Their main source of entertainment was getting high. When he needed to hide from the law or from enemies, Joe came over and stayed at the little apartment that Kay had rented. Soon he moved in with her. Then Joe began taking Kay to bars with long rows of Harley-Davidson motorcycles lined up neatly outside like so many black and silver dominoes.

It wasn't long before Kay was riding with some of the Harleys' owners. Joe wasn't really a biker, and she took up with Big Barney, who was. Kay rode with Barney and his friends for two years.

As she looks back on that period, Kay recalls being scared a lot. She wasn't scared of being hurt on a motorcycle so much as of being busted and having to go to jail. Many of the people she was riding with didn't look too safe, either. "Let's face it," she admits. "Some of them were pretty scuzzy."

But Kay realizes that the danger was part of that life's appeal. "I'm not sure it was sexual," she says, "although I did more sexual things when I was riding with the bikers. For example, we were at Mammoth for a weekend cookout. Barney and I had had one hundred Seconal between us. Of course we got into fights and all kinds of crap because of being so redded out. One of the nights, he thought I was in the woods pouting. In fact I was on top of a hill in a little lean-to getting it on with another guy, whose girlfriend was down by the camp fire."

After taking so many drugs one night that she passed out with the stove on and nearly burned her apartment down, Kay began to wonder if her biker period hadn't run its course. Soon she quit working at the parts shop, broke up with Barney, and began to look for a new adventure.

The opportunity soon presented itself in the form of an amateur topless contest at the Two-Step Club in Long Beach. Kay was on unemployment by then and having trouble making ends meet. Amateur contestants got $25 each, so she and a friend went down to the Two-Step one night, hoping at least to overcome their inhibitions long enough to earn the money.

Just inside the bar's door, Kay nearly backed out. "I was scared to death," she recalls. "I don't think I was so much scared of dancing topless as inhibited and brainwashed; nice girls don't." After stiffening her resolve with some tequila from her purse, Kay entered the Two-Step. Through the smoky haze she could see a half-dressed woman standing on the bar, wiggling clumsily to music from the jukebox. Soon that woman was replaced by Kay's girlfriend, then by Kay herself. "I couldn't be shown up by her," Kay explains of what finally got her dancing.

In later years, Mike the bartender used to kid Kay about her topless dance. He and the Two-Step's owner watched this well-built redhead who was so nervous and so drunk that they were afraid she would stumble off the bar and into the liquor bottles.

But Kay finished her dance and many more as she went on to make her living for the next two years as a regular at the Two-Step. "After the initial shock," she says, "I couldn't get enough of the place. Dancing topless was easy and fun."

This was how Kay rounded out her West Coast sojourn: dancing topless at a nightclub, moving in with the bartender, and partying in her spare time.

With the benefit of several years' hindsight, Kay says reviewing that part of her life is "like looking at somebody else. It's all very vivid in my mind, but I don't think I could do it again. I wouldn't have missed it for the world, but once was enough. The whole situation enabled me to shed my morals and try all kinds of things that I always thought dirty or nasty. It was fun. I'm glad I did them. I'm only sorry it took so much booze and drugs to get me that way."

Kay Collins is an advanced practitioner of the art we all practice to one degree or another: stirring the pot. This refers to activities engaged in more for the sake of excitement than for any apparent goal. Such activities can be conscious or unconscious, blatant or disguised, big or small. Most come under the heading of what Desmond Morris calls "creating unnecessary problems which you can then solve." This could mean stirring up a relationship for the sheer thrill of working things out. Or jaywalking just ahead of traffic to see if you can make it across the street alive. Or putting things off until the last minute to enjoy the thrill of coming in just under the wire.

Something punctual people will never understand is how exciting it can be to dawdle around the house until the last minute, then make a mad dash to the station and leap onto a train with seconds to spare. Or to stay up all night completing a report you've been putting off for six months and then turn it in all red-eyed the next morning. It's not that you couldn't have done it sooner. But where's the challenge?

Throughout the day we all engage in what I call "risklets" — little acts of daring that pump tiny drops of adrenaline. One friend of mine waits until shower water has collected beneath his feet before turning on an exposed light switch in his bathroom. Another man repairs his home's wiring without turning off the current because he enjoys the added challenge.

In response to some risklets I asked about on my questionnaire, 49 percent of those who filled it out said that they have used a fork or knife to get a stuck piece of bread out of the toaster without first unplugging it. Eighty-eight percent jaywalk; 74 percent cut toward themselves with a knife. And like my friend, 24 percent admit to turning on electrical appliances while in a bath or shower.

Here are some other little stirrings of the pot that were listed on the questionnaire, with the percentages of those who engage in them:

- leaving home on a dark, cloudy day without a raincoat or umbrella (79 percent)
- driving a car whose gas gauge registers EMPTY (69 percent)
- striking a match from a folder without first closing the cover (66 percent)
- driving through a STOP sign late at night at an uncrowded intersection (47 percent)
- drinking a beer while driving (43 percent)
- operating a garbage disposal without a lid (38 percent)
- lighting a gas oven that has been on for several seconds (37 percent)
- standing on the platform between two cars of a moving train (36 percent)
- putting off paying bills you can afford to pay until threatening notices begin to arrive (29 percent)
- operating a power lawn mower while barefoot or in sandals (24 percent)
- smoking a marijuana cigarette while walking along the street (24 percent)

Some risklets written in the space marked "other" included: walking at night in tough parts of town; driving through one-way streets or tunnels the wrong way; changing the radio dial while driving; roller-skating in New York traffic; using tools or machinery without proper safeguards; ironing during a lightning storm; drinking beer with the pop-top inside the can; and operating a motorcycle or an airplane "no hands."

Obviously, few such activities are likely to get you sent to Bellevue or San Quentin, or to harm you in any way. But they do move the day along. And your nervous system appreciates the stimulation. "It clears all the cobwebs out of your head," explains singer Billy Joel of why he likes riding a motorcycle. "Terror chess," he calls the experience. "When you get off the bike, it's, 'Whew, I made it!' " Within weeks of an accident that nearly ended his career, the singer was back on his Harley.

To the confirmed pot stirrer, *not* taking such chances involves greater risks than taking them — especially the risk of boredom. We're too quick to assume that when given a clear choice between dangerous and safe activity, an intelligent, informed person will choose safe. And that when people do engage in risky behavior, it's because they're self-destructive or ignorant of the hazards involved.

On the page after a *Newsweek* feature on "The Thrill Seekers," a public service ad promotes literacy. The visual tease of this ad is a photograph of three children climbing over a fence. This fence is posted with a sign reading DANGER! HIGH VOLTAGE! KEEP OUT! "Kids who don't read," began the ad copy, "don't get the message." It's funny; I saw that picture, and before reading the copy assumed that the kids could read, that they did get the message. And that this was why they were climbing the fence.

Those responsible for supervising such dangerous settings are faced with a dilemma. Strong warnings are potent magnets for young bodies in need of a challenge. But when kids accept the challenge and get hurt, suits often are filed arguing that warnings weren't strong enough. As a Federal Railroad Administration spokesman noted about a suit filed by the parents of a child severely injured in a railroad yard, "You knew it was dangerous. The children knew it was dangerous. That's why they were there."

The fatality rate for the fifteen-to-twenty-four-year-old age group is currently the only one going up instead of down. Accidental deaths now account for 80 percent of all fatalities in that age group, up from 50 percent in 1950. For middle-class youths, more such accidents occur in cars than in any other setting. The reason for this carnage is not that adolescent drivers are any less capable than older ones. Rather, it's that they belong to a group with lots to prove and few tools better than cars with which to prove it. Trying to reduce their accident rate by improving driving skills or warning that they could die by driving recklessly is not only an ineffective deterrent but may even make reckless driving that much more appealing.

David Klein of Michigan State University is one of the few safety experts to take seriously the appeal of dangerous driving to young men in particular. As Klein points out, what to adult eyes looks like reckless, thrill-seeking, and self-destructive behavior is something else altogether to a teenaged driver. The teenager is simply trying to conform to group standards and prove himself worthy of membership. If it takes reckless driving to do so, then this is what it takes. But recklessness isn't the goal; the goal is to be found worthy — of good character — by the people who really matter: your peers.

To young drivers, cars have become the best means possible to engage in what's been archly termed "expressive self-testing." The primary inspirations for such testing are one's parents (boring), other adult drivers (boring), friends (interesting), and the Dukes of Hazzard (*very* interesting). From sources such as these, young men of driving age have learned, in David Klein's words, "that the 'real man' is one who is tough, ingenious, and willing to take risks. Yet what aspects of his life can be coped with effectively through toughness, ingenuity, or risk taking?"

The answer, for too many, is driving.

And Klein is a pessimist. Rather than teenagers becoming more like adults in their driving habits, he sees adults becoming more like teenagers. Certainly car ads are geared in that direction, with their appeals to excitement, exhilaration, and *awesome* power. With adults no less than with teenagers, it's clear that scare tactics are something less than effective when it comes to improving in-car behavior. After years of lurid warnings about what might happen to us if we didn't buckle up, the use of seat belts has actually declined. Rational as they are, such warnings are based on a limited, mistaken, and ineffective concept of what motivates human behavior.

It's plain by now that the vast majority of those who don't use seat belts, or who smoke, know the fate they're tempting. It's not as if they just happened to *overlook* the warning on their package of cigarettes. If it's not ignorance that motivates such willing self-exposure to danger, what is it? Delusions of immortality? I'm sure that has a lot to do with it. Subliminal death wishes? Doubtless that's true of some. But we're talking about over three-quarters of American drivers who continue on their unbuckled way, and 53 million Americans who blow smoke at the Surgeon General's warning. Are they all self-deluding masochists?

To a nonsmoker, the regular inhalation of tar and nicotine into one's lungs may only seem explainable by the self-destruction rationale. But as an ex-smoker, I can assure you that the rewards for this activity make far more sense from the inside looking out than from the outside looking in. Like so many smokers, I acquired this habit during my early teens as a down payment on growing up. I can still remember how terrible my first cigarette — and quite a few thereafter — tasted at age twelve. Why did I keep smoking? The usual reasons. To look older. To earn my place in a community I valued. And mostly because I wasn't supposed to.

As an adult, the realization that smoking could kill you becomes more of the same in a way. Not that you think you'll be the one to die, but knowing you might can make smoking cigarettes *more*, not less, appealing. Even if we don't imagine it's a risk we could lose, the danger of smoking is basic to its appeal. Not the danger as such, but the rewards for braving this danger. Camaraderie, for example. The sense of brotherhood smokers share is something nonsmokers will never understand. But the next time you're on a train or plane, notice who's having the most fun: playing cards, engaged in spirited conversation, wandering the aisles looking for action. It's always passengers in the smoking section. Like those of soldiers preparing for combat, the rituals of smokers — the offering and receiving of cigarettes, the sharing of matches, the putting of lips close to match and hand — build little human bonds. Such rituals are perfect icebreakers. ("Got a light?") Even more important is a simple awareness smokers share about the limitations of human reason. Members of this brotherhood not only smoke cigarettes together, they share the knowledge that they're willing to risk death to do so. This knowledge promotes rapport. As a smoker, you show your mettle — not only in daring death, but in flouting the growing taboo against smoking. Add the camaraderie of deviance to that of defying death and you have powerful rewards for those who smoke cigarettes.

These observations all come from an ex-smoker who doesn't miss that habit a bit, but does miss terribly the gang smoking cigarettes made him part of. Although it's been years since I last lit a cigarette, I still think of myself as allied with those who do. They're my kind of people.

During my first visit to an Atlantic City casino, I was struck by two things: how many of those who were there smoked, and how few smiled. On the faces of those huddled over slot machines, craps, or blackjack tables, or merely roaming the packed aisles, smiles were as rare as frowns at a beauty pageant. Intense, purposeful looks were the order of the day. After one young man threw up his drinks, his fellow gamblers were so intent on getting to the next game that many walked right through the fruits of his labor.

When I pointed out the grimness of this setting to my gambling friend Zack, he considered me as the *naïf* my comment suggested. Well, of course no one's smiling, Zack finally responded. Happiness isn't what people are here for. Gambling's too intense for that.

When I observed that some of the bunny cocktail waitresses seemed to really have to struggle to make their breasts stand out, Zack replied, "Oh yeah?" He hadn't noticed. This is not the sort of thing Zack usually overlooks. But, as Zack explained, when he's caught up in gambling, a tornado could strike the casino and he'd only take note if it blew away his cards.

Now that he mentioned it, I'd noticed that the closer we got to Atlantic City, the more tense with anticipation Zack had grown. Normally a heavy smoker, he now lit cigarettes in chains. After we entered the casino, he made a beeline for the first empty seat at a baccarat table, lost some money, switched to blackjack, lost more money. Ten minutes after we arrived, Zack was putting his last $20 into quarter slots, hoping to win back a grubstake. Soon that was gone as well. Our evening at the casino consisted of three hours of driving for fifteen minutes of gambling in which Zack lost money he couldn't afford to lose.

From my perspective the evening was a fiasco. But that's the perspective of someone who limits himself to $2 at quarter slots (when nickel ones aren't available). To Zack, losing his money wasn't that big a catastrophe. What *really* bothered him was losing it so fast. Then he had to stop gambling.

To the nongambler, winning money appears to be the main reason for placing bets. Either that or the self-punishment that some psychiatrists say is the underlying reason for placing bets you know you're likely to lose. To gamblers, however, neither money nor masochism has much to do with the real attractions of gambling. To them gambling is its own reward.

"Oh, it isn't money that's dear to me! . . ." says the hero of

Dostoyevsky's autobiographical novel *The Gambler*. "Even as I approach the gambling hall, as soon as I hear, still two rooms away, the jingle of money poured out on the table, I almost go into convulsions."

As he had already observed, "It is true that only one out of a hundred wins. But what do I care about that?"

To a confirmed gambler, winning is better than losing primarily because the more you win, the longer you get to play. This is why so many gamblers find it hard to pick up their winnings and leave. To them that's the real loss. Then they're out of the action.

As sixty-year-old Vincent Coda pointed out after he won $7.1 million in New York's Lotto game, "It will kind of take the fun out of playing the lottery."

Gamblers are fond of saying that the next best thing to winning is losing. And they're right: both winning and losing bets arouse feelings that are far more vivid than those enjoyed in the course of an average adult day. Some gamblers even find more to be said for losing a bet than winning one. As tragedy is to comedy, suggests actor-gambler Walter Matthau, when compared with pleasure the pain experienced by confirmed bettors is "bigger, larger, stronger. Therefore more interesting."

Aside from the 10 to 15 percent of gamblers who are compulsive, one could argue that for someone who needs regular stimulation there are worse alternatives than placing bets. Canadian psychologist Igor Kusyszyn has long argued that by dwelling exclusively on gambling addicts, his colleagues have paid too little attention to the very real rewards enjoyed by gambling hobbyists like himself, rewards he puts under the heading of "self-stimulation, self-testing, [and] arousal."

A University of Southern California graduate student named William McGlothin once spent several months among thirty-one women who were regulars at legal card clubs outside Los Angeles. These women, whose mean age was thirty-seven, gambled 13½ hours a week on the average. Most admitted to losing more often than winning. Since they seemed aware of the small potential for profit from their pastime, observed McGlothin, there must have been other reasons for engaging in it. He thought such reasons were likely to be neurotic. But when McGlothin administered a standard personality test to the thirty-one women and compared their results with national averages for those of their age and status, he found that "the women in this study are significantly *better* adjusted, on the average, than are the female adults in the general population" (emphasis added).

In speculating about why his predictions were confounded, McGlothin could only suggest that, far from underlying neurotic maladjustment, "to the extent that the game of poker offers a stimulating activity to occupy the participant's time and interest, it may well be an adjustive factor. . . . Several of the women in this study indicated that they had played poker for more than twenty-four hours at a single session. An activity that can maintain interest for such long periods of time is certainly a 'stimulating activity' for these individuals."

The women McGlothin studied were in legal card houses. Those who must break the law to gamble can find the action that much more appealing. For many, being "on the other side of the law" is central to the appeal of pot stirring — even if this only means betting on numbers or driving five miles over the speed limit to get there.

There's a wide range of petty crime available to the average citizen that at minimum risk of apprehension conveys the satisfaction of being an outlaw. In Pennsylvania, a popular pastime is driving to Maryland for cheaper liquor, then "smuggling" this back, half-dreading, half-hoping it will be necessary to try to shake agents of the Pennsylvania Liquor Control Board off your tail. In the Southwest, digging up Indian artifacts is a criminal activity engaged in by a wide range of respectable citizens. One father of eleven, an official of the Mormon church who was caught and convicted of this crime, said that for him pot hunting was like looking for buried treasure. "It's fun and exciting in a way you can't get in no other way," the man explained. "It's also a challenge to outwit the B.L.M. [Bureau of Land Management]."

One poor Louisianan didn't realize he was a pot stirrer until he won an eighteen-year crusade to have his hobby of collecting antique slot machines legalized. After the legislature passed a bill to this effect, the man lost all interest in his hobby. Eventually he sold the slot machines. Collecting them, he explained, was just "not a thrill anymore."

An enterprising industrial psychologist once looked up thirty-two store employees who had been fired for stealing from their employers. After assuring his subjects that he was more interested in understanding than judging their motives, Lawrence Zeitlin got some revealing explanations about why they stole. Many cited "boredom" and other frustrations at work. The majority reported strong satisfaction from "getting away with it." Only six said that profit was their goal. Many gave their contraband away. Few sold any of it.

Based on this two-year study, Zeitlin concluded that after growing dissatisfied with his job, the average retail employee is more likely to steal than to quit. As he explained, the challenges provided by such theft "represent a significant enrichment of the individual's job. He can take matters into his own hands, assume responsibility, make decisions, and face challenges. The amount he gets away with is determined solely by his own initiative. He is in business for himself."

With petty crime in general, profit is seldom the actual goal. Among young delinquents especially, a relative indifference to the proceeds of their crime has often been noted. After surveying what research exists on the underlying causes of delinquency, criminologist David Downes said that motivations of excitement, virility, and the search for thrills recurred "with startling regularity." Citing one study in particular, Downes concluded that "in courting danger and provoking authority, the delinquent 'is not simply enduring hazards; he is also creating hazards, in a deliberate attempt to *manufacture* excitement.' "

Reformed criminal Ray Johnson once said of his delinquent phase: "When I look back at some of the risks I took, I see that they were crazy, but at the time I was just zeroed into the excitement. When I was very young, I had my own car and I'd park it, lock it up, and steal a car just for the excitement. I'd stop and steal a car and go from point A to point B and expose myself to all the risks, police chasing me and shooting at me."

Of his own crime-studded past, singer Merle Haggard recalls, "I got into everything I could get into, just for the excitement of it sometimes." Haggard was first arrested on suspicion of armed robbery when he was fourteen. Over the next eight years, crimes charged to him included car theft, check forging, safe-cracking, and escape from prison. Haggard spent nearly three-quarters of those years behind bars, 2½ of them in San Quentin.

"Wild hair, that's all it was," the singer explained to reporter Paul Hemphill. "I was curious, and I wanted to feel like a man. Like while I was in jail, I could smoke if I wanted to and I didn't have to eat if I wasn't hungry. It's really hard to say what makes a kid do that, but it's certainly not as unappealing as it may seem."

Concluded Haggard: "I wouldn't trade the experience."

With a single exception, crime is primarily a male rite of passage. The exception is shoplifting — the gentle crime.

Just over half of the women who filled out my questionnaire said they'd shoplifted at least once in their lives. This was little different from the rates reported by men. Other surveys have found the same thing: that women shoplift at least as much as men, and in some cases even more.

The popularity of this form of crime among women is partly just a matter of opportunity: the merchandise is there to be taken in settings they frequent. But equally important is the fact that shoplifting bends traditional sex roles without breaking them. It's a crime, true, but not an *aggressive* crime. When it comes to shoplifting, stealth counts for more than hubris. As a psychiatrist who has treated women and girls who steal merchandise points out, this is one of the few risks available to those who live in otherwise orderly environments.

More than any crime, shoplifting is likely to be engaged in by those with no pressing need for the merchandise they steal. Those caught in the act typically have enough money on hand to pay for the merchandise they've taken and often try to do so. The items most commonly taken are hardly basic necessities. Budget costume jewelry is the item most likely to be stolen from a department store, leather goods from specialty shops.

The head of security for Woodward & Lothrop Department Stores in Washington, D.C., once constructed a profile of the typical Woody's shoplifter. Based on 13,000 cases over six years' time, he found that 80 percent of them not only had enough money, but had enough money with them to pay for the merchandise they'd stolen. Many were wealthy. Less than 1 percent had criminal records. Boredom and frustration were their primary motivation, he concluded, particularly among the bureau-crats and housewives who dominated his profile. "I associate it with a sexual climax," suggested the security chief. "They're taking that thing and their heart is pounding. And then they get out of the store and have a totally relaxed feeling. They got away with it! It's a terrific relaxation, a high, and all that day's tension and frustration [are] gone."

The sexual analogy is commonly used by shoplifters them-selves. "I got an orgasm every time I slipped something in my handbag," one woman has admitted. "I just really liked the sly, furtive quality," added a woman in her twenties about the fond-ness for shoplifting that she developed in her teens. "There was something almost sexual about it — like doing it with your boy-friend before your parents came home."

The rites American girls have been left to devise for them-selves have traditionally revolved around sex. Giving up virgin-ity is the big one, of course. But since widely available birth control has reduced the stakes of this rite, one approach has simply been to retain that challenge by forsaking birth control.

When they polled 106,000 readers about their sexual practices, *Cosmopolitan*'s editors were startled to discover that 16 percent of them used no birth control whatsoever. In a study of the motivations for such nonuse or careless use of contraceptives, two Stanford University gynecologists found one to be a love of risk transcending the fear of pregnancy. "In some individuals," explain Eugene Sandberg and Ralph Jacobs, "sexual pleasure is accentuated by or principally derived from the thrill in risk tak-ing." Because contraception limits this appeal, the result too often is what the gynecologists called "coital chicken."

In my own poll, a number of women listed sex without birth control as a risk they were taking or used to take. While most said the latter, one twenty-five-year-old secretary called making unprotected love a risk she'd take now but wouldn't have taken when younger.

"I was aware of other methods of contraception," a woman once explained about her need for an abortion. "Marvin would pound them into my head, but I still went my own way. I *dared* fate. I just dared it. . . . It's like being a maniac driver on the freeway, it's asking for trouble. You know, I think we control our fate, but some of us have to go the limit, just to see what will happen."

The woman making this confession was one of a number of abortion patients being studied by sociologist Kristin Luker. Among the reasons given by her subjects for using birth control sloppily, if at all, was the challenge involved. Although this reason was not commonly stated, Luker found women among her patients who told her that making love lost its pleasure for them when it didn't include the risk of getting pregnant.

Obviously, in an age of legalized abortion this risk isn't what it used to be. Some who "lose" this gamble and have to get abortions refer to a subtle appeal of the penalty itself. One young woman says that for many friends in their twenties and thirties, having an abortion has almost come to be expected, and even welcomed — as a rite of passage. This rite incorporates "a desirable tinge of tragedy," writes Leslie Savan, one that "seems to increase our participation in the great themes of life and death."

The stereotype of postabortion women is one of depression and mourning. But after intensive interviews with a group of unmarried adolescent girls over the several months after each had aborted a fetus, one survey found that more than half of those interviewed said they returned to or surpassed their preabortion emotional state. Among those who felt this way, some reactions included: "Life is better now"; "I feel more grown up, more responsible"; and "My fiancé and I are closer now and we both matured." One seventeen-year-old girl from a strict Catholic family, who took a lot of drugs during her freshman year of college (and got pregnant while high), found that the abortion experience jarred her into moving out of the drug scene, becoming more serious about her future plans, and giving up a poor relationship with a boyfriend for one more seriously committed.

By mentioning such cases I don't mean to endorse abortion as a rite, a maturing experience, or even to endorse abortion at all, but simply to point out that in the absence of better rites, we pass what rites we can.

When it comes to keeping pots stirred, one challenge posed by legalized abortion, modern birth control methods, and loosened sexual taboos is the need to make sure that guilt, danger, and furtiveness aren't lost to sex altogether. Resourcefulness is called for. Some couples find that the risk of making love in public or semipublic settings can replace outdated ones of pregnancy and shame. A thirty-one-year-old wife and mother wrote in as a risklet on her questionnaire, "Making love outdoors, risking discovery." Others have given me similar reports about stimulating sexual adventures while half-submerged in the ocean with lifeguards looking on; on motorcycles; in moving cars; and in elevators, airplanes (both undercover and in the lavatory), and on a Xerox machine making copies after hours at the office. A similar poll of college women turned up one who'd made love on the floor of an all-night grocery. "The chance of getting caught mad it exciting," she explained. In the ultimate sacrilege, another student got high on marijuana and proceeded to have sex with her boyfriend in the car of a monorail traversing Disney World.

This might be called the Jenrette syndrome in honor of former Congressman and Mrs. John Jenrette, who fulfilled a lifelong dream of his by making love one night on the steps of the Capitol. In the most noted section of her memoirs, Rita Jenrette described the action:

> We walked hand in hand up the steps to the House side of the Capitol. John then led me into the shadows of the large white columns that adorn both sides of the entranceway that members customarily use on their way to vote.
>
> I looked into John's deep-blue eyes as he pulled me toward him. We embraced passionately; John unbuttoned my fur coat, and I fumbled with his zipper. I was wearing my blue skirt, and John slowly raised it above my thighs.
>
> We wrapped my coat around us, and we made love standing in the shadow of the large column. I remember thinking how cold, very cold, it was but how warm it was next to John.
>
> We giggled like school kids as members of Congress walked by: Moe Udall, Rick Nolan, Pete Stark, John Cavanaugh, Tom Downey, Bob Carr, walking in and out, voting.
>
> Tip O'Neill walked by, and we waved. He said, "Hi, John. How are you?"
>
> This was the one romantic moment in the responsibility-choked first two months of our marriage. We had rebelled together, done something deliciously scandalous.

Just as reviewers dwelled lovingly on this moment in Rita Jenrette's memoirs, movie critics will always keep us alerted for the latest episodes in what Pauline Kael has called the "sex-in-public mania." A moviemaker can hardly go wrong by taking part in this mania. Recent movies that have included sex-in-public episodes include *Risky Business* (on a subway), *The Man Who Loved Women* (in a car; in a car in a car wash; at the races), *Reckless* (on the floor of a high-school boiler room), and *Don't Blame It on Rio* (at the beach). Jacqueline Bisset has sort of specialized in this type of scene by first making love in an airplane lavatory in *Rich and Famous*, then coupling in a glass elevator in *Class*.

In fact, such movies record fantasies better than realities. We're not in much greater danger than ever of stumbling across couples copulating in elevators. But this is an interesting thought. I once asked a number of men and women to describe for me any fantasies they might have had involving making love on elevators. Most had no trouble at all visualizing such an episode, men or women. If anything, the elevator fantasies reported by women were more vivid, detailed, and daring than those of the men. One twenty-four-year-old editor said that she liked to imagine herself squeezing into a crowded elevator after a hard day at work:

> I'm in the second row from the back. There is a man behind me, but I can't see his face. As the elevator starts down, I lurch back and feel his hand on my behind. More people crowd on and I'm flat against him. I can feel him pushing aside the flap of my wrap-around. I'm not wearing any underwear. I start moving my hips against him. He seems to be built. Then the elevator jerks to a stop. I lean forward. He pulls me back. I can feel him enter me. I look at people around us. Each time the elevator stops and starts, his penetration grows deeper. . . . Only two floors to go. I wish it were 200. The breathing behind me is heavy in my ear. As we arrive at the ground floor, we both climax. The man pulls out of me. My skirt falls into place. I can hear his zipper being pulled up. The door opens onto the lobby. I smile to myself as we leave the elevator. I've never seen his face.

Since few of us will have the opportunity to make love in elevators, or on the Capitol steps, we look for sexual action where we can. According to polls, the extramarital option is more popular than ever for married Americans. As with so many other forms of pot stirring, process is more important than product here, the trip greater fun than the destination. When the substantial portion of married men and women who have affairs are queried about their reasons for doing so, "boredom" ranks high as a motivator. And this does not refer just to sexual boredom. After conducting hundreds of interviews for his book *The Affair*, Morton Hunt concluded that "it is the simple, natural, regrettable experience of boredom — sexual, emotional, or both — that is by far the most frequent cause of infidelity." As Hunt pointed out, however, this is seldom admitted — even to confidants. It just doesn't seem reason *enough* to forsake marital vows, so all manner of more acceptable rationalizations are devised. But in the confidence of his interviews, Hunt found that over half the men and two-thirds of the women reported that some form of tedium at home was their main reason for stepping out sexually in the first place. For repeaters, the figures were even higher.

So here is a case where danger may not stimulate good sex so much as sex stimulates good danger. This is because extramarital sex in general has less to do with the search for better orgasm than the need for a little variety. Its illicit demands only add to the charm. This is the best opportunity many will ever have to star in a spy thriller. If it were possible to have all the intrigue but skip the fuck, a lot of affair seekers would be just as happy. But this can't be. Sex to an affair is like money to gambling; it gives the occasion stakes. It's novel if not better sex, a coupling filled with the perils of exploring new territory. As a cuckolded husband in Herbert Gold's novel *He/She* understands too painfully, "My wife has gone off to spend a weekend with her lover. Of course he will smell new and fresh, and the grain of his beard is different under her fingertips, and his bed will be strange and exciting, and his weight other than mine, and when she instructs him about what she likes, it will be a voyage of discovery for them both."

By keeping us aroused and alive, even such apparently "negative" forms of risk taking can serve positive ends. No less than fighting a flood can something like having an affair be cathartic, intense, and ritelike. Assuming otherwise is morally presumptuous. And seeing only the potential for catastrophe in many

87

forms of pot stirring misses half the fun. As Garson Kanin's father asked when told of a man who reached the age of 106 by never drinking, smoking, or traveling too far from home: "What for?"

Although much stirring of the pot would be meaningless if it were licit, I like to think that providing better challenges and rites for our children would reduce their need to stir the pot later on. Certainly providing better tests than a driver's test couldn't hurt. To some degree at least, good risk can drive out bad — so long as it's genuine.

Take Kay Collins.

After five years of her doper-biker-topless life in Long Beach, Kay had grown physically and emotionally exhausted. When her boyfriend Mike suggested that they go back to her Iowa home-town of Stillwater for a while to rest up, she agreed.

For Mike, a Californian, Iowa was novel and challenging. For Kay it was only challenging. The risks she was faced with back in Stillwater were of a different order altogether from those in Long Beach. One challenge was trying to take over and run her father's business, a cafe. Another was coping with Mike's wish to get married, an idea that scared Kay more than the fastest Harley. And overall, there was the challenge of simply trying to be herself in the small midwestern town where so many people had watched her grow up.

The cross-currents Kay felt in Stillwater came together for her in one particular episode. As she describes that incident: "A friend of mine picked me up after work. I can't remember if Mike and I were together then or not [they separated for a time]. My friend had a Jag and we were cruising around Stillwater getting loaded. We went to find out where the cop was and proceeded to race around to the other end of town. He took one curve so fast and it felt so neat I almost had a climax. But I didn't be-cause we were in Stillwater and that wouldn't be a nice thing to do."

With such exceptions, the risks in Kay's life were very differ-ent from those in California. One was trying to run the bar alone after she and Mike broke up. She couldn't, and embarked on a new adventure: working as one of Iowa's first women on a high-way crew. Her male fellow workers weren't too keen on the idea, and not shy about letting Kay know. Only after nights of crying herself to sleep, and finally staring down her worst tormentor, did Kay win grudging acceptance on the work crew.

Then Kay discovered she was pregnant. This, in her words, was "the ultimate risk."

Her pregnancy wasn't planned. Kay even thought she was barren. When proof arrived that she wasn't, Kay toyed with the idea of getting an abortion. Although back together, she and Mike weren't getting along. Her career on the highway was in full swing. And Kay was terrified that all those drugs she'd consumed out in Long Beach would result in a deformed baby. "But I knew deep down that I would not be able to do anything to the baby," she concluded, "because it might be my one and only chance, and like everything else I do, I wanted to see what it was and what it looked like. I must have an enormous amount of curiosity."

Being pregnant was not a happy experience for Kay. Neither she nor Mike had any idea of where their lives were headed. Their finances were in a shambles. How they were going to support two people, let alone three, was a mystery. "But when that baby was born," Kay found, "it was the most wonderful, beautiful, most fantastic high I have ever had in my life. At the time she was born, we had absolutely *no* money coming in and were three months behind on some bills. But during the three days in the hospital, I didn't think of that once. All I thought about was how lucky we were to have such a beautiful little girl and that she was all ours.

"And I was scared to death I would not be able to take care of her."

Kay's daughter, Molly, is now almost four. Her mother has proved up to the task. Kay finds motherhood suits but also confuses her. If she gives things up for the sake of her daughter — especially risks she might take — is she being true to herself?

"I don't take nearly the risks that I used to," she explains, "because I want to see Molly grow up and I want her to have me while she is still growing up. Now that I am a parent I realize the risk of losing her. That is the one that hurts the most. I can't imagine what my parents must have felt when my brother Mike died. I thought I knew at the time, but I didn't. Losing Molly to school will be the first biggy. I am sure I will be one of those mothers who cry.

"Physical risks scare me now becuase I don't want to get hurt and be maimed for life. Like motorcycles make me real nervous. If I trust the person driving implicitly, I will go for a short ride. But I always am glad to get off.

"There are times when I miss the other life. I miss the feeling of being carefree, not a whole lot of responsibility. There is no comparison between the risks of being a mother and running around. The running around was always very shallow and empty. I always felt alone. . . .Being a mother has rewards that are so full they're hard to describe. . . .

"I know there are still a lot of risks ahead of me but I don't know what they are. Mike and I are both the type of people for whom the chase is the most fun. As soon as things get easy and good we tend to get bored and search out something new.

"Looking back on my life, I don't think I would change much. I have been really lucky because I have gotten to do most of the things I have wanted to or I still have hopes for others. I have no desire to go back to age seventeen. I like being a little older and wiser. Being older is a nice feeling.

"All of my running around is out of my system for now. I don't think I have lost it completely, but I have put it on a back shelf till Molly gets going on her life. Then I can get crazy again. I am absolutely looking forward to being a crazy senior citizen."

They sold the cafe. Together Kay and Mike started a new business: designing and marketing children's playhouses. Their "experiment" in living back in Iowa is now in its seventh year.

Our most recent Christmas card from Kay Collins had a picture on the front of a smiling Santa holding the Equal Rights Amendment in a ribbon-tied package. Inside Kay had written: "I have a new project in life. I have joined the women's movement!"

As the case of Kay Collins suggests, there are saving graces to being a stirrer of the pot. Although often risky, their activities tend to be more mischievous than dangerous. And because pot stirrers are novelty-oriented, few such activities last for very long. These are experimental people. "Action" takes many forms, the more the better. A big tray of exciting appetizers tempts them more than a substantial meal of danger. There are others — some call them "thrill seekers" — who go for the danger.

THE SKYDIVER

When he heard that a skydiver had died that morning trying to land on the Gateway Arch in St. Louis, John Finch called his friend Ken Swyers to find out who the "numb nut" was. If anyone knew, it would be Ken. Not only was Swyers among the most experienced skydivers in the Midwest, but as the Area Safety Officer, he was in touch with all kinds of fringe jumpers.

The phone rang for a long time at Ken and Millie Swyers's. Finally Millie's fifteen-year-old son Mike answered. "Mom and Kenny aren't home," he told Finch. "They went somewhere real early this morning."

With a knot growing in his stomach, it occurred to John Finch who the Arch casualty might be.

He remembered Swyers's cryptic remark to him the night before. When Finch had asked if he wanted to car-pool down to a skydiving center the next morning, his friend declined. Ken said he had some "personal affairs" to attend to. They were with some skydiving friends watching Robert Conrad's "Daredevils" special on television. Swyers had been especially caustic about the jumper who highlighted that program by free-falling for a mile before landing on the diving plane from which he had leaped. In his opinion, this was reckless hotdogging done more for cameras than for sport.

In fact — as Finch later discovered — when another friend offered to videotape Ken Swyers as he landed on the Arch the next morning and send the tape to "That's Incredible!," Swyers declined. If this friend wanted to tape the event, Ken told him, that was his business. But for himself, appearing on television had nothing to do with his reasons for making this jump.

What *were* his reasons?

Thirty-three years old at the time he "went in" (a skydivers' term meaning "died while parachuting") on November 22, 1980, Ken Swyers was generally recognized not only as one of the most skilled skydivers around, but one of the most cautious. As the Area Safety Officer (appointed by the United States Parachuting Association), Swyers was notorious for not letting jumpers go up if conditions weren't right, or if they seemed ill prepared. In the late seventies a relatively inexperienced jumper had leaped to her death from a plane for which he was Jump Master. Swyers had questioned letting the woman go up in the first place because she seemed reckless. In retrospect, he figured she was probably suicidal. After that incident, he grew even more hardhearted about grounding would-be jumpers who struck him as careless. On a safety scale of 1 to 10, says John Finch — a 700-jump veteran who rates himself a 9 — Ken Swyers was definitely a 10.

On a typical Sunday, Ken and Millie would return from a weekend's jumping at the Archway Sport Parachute Center in Sparta, Illinois, with a trunkful of reserve parachutes that other skydivers hired him to "rig," or repack. Licensed to do this by the Federal Aviation Administration, riggers are the accountants of skydiving. For this task, one wants hands that are more careful than colorful, and steady rather than dashing.

Considering his reputation, when word quickly spread among skydivers that it was Ken Swyers — *Ken Swyers!* — who had died going for the Arch, that community was dumbfounded. It was as if the president of the Women's Christian Temperance Union had shown up in the drunk tank. Or Ralph Nader had begun a second career doing motorcycle stunts.

Talk of an Arch jump had been a staple of skydiver bull sessions for years, usually with one beer in hand and a couple under the belt during the general high spirits and tomfoolery after a hard day's jumping. What the World Trade Center represented to Philippe Petit in New York, the Gateway Arch stands for to adventurous skydivers in St. Louis: a colossal dare to the imagination. During its two decades of life, this 16,678-ton cement-

and-steel Eero Saarinen–designed structure — 638-feet high at the apex — has become the spiritual heart of its host city. In St. Louis you cannot escape from the Arch. It surrounds, engulfs, and entices you. Not only can the Gateway Arch be seen for thirty miles around, but its image dominates postcards, advertisements, television logos, and the sides of St. Louis's shopping bags. The jacket patch sold by the Archway Center has a parachutist free-falling between the legs of the Arch.

Looking up from its base, it's not hard to understand how this structure ignites the fantasies of skydivers. Like a huge horseshoe magnet, the Arch pulls your eyes upward and demands that you contemplate scaling its heights, then leaping to the ground. The main reason no parachutist has successfully done so is that 638 feet is at, if not below, the minimum altitude in which even a skilled jumper could hope to billow a canopy (particularly without the help of a plane's backwash). Even for one willing to take that chance, getting on top of the Arch in the first place seems nearly impossible. Elevators carry tourists and staff up the Arch within its hollow core. But once aloft inside, how does one get outside and over the top onto its stainless-steel roof? It's at this point that talk of an Arch jump among skydivers usually turns to other subjects.

For years Ken Swyers had mused along with everyone else and been stumped by the problem of getting out from inside the top of the Arch. But gradually, without his making it public, Swyers's interest began to change from going up the Arch and out to simply coming at it from above; landing on the Arch with one parachute, then leaping off with another.

Only his closest friends knew how consumed Ken was by this monument. His "grail," John Finch called it. Millie can't remember a time when floating from the Arch beneath a parachute didn't dominate her husband's fantasies. One of her earliest memories about Kenny — from just after the time they met through a mutual friend in 1974 — was how fascinated he was by this structure. The Gateway Arch and skydiving, which he'd just taken up, seemed to be the locus of Ken Swyers's existence.

For a year after they met, the two were just pals. One of their favorite ways to pass time was sitting with their backs resting against the massive south leg of the Gateway Arch soaking up sun. Long after their friendship felt solidly in place, Ken surprised Millie by asking her out. On their first date they went to the Shriner's Circus, which includes a parachute exhibition. Next they watched the Army's Golden Knights parachute team put on a show. In one form or another, most of the rest of their life together would revolve around skydiving.

This usually meant spending every weekend at Archway and most evenings working on gear. At first Millie had a hard time accepting her boyfriend's need to risk his life several times a week when the skies were clear. Skydiving was a formidable rival: exciting, glamorous, and seductive. Three years after they were married on June 13, 1975, Millie even tried joining her husband in his hobby. This lasted for exactly eight jumps. On her eighth and final leap, Millie landed badly and broke her ankle in several places. After the bones were set at a nearby hospital, she returned to Archway, where Ken was teaching a class of fledgling skydivers. He offered to stop and drive her home. Although she was in quite a bit of pain, Millie knew Kenny wanted to stay. She declined his offer. Only after the sun had set and Ken's class ended did they go home. Millie still has mixed feelings about the whole episode. Her ankle really hurt.

Three years later, Millie Swyer's slim ankle is still somewhat swollen and discolored. The pin that held her bones together until they healed is displayed on a shelf of her living room in the Overbrook section of St. Louis. Next to it are a number of plaques and framed certificates with Ken Swyers's name on them, as well as pictures of him in various stages of skydiving. Prominent display is given to the Golden Wings he was awarded for his 1000th jump.

Prominence is also given to a collage of clippings reporting the day of September 20, 1978, when Ken Swyers and a fellow jumper set a world record of fifty consecutive jumps by parachutists repacking their own canopies. Millie still remembers the aftermath of that day, how sore and stiff her groaning husband was during their hour's drive back to St. Louis. She spent the evening rubbing his body with liniment. Millie also remembers Kenny's gratitude; not so much for the liniment and rubs but because, as he put it, "You fell back. You let me do what I had to do."

For the next few days her husband was insufferable. The man who typically answered the phone "Big Ken Swyers, Superstar" now became "Big Ken Swyers, Superstar and World Record Holder." In his case, "big" was not technically accurate. Ken Swyers stood 5'9" and weighed 150 pounds. What was big about this man was the impression he made on others. With his bright red hair, full moustache, and piercing hazel eyes, Ken Swyers was hard to miss. Also, the air about him always seemed to vibrate a little. Swyers was big in style, big in presence, big in his aspirations. More than one friend has said wistfully that if Ken Swyers had landed successfully on the Arch, he would have been impossible to live with. Millie told him that a new wing would have to be added to their home to house his ego.

When the *Guinness Book of World Records* declined to list his fifty jumps, Ken was crushed. The record keepers' explanation was that they had no such category. "Well, make up a goddamned category!" Swyers had shouted when he got the news. But they wouldn't. Worse yet, six months after he set the unrecorded consecutive-jumps-in-a-day-while-repacking-your-own-parachute record, another jumper broke it. After that Ken took to answering the phone, "Big Ken Swyers, Superstar, ex-World Record Holder."

A few weeks later, Swyers added "Prez" to his greeting. This referred to his election as president of Local 2352 of the International Brotherhood of Electrical Workers at the Westinghouse plant where he had assembled industrial fuseboxes, meters, and circuit breakers since May 1972. His coworkers remember their union local president as a man in perpetual motion. Ken was a runner, one pointed out, but never a jogger; he *ran*. The man's metabolism just seemed to require constant activity. At the same time, Swyers was hard to ruffle. "He always had control of himself, it seemed," recalls Matt Klutho, twenty-five. Many attributed Ken Swyers's vaunted cool to his years of facing down death as a skydiver. Although considered one of the plant's best wirers, when Swyers did goof off at work it was usually to hide out and talk skydiving with his pal and sometimes jumping colleague John Higginbotham.

Millie says that her husband was basically bored by his work. The highlight of Swyers's Westinghouse career came on the day he parachuted into a company picnic in his trademark black out-fit. It wasn't an easy jump. No jump over a city is. The variety of temperatures and heights in the buildings below creates treacherous wind currents. Also, should a parachutist get blown off course, his options are limited with a city beneath his feet. Unlike the vast, empty farmlands where most jumping takes place, urban targets force fast choices between the best empty lot or park or parking lot to land on if necessary. These targets appear to be the size of postage stamps until you're just above them. Yet they must be hit with pinpoint accuracy. And should it be necessary to "cut away," or release your main canopy, because of a malfunction and open your reserve parachute, the chances of retrieving this expensive piece of gear are slim. As one skydiver puts it, your best bet of ever seeing that fabric again is in a dress worn by someone below.

Losing his parachute would have been particularly hard on Kenny. A gift from Millie, this canopy was state of the art: a rectangular model known as a "para-sail." Para-sails have only been in use since the late seventies. They are designed to give fast and accurate landings to any jumper skilled enough to ma-neuver them. To go along with such advanced equipment, sky-diving techniques have changed as well. The latest craze has been for what are called "stationary jumps" from high, fixed settings. These settings include radio towers, bridges over gorges, and mountains with sheer cliffs, such as the 2000-foot high El Capitan in Yosemite.

Within the skydiving community there is great ambivalence about this type of jump. Contempt for the " 'That's Incredible!' Fever" assumed to motivate them is mingled with animated dis-cussion of those daring enough to attempt such jumps. Skydiving publications mix editorials denouncing stationary parachuting with photo spreads illustrating this practice. Archway's owner Dave Verner says that after 4000 jumps he still finds leaping from airplanes thrilling and can't understand those who look for fixed objects from which to jump. Yet on the ceiling of the jump center Verner owns, many such feats are recorded in black felt pen, including "HORAT, *2nd off El Capitan*," for a local jumper who is the second parachutist known to have made that leap.

In heated debates on this subject that took place at Archway,

Ken Swyers tended to line up with the dubious. He had particular contempt for stationary jumps made with television cameras rolling. Yet Millie also recalls how excited her husband got while watching a television program with a segment on such jumps. And before the practice was banned in the fall of 1980, Kenny told his wife that if they ever got to California, he figured he'd have a go at El Capitan.

What really tempered Swyers's enthusiasm for such jumps was the fact that most had already been done. Stationary leaps that were daring and unprecedented just a few years before had become routine. Few unexplored territories were left to conquer. The Gateway Arch was one.

At some point — Millie is still not sure exactly when — a shift began to take place in her husband's approach to the Arch. Sometime in late 1979 or early 1980 Kenny's musing about parachuting from the top of this structure took on a tangible tone. His talk began to sound less like speculation and more like planning.

Although Millie didn't know it, because her husband chose not to tell her, Ken already had confided in John Higginbotham that he was thinking of having a go at the Arch that June. He even had an occasion in mind: the annual Shriner's Circus. For the past three years Ken Swyers and Dave Verner had done an exhibition jump into that circus in Busch Stadium. Busch is located four blocks from the Gateway Arch if walking, and two as the crow — or a skydiver with a para-sail — flies. Whether a parachutist floating to the ground overhead lands in the stadium or near the Arch — or *on* the Arch, for that matter — depends merely on a twitch of the fingers working the parachute cords. As Ken wondered aloud to Higginbotham early in 1980, why not just twitch a finger the "wrong" way, land on the Arch, and explain later that it was an accident? That the winds blew him off course?

Higginbotham, or "Hig" — a burly, bearded ex-high school basketball player — thought Swyers's idea was absurd. This wasn't easy for him to say. When John Higginbotham had made the first of his own eighteen parachute jumps, Ken Swyers was his teacher. But Hig learned enough from those jumps to know that the crosswinds, the precision called for in landing, and the limited height to open a reserve parachute after leaping off of the Arch made such an attempt nearly suicidal. But his friend and mentor wouldn't stop scheming. Eventually Higginbotham gave up arguing and helped him scheme.

Mostly this involved doing reconnaissance of the grounds surrounding the Arch. These consisted of the Mississippi River east, several acres of park surrounding, and the city of St. Louis west of the Arch. The two spent long hours sketching this terrain and discussing how to get at the Arch, and how to get away.

After he and Ken had been plotting for a few weeks, Hig let slip to Millie what they were up to. She and her husband were so close that Higginbotham just assumed Millie was in on the secret. She wasn't. Millie was furious, outraged. In tears, she told her husband that if he *ever* planned a serious attempt at the Arch, she *had* to be involved. If Hig's your partner, she told him, go live with *him*. Her greatest fear, Millie told Ken, was that he would go in while trying an Arch jump and she would get the news by phone.

After aborting the idea of an Arch jump in June because he didn't want to jeopardize the Shriners' goodwill by going for Gateway instead of Busch Stadium, Ken put Millie on his team. Already on board were Hig, a fellow skydiver nicknamed Bigfoot, and Matt Klutho from work. Each team member had a task. Matt's job was to gather up Kenny's main canopy after he threw it off the top of the Arch. Hig was to take photographs, Bigfoot movies. Millie was the getaway driver. Parked by a church 100 yards from the Arch, she was then to speed over and pick him up once his jump was completed.

Just before sundown on a clear, crisp day early in the fall of 1980, a parachutist was seen leaping from an airplane overhead into a fast wind. As he descended, the jumper seemed to have trouble maneuvering his rectangular parachute through the crosswinds. Finally this figure came to rest on the grass adjacent to the Arch. Gathering up his canopy, the parachutist dashed to a car that had pulled up nearby and sped off.

Since few visitors remained at the park by the time of this jump, Ken Swyers's first attempt at the Arch was witnessed by only a handful of people other than his ground crew. The traffic reporter for a local radio station did mention over the air that he'd seen a parachutist land in the park. No other notice was taken.

Swyers and his team were quite discouraged by the failure of their mission. Later they gathered at Ken and Millie's to review what had gone wrong. The main problem was crosswinds. Ken just couldn't maneuver through them onto the Arch and decided not to try. Everyone understood, and everyone felt depressed; Ken Swyers in particular.

It wasn't until late November that conditions were right for another jump. In the meantime, those planning this attempt debated how it would best be made. Hig wanted Ken to ride a wind in from the east. That way, if he couldn't get his footing on the 17-foot-wide metal surface, Ken would be blown off the side before his canopy collapsed and he'd just continue on to the ground. But Swyers himself wanted to come in from the south. Even though this risked his being pulled down the north leg of the Arch if he couldn't get his footing, there was less turbulence to contend with from that direction, which would make for a softer descent. Also, coming in from this direction improved his chances of actually *landing* on the Arch rather than being blown off the side. Hig's approach made surviving more likely, success less so. Kenny's plan improved the odds for landing and leaping off the Arch at added risk to his life. This was the approach he decided to take.

Debated also was what Ken should do once he was on the Arch. Cutting away his main canopy before opening the reserve parachute was the obvious choice. Merely pulling apart the Velcro strips attached it to his rigging and letting the para-sail float away would minimize the danger of Swyers's being twisted about and pulled off his feet by the billowing canopy. But his para-sail was Kenny's pride. The risk of losing this favorite possession — one that had cost his wife weekends of extra work at Archway — was not one he wished to take. Ken figured he'd have the few seconds necessary to deflate Millie's gift, wrap it in his arms, then detach the canopy and throw it to Bigfoot below.

On the morning of November 22 everything was in place. Ken Swyers rose early that morning and tested the winds with a crepe-paper trailer. They felt strong but manageable. The day was relatively clear. A pilot had been lined up to fly Swyers from an out-of-the-way airport to which his illegal expedition would be hard to trace. When Hig called, Ken told him all systems were go; he'd see him on the ground. "The force be with you," said Hig.

As Swyers and his pilot approached the Arch, the winds picked up. By the time the Gateway Park appeared below, they exceeded 25 miles an hour. Few skydivers like to risk jumping into a wind greater than 20 miles an hour. Dave Verner says that any velocity over 22 means you should just "head west" — go home. But Ken had thought it over and decided in advance that jumping into such a strong wind might even work to his advantage by slowing him down and making the landing softer.

At 8:49 A.M., a twenty-three-year-old advertising art director named Terry Knight — herself a skydiver — was leaving her apartment across the river from the Arch to drive down to Sparta. Glancing up before entering her car, she was startled by the sight of a black-garbed figure beneath a wide black para-sail floating rapidly toward the Arch. It took only seconds for him to draw within a few feet of the radio beacon on top. From her vantage point less than a mile away, Knight could see this figure land partway down the Arch's north leg, where the surface was still relatively flat. His canopy began to deflate. Then she saw the wind take charge of this canopy and begin to reinflate it. In the process, the black-clad figure was being spun about. He couldn't seem to get his footing. Knight could see that he was tugging frantically at the ripcord of his reserve parachute. Then she saw this figure jerked off his feet and thrown onto his back. After that he began to slide down the north leg of the Arch, headfirst. His reserve parachute became a white streamer following behind. Then Terry Knight turned away.

On the ground, Ken Swyers's crew had lost sight of him after he neared the Arch. From their angle — looking straight up — they couldn't tell if he had landed on the Arch or not. "Where's he at?" they began yelling to each other. "What happened? Where's he at?"

Matt Klutho saw a woman approach the Arch from a distance, stop, point to the top of the Arch, and scream. Then they all heard an eerie, metallic sound as if a huge shovel were being

101

scraped across a gigantic tin roof. This was followed by a loud thud on the concrete at the base of the Arch. This sound reverberated up the Arch's metal skin and echoed through the hollow of the museum underground. Finally all was quiet.

The silence soon was broken by screams, shouts, and the pounding of feet running toward the north leg of the Arch. Among those running were Hig, Matt, and Bigfoot. But not Millie. Millie didn't run. From the parking lot 100 yards away she had lost sight of her husband as he floated toward the Arch. Millie held her breath as she waited to see his reserve open, or even his body come tumbling off the side. She saw neither. Then Millie heard the big sounds, followed by the screams and the stampede of those running toward the Arch. She let out her breath. Millie knew what had happened. What was the point in running? Instead, she walked the 100 yards to the Arch. When Millie got there, she pushed Bigfoot aside as he tried to block her path and went directly to kneel by her husband's crumpled body. It lay just a few feet from where they used to sit taking in the sun. Still attached to his body by the Velcro strips he never pulled apart was his para-sail.

After kneeling to murmur a few words in her husband's ear, Millie covered his battered face with her jacket to keep it from being so exposed to the crowd that surrounded him. Then she stood up to face a policeman in uniform, who said he had a few questions to ask. The first one was, "Why did he do it?"

At thirty-five, Ken Swyers's widow is a lively, engaging woman with short frosted hair, a full mouth, and wide, dark eyes that hold yours with a direct gaze. She's about 5'3". Although not pretty in a Hollywood sense, Millie Swyers is unusually attractive. When she can't think of what to say, Millie purses her mouth, raises her eyebrows, smiles, shrugs her shoulders, and holds her hands palms up. During one conversation about her husband, Millie observed that she seemed to be shrugging a lot. I said it was becoming. "Becoming a nuisance," she replied.

I'd felt timid about contacting a skydiver's widow, especially one present at his death, so a woman doing research for me agreed to make the first call. At first Millie demurred. She didn't want to be talking with any writer who might make her husband out to be some "disgusting, muscle-flexing daredevil." But after consulting with friends at the Clayton Community Church where she's a member, Millie Swyers decided to trust in the Lord and take a chance that I would be an instrument of His will.

Millie says her faith as a Christian is what got her through the aftermath of Kenny's death: the reporters, the television cameras, the bitter recrimination from many fellow skydivers, and uncomprehending grief on the part of his family. Even with time to reflect, she has no regrets about backing up her husband, going along, helping out, supporting him in what he chose to do. November 22, 1980, was Kenny's day to die, Millie figures. If it hadn't been the Arch, it might have been in an auto accident. That would have been worse, his body all tangled in steel. This way he went in doing what he loved.

According to his widow, skydiving gave Ken Swyers something he found nowhere else: fulfillment, satisfaction, and a strong sense of identity. "If he hadn't jumped, I'm sure he would have been a different person," she said. "Maybe I would have liked that person better. Maybe I wouldn't."

The period just after Ken was discharged from the Army in 1968 but before he took his first factory job in 1970 is one during which Millie says she's glad she didn't know him. Everyone who's familiar with this phase of Ken Swyers's life gets kind of vague when they talk about it. Phrases like "setbacks," "skids time," "footloose," "sowing wild oats," and "Kenny's hooligan days" are used to brush over that time. More specific comments such as "cruising the back roads" come up now and then, as do "running from the cops" and "picked up for racing."

Just before Millie met him, Ken traded his rowdy phase for the skydiving one. Before ever strapping on a parachute, Swyers had tried and lost interest in scuba diving, weight lifting, and the martial arts. But no activity held his interest like leaping into the void. From his first jump on July 13, 1973, until his last one more than seven years later, Ken Swyers parachuted to the ground from an airplane over 1600 times.

Like everyone else who knew him, Millie appreciated what this sport did for her husband. Skydiving gave his life focus, and purpose. Unlike wiring boards for Westinghouse, parachuting was a skill in which he took pride. It was also a skill he was eager to pass along. The ranks of skydivers in the St. Louis area are filled with those who learned how to jump in a class taught by Ken Swyers.

Since Kenny had just taken up skydiving when they first met, his interest in skydiving and his interest in Millie seemed to grow together. To her this was no coincidence. "It gave him confidence in our relationship," she said of his sport. "If he could hold the skies, he could hold me."

Millie said her husband struggled constantly with his basic timidity. As he put it, the fear is always there. Either you learn to control the fear, or it controls you.

Millie thought her husband's biggest fear was of letting others see how he felt — especially when he felt afraid. Long after they met, Ken told Millie about some vivid memories from his childhood that he'd never discussed with anyone else. One was the time that he and his best friend, Harry, killed a bird with a BB gun. After burying their prey, the two boys vowed never to kill one again. Later, when they were eight, Ken and Harry ran away from home and stayed overnight in an abandoned shack in some woods. The next morning — as a nearby well was being dragged for their bodies — they returned. Ken told Millie that he still could picture the expression on his mother's face as he walked through the door.

The next year, Harry's family moved to California. For the rest of his life Ken could recall the day his best friend came to say goodbye. He was lying on the floor of his family's living room, reading the funny papers. When Harry walked in Ken refused to look up. Finally his friend left. Ken knew that he seemed hard-hearted. But he also knew that if he saw Harry's face, he'd burst into tears. So he didn't dare look up. "At that age," Millie said, "he was already fighting to control that part of himself."

When I asked what she thought was the biggest risk her husband had taken in his adult life, without hesitation Millie replied, "Loving me." Partly this was because she was two years older than Ken, divorced, and had two small boys. But more important than the practical risks involved in marrying an older woman with a family, loving a human being so much that you'd choose to share your life meant giving up some control over that life. "I think what confounded him," she said of their relationship, "was that it was one of those things he couldn't control. I think if he had realized that in time, he would have pulled out. But by the time he did, it was too late." Their relationship nearly ended before it began, Millie added, because once he realized the way things were going, he got "frightened to death" and kept taking off. But Ken kept coming back, until finally he asked Millie to marry him. Ken often told Millie that if he hadn't married her, like so many of his skydiver buddies he would have stayed single. Those who knew this couple comment on how close they were. "Best friends" is the term most often used to describe Ken and Millie Swyers's relationship.

Feeling as she did about him, Millie wasn't thrilled about having her husband constantly leaping from airplanes, but she knew how important this activity was to him. "Anyway," she adds, "if I had wanted him to stop skydiving, I couldn't have. I was married to the man. I didn't own him. Kenny's life was his own. He shared it with me."

Given up by her mother to foster parents when she was three, Millie Swyers has a fine sense of the impermanence of human relationships. Changing foster homes at eleven underlined this sense. After marrying at seventeen in hopes of creating the stable home she'd never had, Millie's subsequent divorce only confirmed her suspicion that things don't last. By the time she and Ken met, she neither sought nor dared hope for anything beyond a day's happiness. Perhaps as a result, they had five largely good years together.

A year after they were married, Millie Swyers accepted Jesus as her savior. Then Ken did as well. For a time their Sundays were given over to worship and activities at the Clayton Community Church. Clayton's membership is made up primarily of those who are looking for a strong, conservative faith but not a conservative way of life. Millie's commitment to Christ gave her life the same focus her husband's got from skydiving — except while Ken felt that he had taken charge of his own life, she had given control of hers over to the Lord. For that reason among others, Ken found his commitment to the church less enduring than Millie's. It also took part of his weekend away from skydiving. Finally Ken Swyers had to choose between Clayton and Archway. He chose Archway. Reluctantly, Millie followed. Although both remained Christians, for the next two years skydiving dominated both their lives.

After years on the line at Westinghouse, Ken had lost interest in his work. Not long before his Arch jump he looked into the possibility of becoming an air controller. Swyers was told he was too old. The cutoff age was thirty. That shook him up. Until that time, said Millie, it hadn't occurred to her husband that he was too old for anything.

What Ken really wanted was to own his own parachute center. He and John Higginbotham went so far as to buy some used skydiving equipment from a defunct parachuting school. That equipment is still in Millie's basement. "It was just a matter of waiting for the right opportunity," she explained about why her husband didn't pursue this dream. "Maybe he wanted too much of a sure thing. He wasn't willing to stake it all."

The picture that emerges of Ken Swyers on the eve of his final jump is that of a capable and ambitious if not enterprising man at an impasse. Millie points to the fall of 1978 as his apex. Within a single week at the end of that September, he won his Golden Wings for making 1000 jumps, set a world record, and became the owner of a state-of-the-art para-sail. Then he was elected president of his union local. After that there weren't too many high points. Like so many of us in our early thirties, Swyers was wondering where he would leave his mark. It wouldn't be at work. He and Millie had tried to have children but couldn't. He was too old to become an air controller. And while Ken talked about writing the Great American Novel, Millie knew he wouldn't. It would mean having to reveal himself. Skydiving remained Ken Swyers's best source of recognition. However, other jumpers were as good at the sport or better. *Guinness* had turned down his world record, which then got broken anyway. He'd won a medal for making 1000 jumps. The next medal was 1000 jumps away. Matching Dave Verner's 4000 was unlikely. He couldn't get up the nerve to open his own parachute center. Kenny needed a goal, something to strive for. Something nobody else had done before.

For a skydiver who usually prepared with such care, Ken Swyers's last jump was not very carefully planned. Many of his colleagues point out the preposterousness of attempting a stationary jump from 638 feet without first having done some test leaps from, say, a hot-air balloon stationed at that altitude. But as far as anyone knows, the only practice jump Ken Swyers did in preparation for his last one (aside from the abortive earlier attempt) involved deliberately cutting away his main canopy over Archway one day and opening his reserve.

As for the Arch itself, Swyers seems to have made no attempt to locate blueprints or plans of any kind to study the structure on which he was staking his life. Among other things, doing so might have forewarned him about the air-conditioning vents on top, whose exhaust may have been what reinflated his canopy. Other than a couple of reconnaissance flights overhead, his plans seem to have been based largely on long conversations with his co-conspirators, Hig especially, which had as much to do with flying to the Arch and getting away afterward as the jump itself. Even Swyers's choice of gear seems to have been casual. The shoes he wore, for example, were a pair of Brooks running shoes with no special gripping qualities to help him get his footing on the Arch's slippery surface. Nor does November 22 seem to have been a particularly good day for the attempt, nor the time of day chosen. Dew was still on the Arch that early in the morning. The winds were too strong. Yet according to Millie, neither she nor Kenny was that scared of this jump. Seventeen feet across is quite a bit of surface to land on, particularly for a jumper as skilled as Kenny. Though the winds were squirrelly, those at Busch Stadium where he'd successfully jumped into the circus were worse. And while 638 feet is not that much altitude for getting a reserve canopy open, Millie was sure Kenny would succeed. He always had, hadn't he?

In a way Ken Swyers's very competence at skydiving reduced the odds of his success. A jumper of less skill and experience might have prepared more thoroughly for such a treacherous attempt. A comment made over and over by fellow skydivers — even those who think him a fool to have tried — was that if anyone could have pulled off an Arch jump, it was Ken Swyers.

This is why better preparation might not have made much difference in Ken Swyers's Arch jump. Under the best of circumstances parachuting onto the Gateway Arch, getting secure footing, unfurling and detaching one canopy then opening a second one and getting it to inflate during a very short trip to the ground was a long shot. A jumper of Ken Swyers's experience had to have known that the odds didn't favor his venture. In a general way, Ken would sometimes discuss the possibility of "going in" with Millie and her kids at the supper table. A few months before he died, Swyers had a mutual friend ask Clayton's minister to give his eulogy if one were ever necessary (the minister did). He'd once told Hig that if he ever went in, they should just "shake the change from my pocket, stick a broomstick up my butt, put a beer in my hand, and go party."

While going through her husband's union notebook shortly after he died, Millie discovered that he'd recently updated an accident insurance policy that she didn't even know he owned. This reminded her of how, upon leaving the house on November 22 for his last jump, Kenny had brushed her arm aside when she tried to hug him goodbye. That wasn't like him. Was it a premonition?

Millie's sure that from the instant he landed on the Arch, Kenny knew this was to be his last jump. She thinks her husband had only a second or two to think it over before he started sliding down the leg of the Arch, and maybe three seconds more before his head hit the ground. She doesn't think he was scared. Battered as it was, his face in death wasn't that of a horrified person. If anything it looked calm; relaxed. Ken even had the slight smile that only an intimate would recognize. "You had to know him to know that smile," says Millie. "It was the kind of smile he'd get when he'd just put something over, done something ornery, and was waiting for everyone else to get the joke."

Some think Ken Swyers wanted to die that day. I don't. Rather than committing suicide, I think what Swyers did was alter the odds of staying alive in a bold attempt to break up the logjam of his life. He knew the odds were against success and chose to take them. To put it another way, Ken Swyers chose not to continue living without the achievement of an Arch jump. He went for the Arch for the same reason that I write books — grasping at a thread of immortality. As John Higginbotham puts it, "He just wanted to do something where he was the first. He wanted to be known for something. He wanted to have his name somewhere."

Soon after her husband died, Millie Swyers began — as she

puts it — "closing doors." Only weeks after Kenny went in, Millie made herself return to the Arch. Six months later, she went down to Archway for the first time since the accident. Normally a garrulous, composed person, the closer she got to the parachute center, the more withdrawn Millie became. Rumors were circulating at Archway that she blamed Kenny's death on skydiving. For her part, Millie didn't know if the anger some jumpers at Archway felt toward Kenny for confirming the suspicion of many that skydivers are death-wishful crackpots would be turned against her.

A few seconds after she got out of her car and wandered over to a startled group of lounging skydivers, Millie was surrounded by an excited mob, all talking to her at once and waiting impatiently for a moment at her side. Dave Verner suggested that she yell at someone, just for old time's sake. Bigfoot said he never believed that she'd actually come back like she said she would. "Bigfoot," said Millie to the man who once tried to protect her from her husband's body, "when will you learn to trust me?"

Returning to St. Louis a few hours later, Millie was excited, giddy, euphoric even. Her words spilled out one on top of the other.

They slowed again as the Mississippi River drew near, and stopped altogether for a moment while we passed by Jefferson Barracks. This is where Ken Swyers is buried in a plain veteran's grave. In the six months since he died, Millie said she'd been there only four or five times — usually on a whim. "We were always spontaneous in our relationship," she explained. "I can't see any sense in getting into a dull routine now."

Now that her living room is no longer needed to rig parachutes, Millie's had it redecorated. Bigfoot took over his former teacher's classes at Archway. John Higginbotham is the new union local president at Westinghouse. At the end of 1980, a St. Louis television station rated the Arch jump one of the year's top ten news stories. And on the ceiling of Archway's office is now written in black felt pen:

Ken Swyers, R.I.P.
First person to stand on top
of the Gateway Arch.

SIX

WUFFO?

*His reasons were his own. He only wished he knew
what they were.*

— IRWIN SHAW
The Top of the Hill

Even if you're not jumping, in order to join a load of skydivers
going up in their airplane, you must first strap on a parachute;
just in case. Protruding from the orange case of this Army-surplus parachute hung over my shoulders was a small rectangular
handle made of metal tubing. If for some reason it was necessary
to leap from the plane, I was told, gripping this ripcord handle
tightly and pulling hard — with both hands if necessary — almost certainly would open up a parachute overhead. I was
warned to protect the handle with my hand at all times to keep
it from being accidentally jerked loose.

For the few minutes before we took off, I wandered about the
grounds of the Archway Sport Parachute Center, patting my
handle every now and then to make sure it was still there.
"That's the one," a young man in an orange jump suit called out
brightly as he walked by me. "Just pull hard."

Our plane was a rickety old single-engine Cessna that looked
as though it may have begun life doing reconnaissance for the
invasion of Normandy. All of its seats had been removed except
the pilot's. This left room for four skydivers in the airplane's

body, and one 145-pound observer with an Army-surplus parachute squeezed into the tail.

The men who were about to jump seemed more preoccupied than anxious. One listened to a Walkman tape player. Another beat a steady tatoo on the plane's metal wall. Other than making my foot fall asleep from being cramped, the flight up to 7600 feet wasn't unpleasant. I've always enjoyed flying. My mood was one of, Hey, what's the big deal? I could probably jump if I wanted to.

After we'd circled slowly upward several times, the pilot leaned to his right and without any warning kicked the door. It flew open abruptly, letting cold air rush in with a roar. Terror blew in with the wind and grabbed me by the throat. As this icy, frigid air howled through the plane, I was certain it was about to blow me back out. I could hardly breathe.

Oblivious to the danger I was in, the jumpers moved up and huddled around the open door. Then they crawled out and gripped the wing's strut as if about to do chin-ups. Each held this position briefly before disappearing. Then only the pilot and I were left in the plane. I was doing my best to make sure that this remained the case. My fingers desperately searched the smooth inner walls of the tail for something to hold on to. The best they could find was a narrow girder that protruded half an inch from the wall. I pinned my life on this girder, pinching it between the thumb and fingertips of one hand while using the other to clutch my ripcord handle like a rosary. My heart raced. My mouth was parched. The open plane door had my full attention.

Finally the pilot leaned over and mercifully closed this door. Only then did my heart finally slow down and my mouth begin to remoisten. But not until we landed and my feet safely touched the ground was I sure I'd survived. Leaping from an airplane for sport is something I could never do.

How can anyone?

Skydivers call those who ask that question "wuffos." On the whole they're quite patronizing of the breed. If you have to ask, they imply, you'll never know. Sensing this, I tried during my time at Archway to avoid asking jumpers about why they jumped. Many told me anyway — eagerly, insistently, sometimes even defensively. Some said it was the adrenaline rush. Others talked of the challenge: of defeating gravity, and holding on to the skies. Still more made reference to the silent beauty of falling through air. Words such as "thrill" were used, and "release." Some just said it was fun.

As I watched them float to the ground — grinning, laughing, shouting, and flailing about beneath their multicolored canopies — skydiving did look like fun. From the ground, anyway. Not enough fun that I'd ever want to try it. I tend to read newspapers from cover to cover, including all the little filler items at the back. This is where skydiver fatalities usually get reported.

Jumpers themselves claim that the ride to the airport is the most dangerous part of a day spent parachuting. If you take precautions, they say, their sport is a safe one. And since they do take precautions, so that it is safe, how could they possibly be wishing for death?

Like most thrill-sport participants, skydivers are painfully aware that Freud's "death wish" notion is a popular explanation of why they do what they do. Based on my own observation of those engaged in such activities, extensive talks with them, and reading of research on high-risk athletes, I don't find wishing for death a persuasive rationale for more than a handful. Such athletes themselves realize that they get the odd suicide or semisuicide in their ranks. Some hotdog skydivers engage in "low-pull" contests to see who can be the last one out of a plane to pull his ripcord. But the vast majority of those who leap from airplanes, climb mountains, dive deep into the ocean, or race down snowy hills on skis take too many precautions against dying and are too intensely engaged in *living* to slip easily into any "death wish" category.

Which leaves the question unanswered: Why do they do it?

Let's start with the simplest premise: that it's fun to float toward the ground beneath a parachute, or share the ocean with barracudas, or search with one's fingernails for cracks in a sheer granite face. To me it isn't; to them it is. We often spend so much time looking under rocks of motivation that we overlook the rocks themselves. As one psychiatrist concluded after an extensive study of skydivers, "Most parachutists jump because they like to jump."

To the vast majority of us who don't engage in such an activity, the dangers of dying or being maimed are reason enough not to. Those who do think about such risks too. But they think about other risks more; especially about the risk of a boring life. When separate groups of skydivers and nonskydivers were asked the same question, "Why would a parachutist pull his ripcord in time to land safely after a period of free-fall?," the contrast in their responses was revealing. The nonjumpers invariably referred first to preventing death. But the skydivers said — usually without hesitation — that if they did not pull their ripcord in time, they would never be able to skydive again.

So obviously important differences in attitude distinguish those who are attracted to such a sport from those who aren't. Death defyers may not be trying to hasten the end of their lives, but they are quite willing to bet these lives as the stakes for an improved version. "The adventurer gambles with life to heighten sensation," wrote Jack London, "to make it glow for a moment."

To outsiders their talk is all about the beauty of their sport, its spiritual dimensions, and the lengths to which they go in search of safety. But among themselves, adventurers mostly talk about close calls; the time when the parachute only opened at the last second, or the belaying rope barely held, or the oxygen tanks nearly ran out well beneath the surface of the ocean.

"You do a lot of 'hangar flying,'" says San Diego pilot Bill McGaw of those who fly small planes. "The hairier the story the better. If it takes place over the Tehachapi Mountains, with the plane flipped on its back, gyro out, and the altimeter gone, and you still make it back — you win that round. Some pilots even have a habit when they get out of the plane of saying, 'I cheated death that time.'"

"Cheating death" is a popular concept among high-risk athletes. Even after having to drop out of a race for mechanical reasons, former race driver Jackie Stewart said he would feel exhilarated by having eluded death one more time. In a study of British racing drivers, Michael Cooper-Evans noted of such an attitude: "While he is racing it seems to the driver that he alone has the authority to decide as between life and death. To exercise this authority in the face of death gives him a feeling of intense power in a world in which to be helpless is unbearable. To flirt with death, yet have the judgment and the control to draw back and return to life, provides a sense almost of omnipotence."

It would be hard to overestimate the appeal that feeling in control of their fate has to those who risk their life for sport. True, the sheer exhilaration of daring death (and unleashing all those opiates) is important to them. So is the concentration this demands, and the euphoric afterglow, which many compare to that following sex. An undeniable sense of *esprit* characterizes the death riskers, of having proved their mettle, as does the intense camaraderie uniting those who do it together.

But none of these attractions compares with the profound sense of control over their own lives thrill seekers claim to feel by repeatedly tiptoeing along the edge of the void without falling in. Voluntarily putting your life in jeopardy makes you the master of your own fate. Once you exit a plane, you are effectively dead until you decide to live by pulling your ripcord. One woman, a veteran of sixty jumps, calls this process "voluntarily saving your own life. You must take positive, direct action. Otherwise you'll die in ten seconds. Doing so is a great declaration of love for yourself. It makes you feel terrific."

This is why the "death wish" rationale seems so laughable to most thrill athletes. By tempting death they choose life — repeatedly. And in so doing, they confirm and reconfirm who's in charge of their destiny.

I have never met a group of people more preoccupied with being masters of their own fate than recreational neck riskers. This is the essence of their relationship with danger. Each time they put their life in jeopardy, the real suspense comes from finding out who's in charge. Is it me, or death? And each time they survive, that question is answered until the next time it's posed.

After years of research about "stress seeking" in general and skydivers in particular, sociologist Samuel Z. Klausner has concluded that at least two-thirds of them look upon that sport primarily as an opportunity to exert authority. As Klausner characterizes this attitude, "He [the skydiver] is out to humble the environment and give it the pleasure of being mastered by him."

To gauge their attitudes toward the sport, Klausner had skydivers develop stories describing pictures of parachutists in action. Said one, "His first free-fall and everything is working out just perfectly. He thinks to himself that he is as free as the birds, but soon he must end this sensation by pulling the ripcord and ride gently earthward. What a great feeling to be able to fall free and remain in perfect control." Said another, "We see him now in a delayed fall, and now he feels all the thrills and feelings of control that he only had hints of before. He now has a feeling of conquest over the normal restrictions of an earthbound man and self-conquest."

It's an important and fundamental characteristic of voluntary neck riskers that danger as such doesn't interest them, only danger they feel they can control. (Thrill seekers tend not to be gamblers. And those who are prefer games such as blackjack or baccarat, where they feel some control, to roulette or slot machines, where they don't.) This is why it's not unusual for high-risk athletes to be more frightened by seemingly innocuous dangers than by those inherent to their sport — a mountain climber terrified of Ferris wheels (I know of one), or a downhill racer more frightened of the lift ride up than the ski down (I know of one too). Hang-glider pilots typically find standing at the edge of a cliff before leaping off more frightening than flying itself, because when flying, they feel in charge.

This passion for control helps resolve the seeming contradiction that most recreational neck riskers set out to take risks, then try to eliminate all risk through fastidious preparation. First they challenge fate, then they try to bullwhip fate to its knees by making their adventure as predictable as possible. In fact, it's not adventure they're after. It's mastery. Danger is simply the ultimate test of their ability to prevail. This is why Charles Lindbergh always hated the "Lucky Lindy" tag hung on him by the press. According to Lindbergh, there was no luck at all involved in his solo flight across the Atlantic, nor much of an element of chance. As the pilot explained, "It went just as I'd planned it."

One man with whom I spent quite a bit of time while working on this project was Philip Bartow. A forty-eight-year-old Seattle native, Bartow has been scaling rocks since he was ten. During that time he's ascended more mountain peaks than he can recall and helped carry out more bodies than he likes to remember. On the whole, Bartow does not think that there should ever be a need to do this. If climbs are planned carefully, participants stay within their limits, and conditions are constantly monitored, he believes anyone can climb without fear of mishap.

To help make this point, Bartow organized the first group of disabled climbers ever to scale Mt. Rainier. This group included climbers who were blind, deaf, missing a limb, epileptic, or some combination. A few had climbed before; most hadn't.

While they were training in Colorado, the news reached this group that eleven climbers had just been killed by an avalanche on the very route they'd shortly be walking themselves. This gave everyone pause. After extended discussion, the group consensus was to proceed — the climbers, because they were willing to risk it; Bartow, because he was sure he could virtually eliminate risk.

Thirty yards from where the eleven bodies were still buried, Bartow's group set up camp one afternoon. To him and to climb leader Jim Whittaker, the first American to climb Mt. Everest, that bit of distance made all the difference. To their experienced eyes, 30 yards was far enough away from the point where the snow of an avalanche was most likely to fall.

With relative ease this group scaled Rainier in four days. Their achievement made national headlines. Disabled and other people alike heaped praise on the climbers for their inspiration. President Reagan received them at the White House. Later he sent Philip Bartow a letter of praise for his accomplishment. It was earned.

What wasn't visible in this dramatic tribute to the human spirit was the planning that made the climb possible in the first place. For nearly two years before it actually happened, Bartow had been scheming, calculating, soliciting donations, and recruiting climbers. As a result of such care, and an assist from good weather, the climb was lacking in mishap. If the deaf hadn't been literally leading the blind on this expedition, it would have escaped notice entirely.

While reviewing the climb for me some weeks later, Bartow expressed no relief, or gratitude to fate and nature that things had gone so well. According to him, it was strictly a matter of planning. Pulling out sheets of paper carefully organized into looseleaf notebooks, he showed me how each day's activity had been scheduled virtually to the minute. These schedules were written in his careful, neatly printed hand. They were made up long before the trip was under way, Bartow explained, well before he had the money lined up, even before he'd selected a team to make the climb. But it made no difference, because Bartow says he *knew* from the earliest stages of planning *exactly* how the trip was going to go. "I felt a year and a half ago," said the sallow, dark-haired climber as he peered intently at me through thick glasses, "that I could close my eyes and see every step that people would take. That's the way I like to run my trips. I felt a year and a half ago I could have directed the movie. A year and a half ago I could close my eyes and run the movie through my head. That's the way you have to do it. I never saw anything but a successful trip."

How could you be so sure, I asked?

Bartow smiled without parting his lips, and adjusted his glasses. "I know what I'm doing," he replied. "I keep things under control at all times. I tell them what to do, when to walk.

"The only uncontrolled variable is human dynamics."

I'm not climber enough to challenge Bartow's certainty. (He can attest that I'm not much of a climber at all.) Yet as sure as Philip Bartow is of his ability to control events on a mountain, I'm just as sure that such a sense of mastery is more clear to him than it is to nature.

Like so many of those who make things happen, Philip Bartow is ultraorganized. His climbing library is catalogued like a real one. The data he collects on climbing groups is organized neatly into files and notebooks. Items calling for special attention are flagged with little yellow slips. Long before it was fashionable, he'd equipped himself with a minicomputer. Today he owns two. Outings he organizes for drug addicts, senior citizens, the blind, and others are subjected to elaborate, computerized research. "Intangibles" are kept to a minimum.

In his carefully planned approach, Bartow is not untypical of mountaineers as a group. Controlling intangibles is the essence of climbing mountains and living to tell the tale. Among the more important intangibles to be controlled is oneself. I've noticed, for

117

example, that trembling — from cold or from fear or both — is rather a taboo among climbers. I think it's seen as an embarrassing bit of evidence that you can't control your own body. Even when no one else is around to see, quivering skin is cause for self-doubt. As climber-novelist James Salter wrote in *Solo Faces* of a fictional mountaineer stuck alone on a ledge overnight during a thunderstorm, "Rand was shivering. It was an act of weakness, he told himself, but he could not stop."

Of his own reaction to nervousness the night before his maiden parachute jump while studying this sport, Samuel Klausner later reported, "A quiver passed from my chest through my stiffly arched back and out the tips of my toes. I cursed my damn body for its lack of control. I commanded it to relax as I struggled against the next quiver."

In such an attitude, we begin to get a hint of what this obsession with control is really all about. When they extol this virtue, control of *what* is always a moot point among high-risk athletes. From an outside perspective, for example, it is easy to assume that a mountain climber's adversary is the mountain. Climbers themselves know that the mountain is merely the battlefield. The real adversary is the climber. As one of them puts it, "You're climbing yourself as much as the mountain." To the world at large the most famous rationale for scaling a peak is George Mallory's flip "Because it's there." But to his fellow climbers, Mallory's more insightful remark was made after conquering Mont Blanc. "Have we vanquished an enemy?" he asked upon returning. "None but ourselves."

Even in the titles of their memoirs, climbers zero in on what they're about, most recently in Rob Taylor's *The Breach: Kilimanjaro and the Conquest of Self*. The nonclimber might be forgiven his curiosity about what it is about the self that so needs conquering. The answer, I believe, can be found in yet another title: David Roberts's *The Mountain of My Fear* (adapted from W. H. Auden's line "Upon the mountains of my fear I climb . . .").

In nearly all high-risk sports, the mastery of fear comes up repeatedly as the principal reward for engaging in it. "I've beaten that fear in myself," a hang-glider pilot once said about his attitude toward heights. "It's a wonderful feeling." About his sense of triumph after scaling the Sears Tower in Chicago, twenty-five-year-old Daniel "Spiderman" Goodwin said, "I have mastered fear." And of his general need for physical adventure, novelist Charles Gaines says, "Partly it's the feeling of mastering fear."

Even the tree trimmer who recently cut down a dying pine for me said he found his work high off the ground rewarding because it was "a way to master your fear." He was thinking about taking up hang gliding.

I began this project with the assumption that thrill seekers were less fearful than the average person. How could they be otherwise? But this turned out to be projection on my part. As I was to discover, most recreational neck riskers are as scared as the rest of us, sometimes even more so. "I'm a very fearful person," climber Edmund Hillary once confessed. "Fear adds to the pleasure."

What distinguishes the high-risk athlete from others is that like all Level I types, rather than running *from* fear, they run *toward* it. Otto Fenichel's concept of "counterphobic" behavior — repeatedly seeking out your major fears so as to master them — is relevant here. I see such behavior every time my son David pleads, "Scare me, daddy. Please? Come on; scare me." It needn't demean the high-risk athletes to call their pursuits child-like. We all should have enthusiasm and such intensity in our lives. Fenichel saw a convergence of thrill seekers and artists in retaining their infantile fascination with fear. Picasso — who called painting a means of "giving form to our terrors as well as our desires" — said that the hardest part of this task was retaining our child's eye.

The idea that a high-risk activity can be a means for confronting fear comes closest to what participants themselves say about their motives. And this is not just a matter of grim self-proving. Samuel Klausner found that the more frightened his skydiver subjects were while going up in the plane, the more enthusiastic they felt upon landing safely on the ground. In fact, the converting of fear into enthusiasm so typified the stress seeker that Klausner thought it was probably a fundamental motivation for courting danger in the first place. In other words, initially you seek physical risk for the satisfaction of mastering your fear. In the process, you discover how exciting, how pleasurable, even ecstatic confronting fear can be. As James Salter wrote in *Solo Faces*, "Dennis had outclimbed his fear. An exhilaration that was almost dizzying came over him."

To some degree we all find a bit of fear exciting. If we didn't there would be no roller coasters or Stephen King novels. But most of us stick to vicarious risk or pot stirring to seek such excitement. If the thought of going further — of putting your neck in a noose for the thrill of pulling it out — sounds preposterous to you, you won't want to ascend the peaks of mountains or descend to the ocean's floor. But you will miss a level of exhilaration known only to those who do.

A climber named Karl Pfefferkorn once fell 75 feet off a cliff in North Carolina in 1980, damaging his spinal cord, breaking his pelvis, and crushing both ankles. Later the climber reflected that although his avocation may have been mad, he still understood its appeal. "The way climbers talk," said Pfefferkorn, "it sounds like they're talking about a combination of sex and religion. But it's better than both. That's the feeling. It's a feeling you can't really explain, and that's what keeps you coming back."

Sexual metaphors are common when thrill seekers try to explain the temptations of putting their necks on the line. An English rock climber, for example, once said that what he liked was "the sheer bodily and sensual pleasure of movement on the rock." As he contemplated a solo trek across the Sahara (undertaken to master his fear of doing so), British adventurer Geoffrey Moorhouse said his terror soon gave way to "an almost sensuous thrill of anticipation."

Earlier I wrote about the power fear can have as an aphrodisiac. In the case of neck riskers, one gets the impression that they carry this process one step further: that for them, living on the brink of extinction is not just a *stimulus* to sex but is itself sexual. Could it be that regularly risking your neck can get you off?

It takes a bolder interviewer than your author to pose such a question directly. But consider what they say anyway, without being asked. Groping about for the proper metaphor, one skydiver said that her feelings while falling to the ground could best be described as "an orgasm in the head." A reporter who asked a number of California skydivers how jumping made them feel found that "orgasmic" was the adjective most often used. One called the feeling of free-fall "the ultimate — better than sex, almost." A psychiatrist who has studied skydivers talks of the " 'erogenous' or sexual pleasure" that many report experiencing, feelings he's sure characterize other sports but ones for which "parachuting is hardly matched."

How does this make skydivers' mates feel? Early in his research, Samuel Klausner's assistant hung around with skydivers' spouses to get their perspective on this activity. After some chitchat about home and children, one of them blushed and stammered, then suddenly blurted out that she needed some advice. "My husband hasn't touched me for the last six months," the woman explained. "Our sexual relations have become less and less frequent these past two years. I am young and I love him, and yet it seems as if I don't know him anymore. He is a changed person. His only interest is skydiving; he spends all his time either working or participating in club meetings. Do you know any way I could attract him back?"

In his own research on high-risk athletes, sport psychologist Bruce Ogilvie has heard similar complaints repeatedly. The wives of race drivers in particular, he says, constantly repeat the phrase, "I'd rather compete with any woman in the world than with that goddamned piece of machinery." The problem is that for most life-or-death athletes, no human relationship can match the intensity of that with their sport. As a result, says Ogilvie, their relationships with others are likely to have "a high turnover."

This could be how they want it. Although high-risk athletes — especially those who band together in clubs — tend to be a gregarious lot, intimate relationships are not their strong suit. "Social workers they're not," says Ogilvie of those he's studied. "Their favored relationships are transitory in nature, requiring only a superficial commitment; they neither seek nor encourage deep emotional ties with others."

In a word, they're loners. To some degree this quality characterizes anyone who participates regularly in an activity that includes the risk of death. It almost has to. Being overly involved with another person creates stakes that are hard to gamble.

Even worse, it requires giving up a measure of control to the person with whom you're involved. This isn't to say that those engaged in high-risk pursuits don't have friends, lovers, and spouses. Many do. But such relationships tend to have a certain *quality*. Amelia Earhart, for example, used to tell friends that to her marriage resembled a cage. Twice she turned down opportunities to enter its confines. When at thirty-two she finally agreed to marry publisher George Putnam, on their wedding day the aviatrix presented her husband-to-be with a letter outlining her terms. Among them were: "In our life together I shall not hold you to any medieval code of faithfulness to me, nor shall I consider myself bound to you similarly. . . . I may have to keep some place where I can go to be by myself now and then, for I cannot guarantee to endure at all times the confinement of even an attractive cage. . . . I must extract a cruel promise, and that is you will let me go in a year if we find no happiness together."

After studying their personal style, no one has ever concluded that risk-seeking athletes are anything other than individualists. With the exception of football players, Bruce Ogilvie has found that "autonomy" is among the traits on which high-risk athletes test highest. Skydivers and race drivers in particular, he noted in a report with two colleagues, "are basically reserved individuals who have rather low needs for close interpersonal relationships. They don't mind having physical or emotional needs taken care of by others but have little inclination to return the favor. They appear very sociable, but their relationships with others are likely to lack depth."

On the surface this observation seems inconsistent with the powerful sense of camaraderie high-risk athletes claim to feel with each other, but the contradiction is more evident than real. As individualistic and prickly as its members tend to be, this brotherhood of shared danger may be the only type available to them. In a study of skydivers' friendships, one psychologist found that the vast majority (83 percent) reported that more than half of their friends were fellow skydivers, and many said almost all of them were.

But it's important to bear in mind that such relationships need not be based on actual fondness. In fact, quite the contrary can be true. Mountain climbers' memoirs bristle with jealousy, spite, rage, and recrimination against fellow team members (feelings that can be exacerbated by oxygen depletion at high altitudes). As one of their number writes, "High-standard mountaineers are extraordinarily individualistic and are only prepared to join together to form an expedition in the first place because they know that, regrettably, they can't get to the top of Everest unaided."

Bonds forged by danger make up in intensity what they lack in affection. But intense as they may be, such brotherhoods of danger are limited in scope. Ties woven by sharing risk with other people are limited to the source of risk itself. Death-defying athletes seldom share anything outside of the sport that brings them together. When the common peril ends, so does their friendship. Ex-skydivers say that relinquishing their place in the brotherhood of jumpers is as hard as giving up jumping itself, if not harder.

Quitting also means that they must try to find a substitute for the arousal of a high-risk sport. If this arousal is sexual, it can be that much harder to replace. One alternative is to replace the sexuality of their sport with that of a human relationship. For many this alternative is unsatisfying. For one thing, it means giving up the sense of self-mastery, of autonomy that their sport won them. For another — to a highly autonomous individual in particular — the sexual reward for braving danger can be more satisfying than that enjoyed with another body.

If courting fear cannot only arouse but resolve sexual passion, one might say this is a powerful reward indeed for putting one's neck on the line. This also poses a paradox. By definition, sexual release demands that one relinquish self-control — if only for the duration of an orgasm. In this respect it's like trembling. Sex may include trembling. A momentary loss of consciousness can even accompany the peak of ecstasy. So how can ultracontrol and orgasmic release both be rewards for putting your life in danger?

The answer is that they can't be. Nor is the issue of control as simple as high-risk athletes make it out to be. In fact, their lust for control may even reflect on the surface an inner hunger to relinquish control.

Could it be that the actual goal of those obsessed with winning control over themselves by defying death is relinquishing the control they've just won? Perhaps it is. Doesn't every overly controlled person yearn for a moment's abandon? And don't we often arrive at the destination we seek by first setting out in the opposite direction?

A psychologist named James Lester once joined an American assault on Mt. Everest. Like anyone who's ever seen mountain climbers close-up, Lester found them individualistic to a fault. But he also observed how fascinated his fellow climbers were by the Sherpas who accompanied them. These Tibetan porters were Buddhists whose approach to life was based on submitting themselves to the will of God, to each other, and to the mountain they were climbing. Lester thought that the tension between their ultraindividualism and envy of the natives' communitarian, fatalistic way of life was central to the fascination Everest had for Western climbers.

I've often felt that deep down, anarchists yearn for someone to tell them what to do. And that my aggressively atheistic friends are engaged in the toughest challenge they can muster to a faith they hope will win. Somehow it never seems that surprising when yesterday's hippie becomes today's Moonie, or revolutionaries start selling insurance.

In a similar process, perhaps the only way high-risk athletes feel free to put themselves in the hands of fate is to first make sure that they've tightened every bolt, double-checked each rope, and reexamined all parachutes.

In a talk on risk taking in sport, Trinity College philosopher (and ex–Princeton basketball player) Drew Hyland suggested that these seeming opposites were closely related: preparation and abandon. In the elaborate, detailed, and thorough preparation of most athletes, he suggests, can be seen their hunger for risk. Most athletes are very concerned with controlling the body they're about to subject to a game. Yet by its very nature, such a game involves chance: uncertainty about the outcome at least, and often physical danger as well. Only after preparing for every eventuality does the control-obsessed person feel free to give himself over to the gamble he's yearned to take all along. Or as Hyland puts it, only after he's eliminated the *preventable* dangers does such a risk seeker feel free, in Nietzsche's words, to "dance on the feet of chance."

If it is childhood abandon and the courting of fear that we are trying to salvage by risking our necks as adults, then feeling *out* of control is far more characteristic than feeling *in* control. The delighted infant being tossed in the air by his father is utterly at Daddy's mercy. And no matter what he says, any skydiver knows that once he exits an airplane, his life is no longer completely his own. He also knows (but seldom admits, even to himself) that this knowledge is central to the appeal of his sport. When we deliberately risk our lives, it's the moment when fate steps in that ecstasy takes over.

The intense pleasure that skydivers and scuba divers and wire walkers say they get from their sport hardly refers to the long, tedious hours of repacking canopies or checking oxygen tanks or tightening guy wires that, by saving their lives, establish that they control their lives. What it refers to is the few seconds or even minutes when they've taken fate on as an equal partner. At times they may even tip the balance in fate's favor.

It's well known among death-defying athletes that most of their casualties occur among experienced participants who go beyond their competence into the realm of chance. This can even involve flouting the very safety measures they've so meticulously taken. During interviews with diving instructors, for example, psychiatry professor Theodore Blau — himself a scuba diver — found that while all insisted this sport was safe if precautions were taken, most admitted to regularly ignoring such precautions themselves. As one put it, "I am a safety-conscious instructor, but I realize that on various occasions I will take risks that would be unacceptable to me if done by my students or by my assistants. I can't really tell you what my feelings were at the time. This is not a sensible attitude at all. I am afraid I make this kind of decision two or three times a year. This, in spite of the fact that I have had friends die after making a relatively senseless decision contrary to their own knowledge of the water conditions."

In a sense, the participants' insistence that safety measures scrupulously followed make risk sports "safe" is for outside consumption only. Those engaged in such sports know how central danger is to their appeal. And they know as well that all contingencies can't be accounted for. Even if this were possible, they would choose to take a chance — just to see what would happen.

However emphatically they deny being gamblers, their attitude is not that far removed from Dostoyevsky's character in *The Gambler* who reports from the roulette table, "Some kind of strange sensation built up in me, a kind of challenge to fate, a kind of desire to give it a flick on the nose, or stick out my tongue at it."

Perhaps it is artists of all kinds who are most sensitive to the delicate interplay between control and abandon in taking a risk. Any artist of consequence knows that he or she must first master a medium — colors, words, camera angles — then be receptive to the guidance of invisible hands. The trancelike state many achieve in the midst of creation is one form of such receptivity. Living at the emotional brink is another. As viewers, or readers, we respond to the edgy contest between control and loss of control in an artist who works at the abyss's edge without falling in. For the artist as for the skydiver, merely giving oneself over to the winds wouldn't do; it's a recipe for disaster in both art and parachuting. But being entirely under control is a form of failure as well because it results in tedious predictability. The best type of daring involves both establishing and surrendering control, taking care and taking chances.

In the end, what lures us to thrill sports and fascinates those on the sidelines is this contest between preparation and fate. Watching Philippe Petit walk a wire you sense his perfect control. But you also know (as he does) that "anything could happen." Knowing that this tension is inherent in his work is what makes Petit scorn any attempt to underline the tension by faking near falls. For himself as well as the audience, he says, "I feel it's always almost out of my hands. That's why it takes you so fully. When I'm working on the wire, I am, in fact, dying every second. But every second I regain from this — my own life. It's a struggle, it's a very fragile take and pull. And I am never safe on the wire."

Because the control part — protecting your life — makes the most sense, and is easiest to put into words, that's the part thrill seekers tell us about. There just aren't words or reasons to describe the out-of-control part, the better part of their activity. More than we realize, these are the moments that provide the real ecstasy in danger seeking of all kinds — the moment when the bet has been made, and someone or something else takes over.

So in a sense we've come full circle. A key reason for taking chances and braving danger is to establish control over our fate by doing so. And this sense is authentic. But the real reward, the feeling that keeps us coming back again and again to created danger, is the ecstatic moment when preparation is for naught and control must stand aside to let fate take over.

Some thrill seekers find this an exciting phase of their lives, but one that they can and do give up for more rewarding (if less thrilling) forms of risk. Others find the ecstasy of danger so seductive that they can't give it up. These people become addicted to taking risks.

SEVEN

MAINLINING DANGER

The fact is that a person can be intoxicated with his own stress hormones. I venture to say that this sort of drunkenness has caused much more harm to society than the alcoholic kind.

— HANS SELYE
The Stress of Life

In late May, 1974, an old wooden boat named *Our Star* left Bermuda for Spain. It was manned by a crew of five young men. A 40-foot motorized sailboat, the *Our Star* was not a sturdy vessel. Among other things, its mizzenmast was fastened only to the deck, not to the keel as is normal for oceangoing vessels. Just before arriving at the Azore Islands off Portugal, the *Our Star* ran into heavy winds and battering waves that nearly ripped the mast from the deck, and the deck from the hull.

"There was one point," Captain Robert Rankin later recalled, "that we were picked up by a wave. . . . I thought we were going over. The mast was almost in the water. The floor came right up in my face. The people below deck were thrown completely across the boat. That was a terrifying moment."

Rankin was the veteran of a single ocean crossing. So was another member of the crew. The other three — Ricky Lee Benedict, Michael Tindall, and Michael's brother Tom — were ocean-sailing neophytes.

Eighteen days after it left Bermuda, the *Our Star* limped into the Azores. The crew then sailed on to Málaga on the southern coast of Spain, where they bought a steel-hulled ketch named the *Quistere II*. Before heading back to the United States in the *Quistere*, its crew made a side trip to Morocco. They arrived there early in the evening of September 5, 1974. The sun had yet to set. On the *Quistere* were two rubber rafts called Zodiacs, which were outfitted with wooden floors and outboard motors. Tom Tindall and Ricky Lee Benedict both got in the larger one, which was 19 feet long. Michael Tindall took the 13-foot Zodiac alone. After the sun went down, these two vessels pushed off from the *Quistere* and made their way several miles inland on a choppy river known to the three men only by charts.

Several hours later they returned. The boats rode low in the water now because each one was filled with dozens of burlap-wrapped bales. The bales weighed 35 pounds apiece. Each one contained seven or eight bricks of a crumbly, greenish-brown substance that court testimony later established was hashish. After transferring this cargo to the *Quistere*, the three crew members took their Zodiacs back upriver and returned with a second load of bales. By now it was daylight.

Their return trip across the Atlantic was so uneventful that the crew sometimes changed course just to relieve the monotony. They also made a significant dent in one of the bricks of their cargo. Late in the afternoon of October 8, 1974, the *Quistere* reached its destination: a coastal area north of Boston called Cape Ann. There they dropped anchor a few miles offshore.

From a house 150 feet off a beach on Cape Ann, a group of men spotted the *Quistere II* on the horizon. Some of this group took a 40-foot yacht out to meet the ship and transfer its cargo to shore. By the time this task was completed it was dark. Those left onshore unloaded the bales and passed them in a human chain to within a few feet of a road. In preparation for this task, Christmas tree lights — taped so a mere pinhole of light shone through — had been strung along a narrow path from the beach to the road. From there the cargo was loaded onto waiting pickup trucks. Most of these bales ended up in Lansing, Michigan. Lansing was the hometown of Peter Krutchewski, who had led the group onshore and organized this entire operation.

Few of its participants saw each other again until 1980 —

more than five years after the *Our Star* first pushed off from Bermuda — when they were reunited in Boston's U.S. District Court. There Michael Tindall was the first of their ranks to be tried on four counts of smuggling drugs.

By now the bearded, laconic Tindall was twenty-nine, married, and the father of two children. He worked as a charter pilot near his hometown of Highstown, New Jersey. Michael Tindall's name was on a long list of past colleagues Robert Rankin had recently shared with Federal prosecutors in exchange for leniency after being caught in a 1978 smuggling operation.

To defend himself, Tindall hired Joseph Oteri. Oteri, a gray-bearded, flamboyant, and highly successful Boston attorney who specializes in drug cases, was convinced his client had been done an injustice. With his partner Martin Weinberg, Oteri entered a novel plea on behalf of his client: not guilty on the grounds of temporary insanity in the form of "risk" or "action" addiction.

Michael Tindall was portrayed by his defense team as a well-behaved all-American boy until he enlisted in the Army at nineteen to serve his country. According to his father's testimony at the trial, before being sent to Vietnam in 1970 Michael was the kind of boy who would think twice before killing a snake. Based on interviews with those who knew him as a child, a defense psychiatrist characterized the young Tindall as the type to "look twelve ways before crossing the street."

Michael Tindall's consuming interest was flying. In the Army he chose to be trained as a helicopter pilot. Given a choice between ferrying troops in Vietnam or piloting a gunship, he chose the gunship. This job was considered among the war's most hazardous. It was said that gunship pilots rarely went home under their own locomotion. Most were carried home, wounded or dead.

In the 129th Assault Helicopter Company, Tindall's commanding officer was Peter Krutchewski. Krutchewski, twenty-five — who later became the war's most decorated helicopter pilot — took the young New Jerseyan under his wing. Before long, Tindall was flying missions on his own. These missions often called for him to attack what were called "free fire zones." In such zones, gunship pilots were to shoot anything that moved. After

first completing such a mission, Michael Tindall landed his helicopter, inspected the bodies killed by his rockets, and threw up.

Over time his work grew easier. In a letter home, which he
wrote seven months after arriving in Vietnam, Tindall described
what that work was like:

> When you're flying over Vietnam at 80 knots at a couple of
> hundred feet and some dink opens up on you, you can't just fly
> away. (I won't just fly away.) You've got to roll in at about a
> hundred feet off the ground and put a rocket in his chest. If he
> shoots at you and gets away with it, you will have every dink with
> a rifle trying to shoot you down. Two of the six ships we have got
> shot up yesterday and we rolled in hot and killed some of them
> but they were still shooting us with 50 caliber and small arms fire.
> We came home, rearmed, picked up the rest of our ships, and
> went back out. As it turned out, our 12 people and six ships
> whipped ass on a batallion of North Vietnamese. We killed about
> 100. Went back this morning. (Nobody shoots at us.)
>
> You wanted to know what was going on over here, so I told
> you. But do not get the wrong idea. I am having a good time.
>
> Got to go.
>
> Love, Michael

Like most Americans who went to Vietnam, Michael Tindall
quickly lost any patriotic reason for being there. The action he
was constantly involved in then became motivated only by the
need to save American lives. Ultimately action became its own
reward. By the last part of his tour, Tindall later told a psychiatrist, "I liked what I was doing. It was exciting and I enjoyed it
but felt guilty. I had this feeling that I needed it. I had complete
control over my team and I needed to go out into the bush.
Everything else was boring. This was fun.

"In the end, . . . I craved it — I was like a zombie when I
went without it. You know, I felt really alive when I got back
from a mission. I had risked my life and made it back. I needed
the stimulation and became listless without it."

Tindall's gunship pilot (and later smuggling) colleague, Ricky
Lee Benedict, told his jury that Tindall and he used to spend a
lot of time discussing the "on-edge" life they were leading. Both

considered facing life and death situations every day "the best and worst of times," said Benedict. Each time they made it back alive, he added, "there was such an adrenaline rush, such a lifting of yourself, that you felt very high, a natural high.

"We couldn't back out, we couldn't walk out, we couldn't leave. And even if we could, I don't think we would [have], because no matter how much we were in disagreeance [sic] with what was going on, at the same time there was a certain thrill to the whole operation, the life-death situation, being in combat every day. It's like an addictive drug. . . . You couldn't wait to get up and fly the next day, to prove yourself again, to test yourself."

Although he could have eased off, Michael Tindall chose to fly missions until the final day of his year in Vietnam. Forty-eight hours later he was in Tacoma, Washington, telling a debriefing officer that he felt a little disoriented. Tindall wondered if he ought to discuss his feelings with someone. The officer said that this could be arranged if the airman would like to stick around for a week or two. Instead, Michael Tindall went to see a friend in California, then returned home.

Back in New Jersey, Tindall's mother had posted a banner on their snow fence reading WELCOME HOME, MICHAEL. Her son brushed past this banner without seeming even to notice it. The returning soldier was embraced by his mother. When she asked what he'd brought home, her son replied, "Four pounds of grass and VD."

Tindall spent the better part of the next two months in his bedroom smoking that grass. Then he accepted an invitation from his brother Tom (also a Vietnam veteran) to join him in Daytona Beach, Florida. In Florida, the Tindall brothers and some other veterans set up their rented quarters in the style of a Vietnamese "hooch." This involved painting the ceiling black with reflecting "stars" and hanging their beds from chains. Within their hooch this group stuck to itself, smoked a lot of marijuana, and watched movies they'd shot while on missions during the war. "They would basically always talk about Vietnam," recalled their landlord, Al Dellentash. "It looked like they were just playing war to an extent."

During his months in Florida, Michael Tindall tried LSD for the first time. He also bought a racing motorcycle, went scuba diving in underwater caves, and flew rented planes low over the Everglades — at times rolling them 360 degrees. "But it wasn't the same as Vietnam," Tindall later told a psychiatrist. "Something was missing."

After he'd been in Daytona Beach for a few months, Michael Tindall was contacted by Peter Krutchewski. Krutchewski had a proposal: that he, Tom, and some other veterans such as Benedict join hands in a "mission" smuggling hashish from Morocco. Without hesitation the Tindall brothers signed on. And on May 17, 1974, the *Our Star* left Florida for Bermuda to prepare for its trip to Morocco.

At Michael Tindall's trial, various experts on "post-traumatic-stress syndrome" testified on his behalf. Dr. Charles Figley, himself a Vietnam veteran, explained to Tindall's jury that such a syndrome can affect survivors of any traumatic experience. But because of their numbers and the unusual intensity of the trauma involved, post-traumatic-stress syndrome is associated primarily with veterans of war. In order to cope with the extreme stress of this experience and its memories, such veterans often repress their feelings into numbness. Only later, sometimes years later, do the repressed feelings surface — at times in bizarre recreations of the trauma that caused them to become numb in the first place. In the case of Michael Tindall, Figley and other defense psychiatrists testified that his smuggling activity was clearly due to post-traumatic stress. For Tindall, they said, smuggling hashish across an ocean provided the opportunity to live again, to break out of his malaise and recreate the excitement he'd grown addicted to in Vietnam. Because the mission involved similar elements of danger, stress, and the brotherhood of fellow veterans under the leadership of his first commanding officer, in their opinion Tindall had little choice but to join it. The smuggle represented his first opportunity since leaving Vietnam to feel alive. Michael Tindall was an "action junkie," psychiatrist Sheldon Zigelbaum told the court, an "action addict," who literally craved the high level of stimulation he found only in war or smuggling drugs. (More technically, Zigelbaum referred to Tindall's "compulsive repetition of trauma-related behavior.") Psychiatrists for the prosecution argued that although Michael Tindall clearly was suffering from a delayed reaction to his experience in Vietnam, this could not be termed addictive. Nor was it sufficient cause to excuse breaking the law.

The jury agreed with the defense. Michael Tindall was acquitted on all four counts by reason of temporary insanity, which took the form of an addictive need for action.

Such a need is hardly limited to ex-soldiers. For years I've heard veterans of stressful experience of all kinds use drug imagery to explain why they feel so listless afterward. A reporter, for example, once told me he had become so "hooked" on the excitement of covering the Middle East, Cyprus, and southern Africa that he suffered extreme depression after being transferred to more tranquil beats. A professor just back from two weeks of research in Belfast said she'd spent the whole time there in such an "adrenaline rush" that she "crashed" upon returning to this country and had to seclude herself for a time while undergoing "withdrawal." And after being defeated in a race for the U.S. Senate, Congressman Toby Moffett of Connecticut admitted that although he was looking forward to spending more time with his family, "I'd still rather be where the action is. You get hooked on it."

As an emergency room doctor once said of his work, "I hate it, loathe it, despise it, curse it, and will stomp anyone who says otherwise, but I'm hooked. I'm really no better than the 'Hey-Man,' guys who see snakes crawling up their legs or steal tv sets to buy smack. I'm addicted just like them. I shoot up the E.R. I crave the adrenaline rush from beating back a coma or stopping a bleeding belly. My head and muscles need the charge. I need the juice. I suppose my stomach even needs the acid."

For a long time such language always struck me as overblown. At best it seemed like an inappropriate choice of metaphor. Now I'm not so sure. Perhaps if you are so disposed, a high degree of stimulation can be as addicting as any drug.

Those so addicted measure the success of any activity by its level of excitement, and failure by boredom alone. Unlike the pot stirrer, they are not just geared to novelty. And in contrast to the thrill seeker, they can't satisfy their need for excitement with intense involvement in a weekend sport. The stimulus addict is to a thrill seeker as an alcoholic is to a heavy drinker. Their need for excitement is constant, elevated, and touches every aspect of their lives. Such addicts seem constantly to provoke crises in relationships with others and grow listless when things are on an even keel; work better in settings of chaos than of order; and sometimes turn to crime even when the income isn't needed because the excitement is.

The stimulus addict's hunger for excitement has nothing to do with good vibrations or happy endings. Even more so than the pot stirrer or thrill seeker, they find ongoing success depressing. This is why it's so easy to label them self-destructive. Some may be. But to those with a compulsive need for excitement, concepts such as failure or success, positive or negative, even living or dying are subservient to the constant need for excitement and fear of boredom. "You can get excited by anxiety," explains a Broadway actor. "I don't know anything about positive anxiety. Only negative. I'm addicted to it."

Graham Greene is an admitted action addict. After winning his early gambles at Russian roulette, he still found that "at fairly long intervals I found myself craving for the adrenaline drug. . . . One campaign was over, but the war against boredom had got to go on."

The British author has long been admired for his courage in seeking out the world's hottest spots to write about. Greene doesn't see it that way. He sees himself as so dependent on excitement that he grows suicidally despondent in its absence. "I hadn't the courage for suicide," Greene once explained, "but it became a habit with me to visit troubled places, not to seek material for novels but to regain the sense of insecurity which I had enjoyed in the three blitzes on London."

This is why the novelist considers his "research" trips to such locales as Indochina during the French war, Kenya for the Mau Mau uprising, and Malaya during a counterinsurgency campaign to have been his adult version of Russian roulette. In such settings Green would often be told by natives that they wished he could have seen their country in peacetime. The honest Englishman says he always wanted to reply, "But all that interests me here is your war."

From such a perspective, the addictive potential of even a horrifying experience such as war has less to do with blood-lust than the incomparable seduction of its excitement to those who are receptive. This is true of only a minority — the ones willing to endure constant nights of fear in order to reach regular dawns of euphoria. But to those so disposed, even sources of stimulation that are initially horrifying can ultimately become addictive.

During World War II, for example, psychologist Richard Solomon found himself assigned to an airfield in Texas. His task was to help develop a .50 caliber airborne machine gun. "I was terrified," recalls Solomon of that experience. "There were stories about it blowing up in people's hands. But after a while it addicted me to thrill seeking. I used to take the gun out in the desert to shoot rattlesnakes. It gave me a very positive feeling about World War II."

In the years since that experience, Solomon has developed a novel and widely discussed theory about how addiction occurs. He calls it the "opponent-process" theory. The essence of Solomon's theory is this: any sensation is followed by another sensation that is more intense and longer lasting but the opposite in feeling from the first. In Solomon's opinion, this is why the brief exhilaration of success is so typically followed by lengthy depression. By contrast, the agony of fear felt in a moment of danger is transformed into extended euphoria once the danger has passed. To earn the euphoria, you must be willing to endure the fear. Those who can — repeatedly — find the process addictive.

To illustrate the opponent process, Solomon uses the example of sauna baths. The typical reaction when first entering a sauna is to recoil from its intense heat. In response many leave, never to return. But those who stick around discover that a few minutes of excruciating heat result in hours of relaxed elation.

Similar illustrations of the opponent process at work include the addictive "high" felt by many runners following the agony of a marathon, and the lift some people get from painfully demanding work. Even human relationships may be subject to such a process. So many of us tolerate or even provoke fights with others as the price of euphoric making up afterward. This is why someone who has a bad effect on us can be more addictive than someone who has a good effect. A relationship with the latter type of person feels more likely to be predictable, tedious, and ultimately depressing, while one with the former holds the promise of regular moments of ecstasy in the calm following constant storms.

A clear dividing line between the stimulus addict and others is at their threshold of boredom. For example, a key distinction made between recreational and compulsive gamblers has to do with the "relief" felt by the latter when the agony of a normal day is relieved by the excitement of placing a bet. "They are intolerant of boredom," says psychiatrist Robert L. Custer of the addicted gamblers he specializes in treating. "They can't sit still. Gambling tends to give them a sensation of being alive. When they're not gambling, they're dead — they don't exist."

It's important to understand that for someone with a compulsive need for stimulation, boredom is not merely tedious; it's agonizing. When Graham Greene describes how he feels in the abscence of excitement, he's referring to a feeling more excruciating than the malaise of kids hanging around a shopping mall. "Boredom sickness" is the term Greene uses to describe that feeling. As he describes its symptoms: "Boredom seemed to swell like a balloon inside the head; it became a pressure inside the skull; sometimes I feared the balloon would burst and I would lose my reason."

Former Weatherman Susan Stern has written a painfully candid memoir describing how she found an antidote for the monotony of housewifery by becoming a street-fighting revolutionary. "Nothing in my life had ever been this exciting," she explained. "Careening from meeting to meeting, from demonstration to demonstration, from man to man . . . I loved every minute of it. I had all the excitement and activity I ever yearned for."

Stern's memoir is a fascinating portrayal of the stimulus addict as political crazy, alternating periods of suicidal depression with the euphoria of violent demonstrations. Although such demonstrations terrified her to the point of throwing up beforehand, she found them unmatched for exhilaration afterward. Breaking glass became her special pleasure: "I swung at the restaurant window with my iron pipe. . . . The window shattered, and I felt high as a motherfucker. Boy, did that feel great." During a later action, Stern ran for several blocks, breaking windows along the way, and "feeling that elation once again as the glass gave way beneath my blows."

137

Like most stimulus addicts, Susan Stern's mood meter seems to have had two basic settings: excited and bored. And as with so many of that breed, her quest for excitement cast a wide net. "I liked oodles of sex," Stern wrote, "mountains of dope. . . . I wanted to live, live, live, live, live, live." Her capacity for uppers, downers, LSD, THC, marijuana, cocaine, heroin, and whatever other chemical she could get her hands on was astonishing. To the horror of straighter movement members, Stern also worked as a go-go dancer. Far from being degrading, she found this work titillating, well paid, and "certainly more exciting and less dehumanizing than secretarial work." She also supplemented her income by stealing from stores and passing bad checks.

In her more lucid moments, Susan Stern seemed to realize that she couldn't keep this pace up indefinitely. From time to time she escaped her revolutionary frenzy by visiting friends in the country, or to serve terms in jail. Afterward she found her pace reduced, speech slowing down, and ravenous thirst for drugs and sex curbed. But in the process Stern grew bored. "What is rehabilitative about boredom?" she asked after one prison term. Stern described the tedium of her time in jail as "murder in the truest sense of the word." Each time she was released from such punishment, after a period of calm her level of frenzy seemed to go up, not down.

Toward the end of her career as a revolutionary, Susan Stern felt on the verge of a breakdown. A doctor warned that her body simply couldn't stand the pace. She tried to slow down but couldn't. "What shall I do?" Stern asked. "Commit myself to a hospital? Ex-Weathermen all over the country have had trouble readjusting to a normal life. I mean when you're a Vietcong one day, and the war is over the next, what do you do, all geared for death, and you got to go on living?"

In 1976, at the age of thirty-three, Susan Stern died of apparent heart failure.

Obviously there is something different in the makeup of a Susan Stern than in that of a less frenzied person, even a less frenzied revolutionary. One problem we have in coming to terms with stimulus addicts is that their problem is defined more by the *absence* of something they find positive (stimulation) than the *presence* of anything toxic. We're so focused on the problems of stress overload that we forget there are those for whom underload — what one psychiatrist has called "the trauma of eventlessness" — is a greater problem.

An emerging perspective on addiction in general is one suggesting that there are "addictive personalities" who are so neurologically understimulated that they can develop a dependence on outer stimulation of many kinds. They are "poly-addictive" — and which stimulus such people choose is largely a matter of circumstances. From this perspective, dependence on a particular substance — drugs, alcohol, action — is only the visible manifestation of a temperament susceptible to addiction in general. With a constant need for stimulation at high levels, and susceptibility to withdrawal symptoms in the absence of such stimulation, the stimulus addict who is out of the action is under a constant threat of severe depression and even physical trauma.

For an extreme action addict, too little stimulation may even hasten death. In his biography of Napoleon, medical historian Frank Richardson speculated that after years astride the political volcano of postrevolutionary France, the tedium of life in exile may literally have killed the French emperor at fifty-three. "On a small island," Napoleon himself wrote before fleeing Elba for Waterloo, "once one has set the mechanism going, nothing is left but to die of boredom — or in some heroic venture to escape from it."

The role of stimulus addiction in political leadership has yet to receive the attention it deserves. Some politicians themselves admit that constant arousal is the payoff, not the price of their work. Winston Churchill once said of his second career, "Politics are nearly as exciting as war, and quite as dangerous." More recently, New York's City Council President Carol Bellamy characterized her calling as "an addiction," one motivated by "a fear of being bored."

Of course, being boredom-phobic is not necessarily a bad trait in a politician. Indeed, whoever is subjected to the grueling pace of political life had better enjoy, thrive in, even *need* that level of stimulation. The late political scientist Harold Lasswell used to say that we're all born politicians, and some of us outgrow it. But this wasn't necessarily a criticism of those who run for office.

On the contrary, it may take a child's love of excitement to survive and flourish in that atmosphere.

The danger is that by accelerating the pace of stimulation in public life, we may be limiting ourselves to those so in need of such arousal that they even regard the day-to-day demands of governing as a relatively tedious price they must pay for the exhilaration of campaigning (this has been suggested about George Wallace, Jesse Jackson, and Ronald Reagan). Worse yet, once in office the political-action addict may create crises to cope with if enough don't present themselves naturally.

Richard Nixon always portrayed himself as being at his best in the midst of crises. Many seemed to be of his own making. Nixon once observed that a political leader "should learn to live with and be stimulated by tension, rather than numbing his spirit with tranquilizers. Eisenhower demonstrated a trait that I believe all great leaders have in common: they thrive on challenge; they are at their best when the going is hardest. When life is routine, they become bored; when they have no challenge, they tend to wither and die or go to seed."

Nixon noted further that "those who have known great crisis — its challenge and tension, its victory and defeat — can never become adjusted to a more leisurely and orderly pace. They have drunk too deeply of the stuff which really makes life exciting and worth living to be satisfied with the froth."

Tempted as they are by life in the eye of a crisis, stimulus addicts have ended up leading nations throughout history, often into war. Depending on the circumstances, this can be a blessing or a curse, or sometimes both. Winston Churchill, after all, was widely ridiculed as an adventure-craving adolescent in a grown-up's body until those qualities began to look attractive when Hitler's bombs were about to fall. And Israel's General Ariel Sharon has won battles for his country at crucial moments because he does so well in moments of peril. But many of his countrymen think Sharon has contributed needlessly to their peril by initiating the type of action at which he thrives.

A study of kibbutz managers in Israel found action seekers so common among them that they dubbed this style "Type C." In contrast to the more familiar "Type A" (who seeks stress but suffers from it) and "Type B" (who avoids stress because he finds it unpleasant), the Type C managers flourish in the midst of chaos. Not only psychologically but physically as well, the researchers found, such managers "show greater coronary risk under relatively tranquil, nonstressful conditions."

This Type C is at least as prevalent as his A and B counterparts in American management. A management professor named Henry Mintzberg once spent a week at each of five major companies observing the heads at work. In contrast to the traditional view of such top executives as working in an orderly, rationalized manner, Mintzberg found that they preferred "calculated chaos." He described a typical moment of their working day as involving "the cigarette in his mouth, one hand on the telephone, and the other shaking hands with a departing guest." According to Mintzberg, few of such executives' activities took longer than nine minutes apiece. Most were open-door types who welcomed more than they shunned interruption. In general, he concluded, this working style was dictated by a need to avoid routine.

Their need for constant excitement is of increasing concern to those treating both the bodies and minds of American managers (to say nothing of those concerned about the state of the economy). From such a perspective, what's often called workaholism too often doesn't involve an addiction to the substance of one's work so much as to its arousal. "If there's one problem that brings people to my office," notes psychiatrist Jay Rohrlich, who specializes in treating those who work near his office in New York's financial district, "it's that they like their work too much. The intoxication of it obliterates whatever else they used to find enjoyable — they don't need to read books; they don't need to go to the theater; they sometimes don't even need to have sex."

Research done in the American workplace has confirmed not only the prevalence but the preference for stress at addictive levels. This craving for excitement often passes for "risk taking." Unlike management styles elsewhere, our cliff-hanger approach too often substitutes the short-term excitement of memo wars, transfers, reorganization, and acquisitions for actual long-term risk. Management psychiatrist Michael Maccoby calls this the style of a "gamesman" whose fear of boredom and need for action transcends any need for lasting results (leading many to shuttle from one company to the next). As Lee Iacocca said as he was about to leave Ford before he joined Chrysler, "If I have any fear, it's what do you do when you've been embroiled in activity and it suddenly stops?"

As with any stimulus addiction, the addiction to work has more to do with the level of arousal than with its quality. Even those who loathe an exciting, stressful job may come to depend on its stimulation. Long after losing their jobs due to a strike called in part to protest their work's stress, air controllers seemed to mourn the loss of this work — stress included. Not surprisingly, when tested on their sensation-seeking tendencies, air controllers came out quite high. A long-term study of male controllers found them generally to be strong, intelligent, dominating, self-confident, and unusually "macho" types, who were conscientious at work but drank too much alcohol and had minor skirmishes with the law on their own time. As with veterans of Vietnam, it might be revealing to keep tabs on ex-controllers in years to come for evidence of post-traumatic-stress syndrome, including criminal activity.

One of the least appreciated motives for crime in general is a compulsive need for excitement. Michael Tindall's lawyer, Joseph Oteri, estimates that whatever their initial motivation, 90 percent of the drug smugglers who make up most of his clientele stay in that business because they grow dependent on its excitement. The rest of their lives seem drab by contrast. Oteri's partner Martin Weinberg adds that the degree of adventure involved is so captivating that leaving the life of a smuggler altogether is "a very brave act. You're left without the accoutrements of success other than money, which isn't much compared with the adventure."

To the average criminal, profit plays the same role as it does to the average gambler: it gives his occupation stakes. The late Willie Sutton once explained that while he loved robbing banks, "to me the money was the chips, that's all. The winnings. I kept robbing banks when, by all logic, it was foolish. When it would cost me far more than I could possibly gain."

So why did he do it?

"I enjoyed it," Sutton said. "I loved it. I was more alive when I was inside a bank robbing it than at any other time in my life."

A *Les Misérables* approach to crime as a direct, desperate response to poverty is simplistic at best. Such an approach can't account for the vast majority of law-abiding poor people. Nor can it explain criminals who are financially secure but continue to commit crimes. Or those career criminals who scorn comparable income from "straight" but routine work. "They tried to give me an alternative," an armed robber once explained from his jail cell, "but it wasn't lucrative enough at the time. There's no way you could offer me a better life than the life I chose. Not just the profit aspect. There's not enough excitement."

In their sixteen-year study of *The Criminal Personality*, the late psychiatrist Samuel Yochelson and psychologist Stanton Samenow found it typical among criminals they treated in Washington, D.C., that money as such had a fairly low priority in their lives. The cases in which their lawbreakers squandered or even gave away the money they'd stolen were "so numerous as to be the rule rather than the exception," wrote Yochelson and Samenow. On occasion the take was even discarded. For careeer criminals, the two believe, it is not income but excitement that constitutes "the oxygen of their lives." Compared to a typical job with regular hours, routine work, and predictable income, crime provides an ideal alternative. When it comes to stimulation, few careers can compare. "Thinking about crime is exciting," says Samenow. "Talking about crime is exciting. Committing the crime is exciting. Even getting caught is exciting. Trying to figure out a way to beat the rap is exciting." Indeed, when not engaged in some aspect of crime, he and Yochelson report, the career criminal is subject to anxiety, psychosomatic ailments, and depression.

Consider the case of Ray Johnson. Although today a thoroughly reformed consultant on crime prevention for the Southland Corporation's 7-Eleven stores, Johnson was a career criminal for most of his adult life. And even though most of those years were spent in prison (he was the first man to escape from San Quentin), like a reformed alcoholic Johnson says that he will never stop missing his crime habit. "Not long ago," he wrote in a memoir, "in the Valley shopping center, I saw an armored car which was unloading square bags of money. Square bags mean currency. Everybody was out of the truck and that was like heaven speaking to me. I went back the following week, same time, and by god, they did it again. I felt the adrenaline pumping and my head was humming. Now I know absolutely that I'm not going to do anything about it, but I can't deny that it really turns me on. It's a pleasant feeling."

Like skydivers, the ranks of career criminals seem dominated by those who have discovered that fear induces excitement. Yochelson and Samenow found that the peak of excitement for their clients is felt just before they commit a crime. This is also the time when their fear of apprehension is greatest. During the crime itself, in the classic Level I pattern, they "cut off" fears and become ultracool and concentrated (presumably due to all the endorphins they're pumping). Afterward, Yochelson and Samenow found, lawbreakers commonly remained in the neighborhood where they committed their crime because walking around unapprehended added to the excitement.

The complementary poles of fear and excitement were on display constantly in a unique drug rehabilitation program organized by Philip Bartow (the man who led the disabled group up Mt. Rainier). In addition to their drug offenses, most of the members of this program were involved in crimes such as burglary and armed robbery. Some had already served long prison terms. Few looked like people I wanted to run into on a dark street outside the program we shared for a few days.

"You put in that book you're writing that I'm scared as hell," an armed robber named Ike told me on our first ride to climb rocks. Ike was muscular, wore a stocking over his hair, and a constant scowl that belied his words.

"Me too," chimed in voices of his companions.

As we parked in the lot of a state forest in Maryland, Ike looked nervously out the van window at a 1000-foot peak nearby. "We gonna climb that mountain?" he asked a counselor named George.

"Yeah," George replied.

"There bears up there?" asked Ike.

Bears were a major concern of this group. So were snakes, poison ivy, bugs, and anything else that might be lurking about. As we hiked up a trail to the rocks, there was a slight rustle in the adjacent brush. "All right," Ike called out, stopping his pace. "What's in there? Whatever it is, don't come out."

One member of the group was a slight, twitchy, twenty-four-year-old named Sunshine, who the others said had fried his brains on LSD. Whenever he inched his way up the rocks, Sunshine kept up a running commentary about how terrified he was. At one point he went completely out of control, trembling wildly, screaming hysterically ("Get me off this motherfucking mountain!") and finally tucking his body into a fetal position when Bartow came to the rescue. Yet in between hysterics, even this young addict was not only game, but eager to try the climbs. Sunshine often was one of the first to volunteer to start up the rocks. By contrast, I always held back to study the situation first and give my fear time to settle down. Feeling afraid obviously provoked different responses in the two of us.

One climbing exercise was calculated to make us lose our grip and fall (tied to a rope, of course). When Ike first fell, he got to his feet, brushed off, then said to the rest of us with a sheepish grin, "Man, that scared the shit out of me."

"Wanna untie?" asked George.

"Leave that thing on," replied Ike. "I'm going right back up." And he did, falling yet a second then a third time before moving on to the next set of rocks. Among the most dubious at first, Ike really was getting into his climbing. As I was trying to struggle my way up a high, sheer cliff he had already mastered, Ike called out, "C'mon, Ralph. If I did it, you can."

On the way down the mountain Ike was as jittery as ever about what might be in the brush. He told me that with a gun in hand he wouldn't be scared of anything on that mountain, not even a bear, not even at one in the morning. Ike showed me how he'd draw a bead on that bear with a pistol.

In three outings I watched this group's enthusiasm and self-confidence about climbing grow by the trip. With five more to go, I was eager to see what results the entire experience might produce. It was not to be. After their fourth outing (which I missed), most of the group — including Ike — were expelled from the program for continued use of drugs.

Marvin Zuckerman, the University of Delaware psychologist,

once worked for a drug rehabilitation program in the same city where Bartow's was located. As have so many who work with them, Zuckerman found addicts extremely ambivalent about being rehabilitated. It wasn't their addiction they were reluctant to give up as much as the life of an addict. Zuckerman found that even those who had kicked their drug habit spoke nostalgically about the risk, excitement, and variety of their former lives. One asked the psychologist: "When I am straight and have a nine-to-five job, where will I get my kicks?"

Zuckerman thinks that crime in general and drug abuse in particular can best be understood as an extreme expression of the sensation-seeking trait. As he puts it, "The concept of risking one's life and freedom for the sheer excitement in criminal activity is incomprehensible to anyone but a high sensation seeker." Since normal amounts of stimulation are experienced as excruciating to such stimulation-starved criminals, the risk of breaking the law can be a means of maintaining equilibrium. As a forger once explained of his reasons for beginning to write bad checks again after a period of obeying the law, "After the apprehension of going straight, there was almost relaxation. I could sleep at night. The tension was over."

In recent years speculation has centered on the idea that those with an exaggerated and chronic need for excitement may suffer from neurological disorders. Violent delinquents in particular have been found to have a common history of brain lesions, in some cases resulting from childhood accidents. But even in the absence of such pathology, it's plausibly argued that those whose need for action is addictive have brains that are built differently than others.

From this perspective, the action addict's nervous system may be one so deprived of natural opiates that at a state that to someone else feels steady, they experience painful despair. One way to ease this pain is with synthetic narcotics. Another is by constantly engaging in activity so stimulating that it ensures a steady flow of natural ones. Unlike the thrill seeker — whose reward comes in the form of euphoria when such opiates are flowing — the addict needs generous and constant amounts of them just to feel "normal" and prevent the agony of withdrawal.

As natural opiates, endorphins were at first thought not to be addicting. We now know better. When administered externally, they've been found to be every bit as addicting as the morphine they resemble. This strongly suggests that some of us can develop a dependence on our own opiates, which, since they are released in response to stress, can ultimately lead to dependence on stress itself.

Whether one is born with such an addictive need for excitement or acquires it along the way is hard to say. Some of those who work in this field believe we're predisposed genetically to produce more or less than our share of natural opiates. But even assuming this to be true, other processes are also at work. It's been found, for example, that fetuses respond almost instantly to the chemicals released by their mothers under stress. Since the brain is still quite plastic at that stage, such prenatal chemical messages could have a lifelong influence on its development. Even after birth there is evidence that the pathways of immature brains can be altered by experience. More specifically, at least among certain individuals, the number of brain receptors that respond to endorphins and other chemicals may be increased or diminished by the types of experiences they have. This could help explain why a known risk factor for lifelong compulsive gambling is a big win during adolescence. And why some Lebanese teenagers who have grown up in the midst of a civil war find that they get bored and jittery during occasional trips abroad to peaceful countries.

So, a plausible rationale for action addiction suggests that *if*, due to genetic, prenatal, or postbirth influences, you are disposed to seek the means to make up for an endorphin deficiency, and if at a receptive time of life you discover that a high level of excitement can release extra endorphins to the point that you become dependent on them, then your chances of becoming an action addict are good. Whether such addiction is to crime, narcotics, war, work, bad relationships, or some combination may be largely a matter of circumstance.

But the important point is that you must be predisposed. I don't think you can grab any Girl Scout off the street and through a lot of action "hook" her on a lifelong need for excitement, any more than a sip of whiskey creates an alcoholic or a single shot of heroin produces a junkie. But to those so disposed, exposure to high degrees of arousal at a receptive stage of life may influence the development of their brain in such a way that it develops a lasting dependency on stimulation simply to maintain equilibrium and avoid the painful frustration of tranquility.

In the case of Michael Tindall, the veteran turned smuggler, I don't think the evidence is as clear as his lawyers and psychiatrists suggested that this man was a *tabula rasa* infected by the germ of adventure in Vietnam. Something that was touched on but never explored at his trial was the fact that before going overseas Tindall was an active member of the Fort Benning Sport Parachute Club. He also volunteered for the hazardous job of helicopter pilot, then chose to pilot gunships rather than ferry troops. Tindall clearly had a taste for excitement that sought expression. The more convincing argument is that this taste became a hunger then an addiction in the unrelenting life-or-death setting of Vietnam.

The Vietnam war generally seems to have produced more than its share of action addicts. This was due not only to its unrelieved jungle horrors, but also to the fact that for those in combat, action during a year's tour of duty tended to be constant. By contrast, the average World War II soldier saw only a few weeks of combat in several years of service. Furthermore, in that war the average GI was twenty-six years old. In Vietnam our soldiers' average age was nineteen. Presumably one's brain is more vulnerable to alteration in its late teens than in its midtwenties. If so, the impact of unrelieved action on many still-maturing nervous systems may have been profound and indelible. Conceivably we have a generation with more than its share of action addicts who served in Vietnam and now are serving prison sentences at a rate twice that for nonveterans in the same age group. Fully a quarter of all 1.5 million Vietnam vets are estimated to have had brushes with the law since returning home. At least one-third may suffer some form of post-traumatic stress. Some, in the Northwest especially, have even retreated to dense forests where they live by their wits in a re-creation of jungle war.

In discussions with Vietnam veterans, and sprinkled throughout their memoirs, this sentiment recurs over and over: I hated the war and hope never to fight in one again; I miss the war.

"Anyone who fought in Vietnam," writes veteran Philip Caputo (later an antiwar activist), "if he is honest about himself, will have to admit he enjoyed the compelling attractiveness of combat. It was a peculiar enjoyment because it was mixed with a commensurate pain. Under fire, a man's powers of life heightened in proportion to the proximity of death, so that he felt an elation as extreme as his dread. His senses quickened, he attained an acuity of consciousness at once pleasurable and excruciating. It was something like the elevated state of awareness induced by drugs. And it could be just as addictive, for it made whatever else life offered in the way of delights or torments seem pedestrian."

In a review of his fellow Marine's memoir, World War II veteran William Styron said that from the first page of Caputo's book he experienced "a chilling sense of *déjà vu*." What Styron said he most admired in his younger colleague's work was Caputo's willingness to explore the "unholy attraction" of war, and his courage in being "never less than honest, sometimes relentlessly so, about his feelings concerning the thrill of warfare and the intoxication of combat."

Although the responses of veterans to war vary greatly, the ambivalent nostalgia felt by Styron, Caputo, and Michael Tindall is probably more widespread than we realize. Because the repulsiveness of war's horrors are more understandable, they're what we're more likely to hear about. To mention the horror's seductiveness risks getting a veteran tagged not only as a killer, but a killer happy in his work. Yet for many — no matter how they felt about participating in a war — life will never be its equal in intensity. Some are just as glad. Others engage in a constant quest for war substitutes. They have become stimulus addicts.

Are stimulus addicts risk takers? Only in the most narrow sense of that word, one that equates risk with derring-do and relentless excitement seeking. But as we've seen, a compulsive quest for excitement may have more to do with needs of the body than those of the spirit. Like most Level I risk takers, the stimulus addict may be avoiding scarier risks than those he takes while constantly looking for action. For those whose risk taking is largely of the high-excitement, Level I variety, far harder risks to take usually await them at the second level.

LEVEL II

RISK TAKING

An interviewer once asked James Michener if he was a risk taker. Yes, the author replied, he was. As evidence Michener pointed out that he'd run with the bulls through the streets of Pamplona in Spain.

A friend of mine once ran with the bulls at Pamplona. When I complimented him on his courage, my friend scoffed. This man was in his mid-thirties, in the process of ending a marriage, and stuck in a boring job with no alternative in sight. His solution was to fly to Spain and run with the bulls. Unlike the risks he faced back home, this activity seemed simple, clear, and not nearly so frightening as coming to terms with his life as a whole.

Compared with running from bulls, coping with one's life as a whole might be considered a second-level risk. These are the risks we most typically avoid with exciting Level I activity, yet they can be by far the more daunting.

As Philippe Petit points out, life-or-death issues have "clarity." Emotional issues seldom do. One reason that so many men march happily off to war (until they get there, anyway) is its promise of a clear and focused danger to replace the fuzzy and diffuse ones most of us grapple with at home.

Such second-level dangers are long-range, ambiguous, and low in stimulation. They involve risk to the ego and risks of boredom, failure, and regret. More than merely the body is at stake.

What risks are we actually talking about? In no particular order: creating ties to others. Building careers. Developing self-

153

knowledge. Tolerating silence. Doing nothing. Not trying to control all outcomes. Being bored. Being boring.

These may not sound like risks. But ask a Level I type in a candid moment what he or she fears most and is trying to avoid by being so active. Grace Slick, the hyper rock and roller who is still going strong into her forties, once confessed to a lifelong fear that people would discover she's boring.

As Americans we're especially prone to equate risk taking with movement, *doing something*, preferably something dramatic. Given our immigrant heritage, it's probably inevitable that we equate taking a risk with making a move. Such action may be good, necessary, and even risky. But sometimes doing nothing can be the bigger risk, especially in a society that frowns on this sort of thing. Our historic restlessness may have made American culture as effervescent as it is. But it's also involved, as historian John Higham puts it, "a flight from travail, from complexity, from the terrors of self-awareness."

Just as action can be risky for a reflective person, reflection can feel dangerous to someone who's active. Sensory-deprivation studies — in which subjects are left alone in barren rooms for extended periods of time — have been found to be particularly excruciating for aggressive, control-oriented men. To such men, having only their own thoughts for company can be literally terrifying. When soldiers were used as subjects in such an experiment, 37 percent found it too unnerving to last the full four days and quit early. In follow-up interviews, those who left early said they were terrified of losing control over their own thought processes.

To some degree we're all afraid of what we might hear should we sit still and listen. Hasn't "Dr. Jekyll and Mr. Hyde" lasted so long as a metaphor because we're all so sure a Mr. Hyde may be snapping, growling, and salivating deep within our own dungeons? Not wishing to risk peering inside to find out probably keeps us more on the go than we realize.

I recently heard a talk given by an advertising man in his midforties who changed jobs every couple of years. He did so, the man said, by virtue of being a risk taker. "It's what makes your heart beat faster," he explained. Because he had a short attention span, the man added, was easily bored, and enjoyed change, he continually took the risk of moving on. But wouldn't a bigger risk be to stay put?

A nurse I know is a classic American "risk taker" in the sense that she moves frequently, changes jobs often, prefers working in the chaos of an emergency room, has gone para-sailing behind a boat in Acapulco, and dreams of skydiving. The most frightened I have ever seen this woman was when at the age of twenty-nine she and her husband discovered she was pregnant. This brought all manner of fears to the surface: fears of commitment, responsibility, and rootedness. The thought of having to stay put terrified her, as did the risk of becoming conventional. Far greater than her fear of physical danger was her fear of becoming one more person on line waiting to buy Pampers. A sedentary person. Not a risk taker. By definition.

Second-level risks are rarely called daring, not in this culture anyway. They're just so *undramatic*. Yet especially for Level I types with an exaggerated need for stimulation, more profound dangers lurk along less stimulating paths — ones that might lead to boredom. If boredom feels like a fate worse than death, as it does to so many first-level risk takers, then the risk of a boring life can feel far more dangerous than the mere risk of one's life.

Among the many adventurous women Grace Lichtenstein profiled in her book *Machisma*, few were involved in lasting relationships. Parenting was a rarity among them. One "risk taker" profiled was a writer who spent years shuttling about the world on different assignments before becoming the superintendent of a small national park in Alaska. Her philosophy, writes Lichtenstein, is "Take a chance, take a flight — it might have great possibilities." Yet as she goes on to observe about this friend, "Marriage, with its compromise of personal freedom while seeking a stable relationship, frightened her more than any 'risk' she had taken before."

There's a fairly predictable concurrence between a taste for high-stimulation risk taking and a fear of lasting ties. Three social scientists once studied both the driving habits and personality traits of a random sample of young men. They found that those who regularly used reckless driving of their cars as a means for "self testing" also expressed the most interest in moving frequently. They did not consider being near friends or relatives an important consideration in selecting a residence. Self-testing drivers also were less likely to be active members of community organizations, and were more interested in national than local news. Whether such an approach involves laudable daring or cowardly avoidance depends on how you look at it. As the social scientists who discovered this relationship pointed out, the same qualities that characterize self-testing drivers also characterized the migrants and pioneers who created this nation: a willingness to take physical risks, to move, and not to feel too bound to others. "Such people," they concluded, "may ultimately colonize Mars."

But are they taking real risks? At a glance, they are. Decisive people willing to take bold steps nearly always look more daring than relfective, sedentary ones. Yet bold decisiveness often reflects a fear of ambiguity, of leaving matters fluid and unresolved. And apparent risks being taken in public often disguise those being ducked at home. Even saintly risk takers such as Gandhi and Tolstoy seem to have had an easier time being daring on behalf of principles and populations of people than in taking chances with the families they neglected at home.

In the introduction to Level I risk taking, I considered the "C-virtues," which were bonuses for taking such exciting risks: control, concentration, calm, camaraderie, and character. There are C-virtues at the second level as well. Among them are feelings of continuity, complexity, and calm — a more lasting, lower-level type of calm than the temporary release of tension enjoyed after taking a high-stimulation risk. In two cases in particular, Level II C-virtues are the direct antithesis of their counterpart at the first level. These are the rewards of commitment and community.

COMMITMENT

As he approached middle age, race driver Dan Gerber wrote that while he still enjoyed the spice of physical danger, "I've come to admire other, more necessary though no less heroic, kinds of risk taking: the risk an artist must take in his work, doing what he isn't sure he can do, the risks of friendship, of marriage, of commitment of any kind."

Commitment might be seen as the antithesis of control. Committing ourselves — to another person, group, or conviction — makes it necessary to relinquish some control over our own destiny. The obvious example is when we tie ourselves to another person and give that person a say in the direction of our lives. But there are others. On my questionnaire, two people — one a young paralegal, the other an older rabbi — mentioned commitment to their vocation as the biggest risk they'd taken. One of the most perceptive responses I got to the interview question "What would be a risk for you?" came from a sixteen-year-old boy who was trying to decide what direction to take with his life. He wanted desperately to become a professional musician. The teenager wanted this so badly that he said the biggest risk he could imagine taking would be to pursue his dream of a musical career and run the risk that it wouldn't come true.

Making a commitment to do what you really want to do involves profound danger. Should you fail, so much is at stake. I don't think we'll ever appreciate the role not risking a dream plays in driving us to second-choice careers and third-choice lives. Among would-be writers, I find it common that those with the biggest dreams of literary triumph are the ones most reluctant to put their writing in the mail (or even on paper) for fear of jeopardizing that fantasy. I've even thought of distributing fill-in-the-blank forms at the outset of writing workshops that would read, "I'd have been a great writer except that _____." We all have something, or many things, to write in that blank, and alternative introductions as well. The more credible our rationalization, the less need there is actually to risk finding out whether our dream has substance. There's a lot to be said for not doing what you really want to do. If you fail at something else, so what? Little was at stake. No commitment was dared to anything you really cared about.

The most profound stake involved in risking commitment is time. With so long a period of time involved — a lifetime, even — suppose you make the wrong choice: of mate, career, or conviction? By keeping things fluid and temporary and by staying on the move we avoid taking this awesome risk.

157

It's characteristic of our leading models of adventurousness — Ernest Hemingway, Joseph Conrad, Burt Reynolds — that sustained marriages or relationships of any kind seem not to be their strong suit. This is one reason that the camaraderie of danger can be so appealing to such men. The intensity of temporary relationships conforms to their romantic ideal far better than ongoing ones. And this is not only because sharing danger promotes intense bonds, but because these bonds end with the danger. Wars cease. High school classes graduate. Plays complete their run. Knowing in advance that relationships will end allows them to be intense while they last.

But camaraderie is *not* the same things as community. Community takes place at a much lower level of intensity. It has to. When people know they'll be with each other for a while, perhaps even for a lifetime, they lower the heat. Community can only be simmered. By demanding a level of excitement that can't be sustained, camaraderie can actually thwart the building of a sense of community in which members gradually come to know one another.

COMMUNITY

Among excitement-seeking utopians, models of "community" are nearly always the short-lived, pressure-cooker versions: Woodstock, the Paris Commune, a weekend workshop where everyone falls in love. But when they try to translate such a model into something ongoing, the venture nearly always fails. Has anyone seen a commune recently?

In the sense that we usually use that term, "risk" and community are antithetical. When mired in the bosom of a group, we supposedly lose our sense of daring. Yet in a more profound sense, community *is* risk — to those who are committed to one. To them the stakes — their most catastrophic potential loss — are not their property or their homes or even their lives, but ties to others in which they have so much time and so many feelings invested. The most devastating trauma of disasters is seldom a direct result of being threatened by bombs, drowning, or having one's home sucked into the sky by a tornado. Such experiences can contribute to *esprit* and a sense of fraternity among those who must band together to cope. The real trauma occurs when the underpinnings of a community are lost along with property and lives.

It's well known to military psychologists that at least 50 percent of the housing of a civilian population must be destroyed before morale can be hurt by bombing during a war. Psychologically speaking, one of the worst natural disasters ever to occur in this country involved a dam that burst above Buffalo Creek, West Virginia, in 1972, destroying most of the homes and residents of that valley. As sociologist Kai Erikson noted in her report on this tragedy, unlike the rebound commonly experienced by communities following a disaster, here "victims outnumbered the nonvictims by so large a margin that the community itself has to be counted a casualty."

As one survivor put it:

> We did lose a community, and I mean it was a good community. Everybody was close, everybody knowed everybody. But now everybody is alone. They act like they're lost. They've lost their homes and their way of life, the one they liked, the one they was used to. All the houses are gone, every one of them. The people are gone, scattered. You don't know who your neighbor is going to be. You can't go next door and talk. You can't do that no more, there's no next door. You can't laugh with friends. You can't do that no more, because there's no friends around to laugh with. That don't happen no more. There's nobody around to even holler at and say 'Hi,' and you can't help but miss that.

In contrast to a sense of community built over a lifetime, the camaraderie that results from uniting to cope with challenge is based on a temporary experience so riveting that it makes dealing with distractions unnecessary. This is its great appeal. But it is the very need to deal with distractions — buying toothpaste, washing dishes, hurting feelings, passing time — that builds lasting community even as it destroys short-term camaraderie. Community is built of details. It must be. Community gathers together whole human beings for the long haul, not just ones sharing for a moment an intense part of themselves. Taking the less intense, longer-lasting second-level of risk poses particular problems for men, the young, and those who would be more masculine and youthlike.

DO MEN TAKE MORE RISKS THAN WOMEN?

Throughout this book it's been implied but never stated that Level I risk taking is part of the traditional male role. And that "risk taking," as we usually use that term, is more likely to be engaged in by men than by women.

At some point our culture determined that climbing a mountain constituted "risk taking," while giving birth to a child didn't. As a result we tend to see risks as the sorts of things men take and women avoid. When polls are taken of traits associated with sex roles, "risk taking" is routinely put in the male column by men and women alike. As one woman so surveyed explained about what she envied most in men: "I want some of that good old *macho* courage. Males get all the interesting roles in movies, because the male role — the cool heroics of a Kojak or a Dirty Harry — is more exciting than the female role."

But this is just one more example of equating stimulation seeking with risk taking. Not surprisingly, men as a group appear to produce fewer of the brain chemicals that promote inner arousal and make less likely the search for outer stimulation. On my own questionnaire, more men than women reported that they were bored "often" (23 percent to 18 percent). In exactly opposite proportions, more women than men said they were "almost never" bored. There also was a revealing contrast in the ways men and women reported dealing with a feared activity. Men by a 24 to 14 percent margin agreed with the statement that since few things scared them, fear didn't usually keep them from doing something they wanted to do. By about the same ratio (29 percent to 19 percent), more women than men said just the opposite: that fear could keep them from engaging in an activity they wanted to engage in. But more women than men (39 to 31 percent) concurred with the statement, "Even though something might scare me, I'll still go ahead and do it." If risk involves action in the face of fear, this response alone gives women the risk-taking edge. Closer to sensation seeking would be the statement, "A little fear can make things more interesting and exciting," which was endorsed by 23 percent of the men and 16 percent of the women.

One of the most consistent findings about sensation seeking by Marvin Zuckerman and others is that it characterizes men more than women, and that from the twenties on, this trait declines steadily with age. Since we do confuse sensation seeking and risk taking, men and the young are presumed to be our leading risk takers. In the chapters to come, I'd like to suggest the opposite: that although they clearly seek more stimulation, the risk-taking capacity of men and the young is less than assumed, while the willingness of women and older people to take risks is greater.

Even without Zuckerman's data, few would question that on the whole men are more likely than women to seek sensation — often in death-defying forms. But more revealing than this broad conclusion is the *kinds* of sensation men and women are likely to seek or avoid. As might be expected, far fewer women than men taking Zuckerman's sensation-seeking scale expressed interest in such activities as "crawling along a ledge on a high mountain side," "starting out in a sailboat on a rough sea," or "being alone in the woods at night." Men, on the other hand, to a much greater degree than women, reported "going to a counseling bureau to seek help" as a dangerous activity they'd rather avoid. Other pursuits that felt more daring to men than to women included "going to meet a new date," "going into a psychological experiment," and "entering a contest before spectators."

So the more interesting question is not whether men or women as a group take more risks, but which types of risk each group is more likely to take.

When she analyzed stories describing the same pictures written by eighty-eight college men and fifty college women, psychologist Carol Gilligan found striking differences between the sexes in their perception of danger. In general, the women described situations involving competition for achievement as fraught with peril, and saw great danger in social isolation. By contrast, the men were much less likely to describe competitive situations as hazardous, but saw much to fear from intimate involvement with other people. "The differences found in this study suggest that men and women experience attachment and separation in different ways," concluded Gilligan (with associate Susan Pollak), "and that each sex correspondingly perceives a danger that the other does not see — men in connecting, women in separation."

Gilligan went on to suggest that from the male perspective, which characterizes most research on life stages, women tend to be "mired in relationships," have problems with "individuation," and are overall not up to making their independent way in the world. By contrast, the most "successful" navigators of life-stage passages — men, typically — tend to be friendless and have a distant relationship with their families. As life-cycle researcher Daniel Levinson once observed of the men he's spent years studying, "In our interviews, friendship was largely noticeable by its absence. As a tentative generalization we would say that close friendship with a man or a woman is rarely experienced by American men."

In the increasing discussion among women about how to take more risks, this manly approach seems to have been swallowed whole — with all of its contraindications. Among business-women especially, such dialogue is based on a concept of risk that can be more implicitly masculine than that held by men themselves. The concerns about risk taking among women in business focus on their tendency to treat work relationships like personal ones, and to approach the office as they would a home. Being family-oriented, they profess having trouble making decisions that could threaten such relationships. This also gives them a perspective on their lives that makes it difficult to accept transfers or to continually work long hours. Taking short-term gambles with large sums of money is a risk women discuss as being especially difficult. So are the risks of competing effectively in office politics, and letting go of relationships that are no longer useful. A typical exhortation made by one businesswoman to others at a workshop on risk taking urged them to avoid "unsuccessful turkeys," even if such turkeys were friends. "Leaving your friends behind isn't disloyalty," this woman told her audience. "You are going to be judged by the company you keep. Seek out the people who can help you. Men have known this for years, and we are playing in their arena."

The irony is that even as women are arming themselves at

such gatherings to storm the Bastille of manly risk, men themselves are slipping out the back to attend seminars on developing a longer-range investment perspective, more sensitivity toward employees, and the ability to create a "family" atmosphere at work. These might be thought of as womanly virtues, and indeed are the very ones women are trying to jettison so they can take more "risks." But not wanting to call them womanly, men prefer to think that such virtues are . . . "Japanese." In this manner they reduce the stakes of daring to violate their sex role. Yet this very risk is one more men would like to take — if only they dared.

One person I interviewed for this project was a television camerawoman. She told me that the American public's thirst for vicarious risk had made her job increasingly hazardous. Quite a number of camerapeople have died while filming stunts for action shows and daredevil-type commercials. The camerawoman made a point of refusing any assignment that she felt put her in unreasonable danger. Every time she's done this, male colleagues have congratulated her — in private — for taking such a risk. They would like to do the same, they tell her. But as men, they can't dare to seem afraid of a dangerous assignment.

AS TIME GOES BY

Late in his life my own father has turned to writing poetry. This is a pursuit he took up soon after retiring from his career as an economist, city planner, and teacher of both. In college he'd originally majored in English. His earliest poetry was written at this time. But midway through college, my father switched his major to Economics. I'd always thought that this was because the depression was on, and English (to say nothing of poetry) seemed like a frivolous response to the times. Recently my father gave me a different explanation altogether. It seems that writing poetry — his real love — had begun to strike him as not "masculine" enough. Economics seemed more so. And this is what he chose for his career. But by his late sixties, no longer concerned about whether he is "masculine" or not (or perhaps just more sure), my father produces a chap book a year of his best poetic efforts.

One of the most consistent findings about changes with age is that conforming to sex roles declines in importance. Over time men and women tend to meet at a crossroad as women allow themselves to become more assertive and men more reflective. An ongoing study of intellectually gifted men who were surveyed from youth into old age at seven-year intervals found that age fifty was typically a watershed after which their pace of activity declined. So did activities associated with being "masculine." From one perspective, this suggests you're less of a man after fifty. From another perspective, the need to prove that point declines as self-acceptance rises.

While attending a number of high school reunions for an earlier book (*Is There Life After High School?*), I was struck by how much more relaxed older gatherings seemed to be, and how much warmer participants seemed to be with each other. This was particularly true of a fiftieth reunion. For them the war was over. They had accomplished what they would accomplish in life. Now they were free simply to enjoy each other's company. And they seemed to, far more so than did those at younger reunions, where competitive fires still burned bright and hot.

With regard to feelings for others, among men especially, the capacity to risk can increase with age. Think about the danger of saying something in high school that might have tipped your hand: complimenting people, say, or telling them you liked them. Such a risk is nearly impossible to take at that precarious time of life. In later years it may be no less of a gamble; but you know you'll probably survive the loss of that gamble, and that the potential gain makes it work taking. At the age of eighty, V. S. Pritchett observed that he was finding that "love itself becomes more mysterious and tender and lasting. . . . I was not an affectionate young man, and indeed I was thought of as fierce — a bolting pony someone once said. But passionate love made me affectionate. I am deeply touched by the affection I now receive — one of the rewards of old age. I suppose I am slowly growing up."

On my questionnaire and during interviews, I was repeatedly told by those well beyond adolescence that chief among the risks they found easier to take with age were those of being open with other people, particularly people they cared about. This was among the reasons psychologist Carl Rogers gave for calling the period of his life from his midsixties on not only his most "satisfying," but the most daring as well. Now in his early eighties, Rogers said he has found his later years filled with feelings, far more so than his younger ones. The originator of client-centered therapy has wondered aloud if this was unique to him, or if it might be a broader aspect of growing old that's been overlooked. "I do not know," he concluded in a talk. "I simply know that my feelings are more easily stirred, are sharper. I am more intimately acquainted with them all."

With his bald head, rimless glasses, and soft-spoken manner, Carl Rogers in his eighties more closely resembles the minister he'd originally set out to become than today's "self-employed psychologist." After putting his stocking feet up on a glass table on the patio of his home overlooking the ocean in La Jolla, California, Rogers described himself as being "pretty conventional" and "uptight" well into middle age. This was despite the fact that he was seen and saw himself as rather daring intellectually. Notwithstanding his rebellious challenge of professional dogma, Rogers looks back on his younger adulthood as that of a basically conventional and emotionally cautious person. In a talk on "Growing Old," which he gave in his seventy-fifth year, the man who was instrumental in taking counseling off the analyst's sofa admitted that for him, doing therapy with clients had always been a way to meet his need for intimacy "without risking much of my person." Not until his sixties, said Rogers, did he feel confident enough to reveal his actual feelings — bad ones as well as good — and to risk being open in relationships with friends and lovers alike. "I think I'm a little more willing to put myself on the line," he said, "because it no longer matters what other people think of me."

So here is one area, anyway, where courage can grow by the year: the willingness to risk our public image to do something we really want to do.

For *Is There Life After High School?* I looked up the high school careers of a number of successful actors. What was striking was how many admitted that they had wanted to be actors since adolescence, but never said so at the time for fear of becoming a laughingstock among their classmates.

The risk of humiliation is firmly in the Level II column, one infinitely harder to take when young. As Erica Jong once noted of her success as a writer, "The difference between the woman I am today and the girl sitting in that creative writing class fourteen or fifteen years ago is mostly a matter of nerve and daring. The nerve to trust my own instincts and the daring to be a fool."

When stacked up against something like climbing a mountain, daring to look foolish might not sound like much of a risk. Yet it could be the one most routinely avoided by taking gaudy Level I risks. In fact, since avoiding the risk of looking foolish is so often the real reason we take lesser risks that appear greater, I've come to think of this as "The Underlying Risk."

EIGHT

THE UNDERLYING RISK

As a young man, George Orwell spent five years on the colonial police force in Burma. After that Orwell endured severe deprivation back home, which he described in his book *Down and Out in Paris and London*. Later he fought for the Republic in Spain's civil war and was wounded in the throat. Throughout such displays of physical courage, Orwell's moral nerve was on display as well in his outspoken commitment to democratic socialism.

But in one revealing episode, Orwell's nerve failed him altogether. This was when, as a policeman in Burma during the mid-1920s, he was confronted by a marauding elephant. The animal had broken free of its chain and was wreaking havoc in the local marketplace. An Indian coolie had already died beneath the beast's feet. As Orwell set the scene in his essay "Shooting an Elephant," the animal had settled down by the time he arrived. The elephant now represented a threat to no one. He also was quite valuable to his owner as a work animal. But Orwell had made the mistake of taking an elephant rifle with him to the scene. This suggested to the large crowd that had gathered there that he intended to use it. Not shooting the gun would result in a serious loss of face.

So, despite his conviction that killing the animal was unnecessary, despite the fact that he wasn't a very good shot, and although he feared for his life by trying, Orwell made ready to shoot the elephant. "I was not thinking particularly of my own skin," he later explained, "only the watchful yellow faces behind.

For at that moment, with the crowd watching me, I was not afraid in the ordinary sense, as I would have been if I had been alone. . . . The sole thought in my mind was that if anything went wrong those two thousand Burmans would see me pursued, caught, trampled on and reduced to a grinning corpse like that Indian on the hill. And if that happened it was quite probable that some of them would laugh. That would never do. There was only one alternative. I shoved the cartridges into the magazine and lay down on the road to get a better aim."

Orwell did shoot the elephant, badly, taking more bullets than necessary and forcing the beast into a slow, agonized death. But he was not laughed at. Later, the Englishman's fellow colonials complimented him on his courage. Orwell himself was more conscious of his actual cowardice. "I often wondered," he wrote years after killing the elephant, "whether any of the others grasped that I had done it solely to avoid looking a fool."

No risk is avoided more often by taking even dangerous physical risks than that of looking foolish. In fact, much apparent "risk taking" is little more than activity engaged in to head off the greater risk of losing face. In such cases we're not *taking* the risk of physical injury so much as *avoiding* the risk of humiliation. Any one of us is liable to accept a friskier horse than we feel able to ride or ski too steep a slope before we'll dare admit not feeling up to it. (It's said that the three most dangerous words in skiing are "Follow me, Dad!") When a young man who feels in danger of appearing cowardly buys a 250 cc Yamaha and proceeds to ride this motorcycle at heart-pounding speeds without a helmet because he thinks this will reduce his risk of being ridiculed, he's taken a more objectively dangerous risk to head off a more feared subjective one.

Such an exchange of risks underlies the misapprehension that teenagers take "big risks". The dangerous acts in which we engage during adolescence are usually motivated by a fear of humiliation if we don't. This is the time of life when we're most likely to risk pregnancy rather than risk the embarrassment of using birth control. Or dare to lose our life by driving recklessly for fear of losing face with our friends if we don't. And can anyone imagine clicking on a seat belt during high school in a carful of friends? I've often wondered how many of us at any age don't take insurance on our lives by buckling up for fear of telling the world that we're fainthearted seat-belt wearers (shoulder belts are especially eloquent in this regard).

Example could be piled on example of occasions in which we'll risk life before dignity. As a woman once wrote to Ann Landers about some necessary surgery she kept putting off: "It's not the operation I fear. It's much worse than that. You see, I have an upper plate. The thought of taking my teeth out in front of all those people in the operating room is humiliating to me. I don't think I can do it."

The risk of looking foolish is not given enough weight as the awesome risk it is because this danger is essentially invisible. What's at stake is so intangible: your face, and not getting egg on it. Yet on the scale of risks difficult to take, this one ranks at the top — to Level I types especially. Branch Rickey used to say that baseball players' concern about being humiliated was far greater than their fear of being injured. Professional athletes in general — who seem so stoic about the risk of being maimed — refer obsessively to the fear of embarrassing themselves on the playing field. After giving football his knees, ex–New York Jet quarterback Joe Namath said that throughout his career he was so afraid of embarrassing himself before a crowd that he wouldn't even join his teammates in singing the national anthem before games. And of being a pioneer in space, astronaut Walter Cunningham once observed, "In this business, it isn't uncommon to be less concerned about getting killed than about making an ass of yourself, especially in front of your peers."

In an earlier time, of course, public shaming was considered among the most severe of punishments. This took the form of stocks (which were still being used in England as late as the latter nineteenth century) and dunking. Even today the Chinese use group criticism and fear of losing face as the basis of their socialist discipline.

As Americans, we may place less emphasis on face and have greater latitude to make fools of ourselves, but the basic human fear of ridicule transcends culture. The exact origins of this fear are unclear. As Darwin first brought to our attention, man is the only animal that blushes ("Or needs to," added Twain). The mechanics of blushing and what sets them in motion are little better understood today than they were in Darwin's time. Certainly what he himself suggested is no less true now than then: "It is not the simple act of reflecting on our own appearance, but the thinking of what others think of us, which excites a blush."

Blushing, and the fear of embarrassment, have been observed in children as young as three. Confronting one's first classroom full of peers headed by a teacher ready to invite you to humiliate yourself before them is what really gets this fear rolling. On my questionnaire, 38 percent of those responding marked "being teased or laughed at" as a significant fear recalled from their childhood, one exceeded only by darkness (44 percent), heights (43 percent), and snakes or worms (39 percent).

Another inquiry on the questionnaire was this one: "Picture yourself climbing to the top of a very high diving board at a public swimming pool. Behind you is a line of people waiting for their turn to dive. Walking to the edge of this board and looking down, you become quite frightened by the thought of diving. Would you:

1. dive anyway, head first
2. jump in, feet first
3. turn around and climb back down the ladder."

Of all those responding, 12 percent said they'd dive anyway, 49 percent would jump (I would), and 26 percent claimed they'd walk back down. While about the same proportions of both sexes said they'd jump (60 percent of the men, 58 percent of the women), more men than women said they'd dive even though scared (18 percent versus 8 percent), while more women said they'd walk back down (32 percent versus 20 percent).

A friend of mine, a Presbyterian minister, once took a wilderness "survival" course. In the midst of this course he was applauded by his companions for sticking with a difficult rock-climbing maneuver that took him far longer than it should have and held up everyone else. At the time he basked in their praise. In retrospect he's not sure his course of action was that courageous. "The bigger risk," he thought, "would be to have to say, 'I can't do it,' and climb back down." But this was a risk he wasn't willing to take.

On the second outing of the addicts' climbing group, I saw a clear example of physical risk being peddled as preferable to humiliation. A new member joined us, a large, rather imposing heroin addict named Tiny. Tiny had been assigned to the program more or less against his will. Heights scared him. On this and the next outing Tiny was cajoled, badgered, and finally shamed into climbing for 15 feet or so. Afterward he cornered one of the counselors and rebuked the man for putting social pressure on him to do something he really didn't want to do. When I later asked this counselor about the incident, he explained that in some cases it's necessary to pressure such a person to extend himself, to take a chance. But I thought that by admitting in front of a group that he was too scared to climb, Tiny had already taken a chance, a bigger chance perhaps than climbing itself.

The military has always depended on the fear of humiliation as its most potent tool for preparing soldiers to risk death in combat. The main reason that small batallions are still the basic unit of military organization in an age of MX missiles is the social pressure such small groups of men put on each other to choose the danger of death over that of embarrassment. And it works. Three and a half decades after the end of World War II, William Manchester says he still could picture his Marine platoon bravely marching into the treacherous jungle, "determined not to shame themselves in the eyes of others."

As they toured the Antietam battlefield where in the Civil War's bloodiest day 23,000 Americans lost their lives, James Jones was asked by his son and a friend why men slaughtered each other and allowed themselves to be slaughtered. Jones replied, "Because they didn't want to appear unmanly in front of their friends. On the average I think that counted more than anything."

Because it does square with our concepts of manliness, risking body before face motivates men more than it does women. Of eighty-eight fears inquired about in a survey, "looking foolish" was one of only three that were felt more often by men than women. Other studies have confirmed that the fear of humiliation is a particularly strong male characteristic.

It's hard to overestimate the degree to which a desire to impress other men favorably, or at least not to lose face in their

171

eyes, motivates male behavior. As with teenagers of both sexes, the major source of the stereotype that men are bolder than women is the physical risks they'll take before daring to look foolish. In a revealing study of driving behavior, 237 Americans were observed behind the wheel as they waited to execute a difficult left turn against traffic into a shopping center. The amount of time this maneuver took each driver was used as a measure of his or her willingness to take chances while driving. The shortest average waiting time — 7 seconds — was recorded for male drivers with male passengers. Next came female drivers with female passengers, men with women, and women with men. The *longest* amount of time — 17 seconds — was recorded in men driving alone. Women alone averaged 12 seconds per turn.

In another study, when high school and college students were paid by the minute to sing "Love Is a Many Splendored Thing" in public, male subjects were far faster to sacrifice income to save face when confronted with an audience of men rather than one of women.

Money in general is a topic rich with the potential for humiliation. I know far more people who will discuss their sex lives, their loneliness, or their fear of dying than will talk about how much money they earn and owe. All manner of financial transaction is dictated as much by the need to protect one's face as one's resources. When *Esquire* gave Andrew Tobias $10,000 to invest for a report to his readers on how these investments had done, Tobias later wrote that the pressures proved far greater than he had imagined. "Not because of the risk of loss —" he explained, "I didn't care a damn about the *money* — but because of the risk of looking stupid."

Market researchers have found repeatedly that minimizing the risk of embarrassing ourselves in the eyes of others can motivate consumer buying habits even more than price or quality. As one summary of such findings explained, "Risk may be perceived in the most innocent appearing products, such as toilet paper and spaghetti, to name two which have been studied. This is because the purchase price is not the sole determinant of perceived risk, and often is not the main factor. A housewife who serves a sinewy roast at a dinner party may suffer a much greater 'loss' than if her new sewing machine (valued at 20 times the cost of the roast) turns out to be a lemon."

In a famous survey for which he seldom gets credit, market researcher R. H. Bruskin once asked 3000 Americans to rank their major fears. "Speaking before a group" was put at the top by 41 percent of those polled. Far back in second place was a fear of heights, cited by 22 percent. Down in sixth place was the fear of death, mentioned by only 19 percent. A case can be made (and is made well in Ernest Becker's book *The Denial of Death*) that our fear of dying is so profound that we deny this fear, or shift it onto less ominous targets such as speech making. But on the conscious level, it's clear that the fear of speaking in public is acute, widespread, and heartfelt.

In Connecticut, an employee filed for disability compensation on the basis of having his emotional health permanently impaired by having to give a speech at a training session. And a DuPont executive once accepted a high-level promotion only on the condition (which he got in writing) that he would never be required to make a speech in public. After retiring as chief executive of General Motors in 1981, Thomas A. Murphy said the part of his job that he was most glad to be rid of was giving speeches. A lifelong public-speaking-phobe, Murphy said that had he realized being head of GM would require him to make a speech a week on the average, he would not have taken the job in the first place. "I never did like to make speeches," explained Murphy on the eve of retirement, "and I don't think I ever will. I dread it. I border on being physically ill. Particularly if I have enough time to think about it."

The heart rate of a group of physicians about to speak before an audience of their peers was once measured. The average was 154 beats per minute. (The normal adult resting rate is between 60 and 80 beats a minute.) Two subjects' hearts beat at the rate of 187 per minute. This average rate exceeded that of a group of skiers tested after vigorous cross-country competition, and was comparable to that of a driver during an auto race. A similar study done in England with a group of twenty-one men and two women (including seventeen doctors) recorded an average heart rate of 151 beats per minute and a maximum of 180 while making a presentation before an audience. A range of stress-released chemicals was found at high levels among subjects in both studies.

In such surveys, the relative amount of experience in public speaking had no bearing on the degree of nervousness experienced by subjects. In fact, one extensive study of the fear of speaking in public found that the *least* useful remedy was a course in public-speaking techniques. Far more useful were remedies based on relaxation exercises. This suggests that mere inexperience is the least part of the risk we feel when making a presentation in public. The risk, the fear, goes deeper than that.

BRAVING AN AUDIENCE

"Performance anxiety," more commonly known as "stage fright," is the heading under which psychologists place this fear. Even the knees of veteran performers can buckle under its weight. A list of those who suffered near-crippling stage fright at some point in their career is like an honor roll of actors: Sir Laurence Olivier, Lionel Barrymore, Maurice Chevalier. "I would say that one of the fundamental emotions of my life has been terror," John Houseman once confessed. "Sheer terror."

Like Houseman, some of the most visibly suave performers have been among the most frightened. Throughout his acting career, for example, David Niven found that performing unnerved him so much that he needed to drink Mist o' the Moors beforehand to keep from trembling, and grease his parched lips with Vaseline to keep them from sticking to his teeth as they had during his Broadway debut. "It's sheer fear," explained Niven. "All this urbanity, casualness, and relaxation people say I have is deliberate deception and a cover-up. The really great stars were all scared — Cary Grant, Clark Gable, the lot."

Cornelia Otis Skinner once compared performing for an audience to being at a dinner party knowing that the next morning you'd be reading in the newspapers exactly what each of the guests thought of you. To make matters worse, millions of other subscribers would be reading the same thing. On the eve of an opening night early in her career, the actress asked her actor-father, Otis Skinner, when she could expect to outgrow her stage fright. He snorted. As she later recalled, "He looked at me with a quizzical compassion and said, 'I have been in the theatre for fifty years and I've *never* outgrown it. Any actor who claims he is immune to stage fright is either lying or else he's no actor.' "

Within their own ranks, performers have levels of daring. By common consent, stand-up comedians are at the daredevil, even the kamikaze, level. Many an experienced actor has observed that standing alone before an audience telling jokes is not something they could conceive of doing. Even as opposed to being part of a comedy troupe, Tim Kazurinsky of "Saturday Night Live" once said, "I could never do stand-up. It terrifies me."

"Saturday Night Live's" Joe Piscopo has also done both stand-up and legitimate theater. He calls the latter "a breeze" compared to the trauma of telling jokes in public. In a play, Piscopo points out, you've got a script, props, costumes, and a supporting cast. In stand-up you've got only yourself. "If you get rejected," says the pug-nosed actor, "it's the biggest rejection in the world. It's you on stage. Only you. It's you they're rejecting."

Piscopo is renowned among his fellow comics not only for his talent and his success but for having had his nose broken by an irate audience member. He himself doesn't like to discuss the incident. But even that experience, says Piscopo, pales beside the horror of telling jokes and not getting laughs. "Infinitely worse," he calls the latter. "The rejection will kill you. The audience can be cruel. It devastates me for at least a day."

One night at a comedy club in Manhattan, I watched a twenty-nine-year-old brokerage clerk named Chuck take the stage to tell jokes for the first time in his life. Wearing a red tie and suspenders over his v-neck sweater, with his trimmed hair and moustache Chuck resembled the actor Billy Dee Williams.

As he nervously clutched a lit cigarette, Chuck told an audience of fifty that when he began working for the Dean Witter brokerage, he said confidently on his first day, "When Dean Witter talks, people listen, right?" That earned him a ripple of laughter, as did a couple of lesser lines. Then Chuck paused. After a few seconds of silence he murmured, "What do I say now?" His eyes darted about the audience. "Oh, my God," he gasped. "They're all staring." Chuck then looked around the room like a

fugitive cornered by the police and puffed fiercely on his cigarette. "At this point," he finally admitted, "I've run out of my
lines. So to keep from making a fool of myself, I'm going to turn
it over to the next one." At that Chuck fled from the stage to a
polite smattering of applause.

At the club's bar a few minutes later, Chuck was still suffering
the aftereffects of his ordeal. "Oh, my poor heart," he gasped.
"It's going into fluctuations. My poor stomach. I had a butterfly
so big I felt it would fly away with me."

After his panting slowed down, Chuck told me that his coworkers at Dean Witter had urged him to audition that night
because he was so funny around the office, always threatening to
call people's mothers when they were bad. Quite a few of them
had been in the audience. They accounted for most of his laughs
and applause.

"I know I moved around too much up there," said Chuck as he
lit another cigarette. "But if I hadn't moved around I probably
would have broken wind, stuttered, anything to keep from falling down. I thought I might faint into the crowd. I have a stain
on my sweater. I thought people might notice the stain on my
sweater."

What had he felt on stage?

Chuck winced at the memory, then replied, "What if people
hate me? Want to stab me? Shoot me? Can you imagine the
thought of being rejected? I think I'd sit up there and cry. I'd
quietly leave, pinky in the air, slashing my wrists as I went."

To describe how they feel while performing, actors constantly
use the term "naked." Even with the disguise of a role to hide
behind, the actor reveals feelings if not facts in any good performance that are potentially embarrassing. Dancer Paul Taylor
has said that what drove him from performing to choreography
was the simple fear of being "*seen.*"

For performers in general, suggests psychologist Martha
Friedman, the feeling that everyone in the audience has X-ray
eyes searching out the least bit of lint in our navel is a hard one
to avoid. At worst the thought becomes that, since such eyes can
see you as clearly as you see yourself, your inadequacy as a
person is now on public display. "Then," she said, "the jig is up.
There are people out on stage singing, who fear as they're sing-

ing that they'll be found out, that they put one over on the producers, the audience, and critics. That they'll be pulled off the stage with a hook."

Friedman made these observations during a course on "Stage Fright," which she cotaught at New York's New School for Social Research with fellow psychologist Penelope Russianoff. Attended by forty performers and would-be performers, the course emphasized ways in which our fear of unfavorable reviews begins at home. Friedman suggested that "don't show off" is a particularly potent parental message that plants lifelong seeds of performance anxiety. She mentioned the case of one performer who told her of being stopped in the middle of reciting a poem by his mother saying, "That's enough. Don't show off."

Early in the course, a collection was taken from among its students of inhibiting messages they still hear from childhood. Among those contributed were: "Dummy!" "You did it again!" and "How could you be so stupid?" Even worse were such double messages as, "You'll do better next time," and "It's horrible to fail, but to be expected." Friedman added to this list: "Do what you want to do, but make me proud," and "It's okay to make a mistake, but don't tell your father."

In a thick European accent, a gray-haired musician recalled for the class a sign reading SHAME ON YOU that her mother had pinned to the back of her dress for a full day after she wet her pants. Another woman, a fortyish blonde, remembered that when dancing as a little girl, one performance wasn't up to her usual standard. This led her mother to ask, "What happened?"

"And I never knew what happened," concluded the dancer.

Martha Friedman — a cheerful, grey-haired woman who obviously enjoyed the performance of teaching — pointed out that many such messages can lie dormant for years. All it takes is a curtain rising or facing a single audition to get them spinning again with a vengeance. And that's when our knees go weak and we feel like throwing up.

But knowing this doesn't cure anxiety about performing. A case in point was Friedman's colleague Penelope Russianoff. An imposing, dark-haired woman who stands six feet tall, Russianoff is best known in New York's professional circles for the New School courses she's taught for years on subjects such as

"Risking Intimacy" and "Risking Change." To the public she's better known for her books (*Why Do I Think I Am Nothing Without a Man?; Women in Crisis*) and her appearance as Jill Clayburgh's therapist in the movie *An Unmarried Woman*.

When director Paul Mazursky offered Russianoff this role, she demurred. For one thing, the character was bisexual. As Mazursky warned her, viewers would assume she was typecast. More importantly, Russianoff risked making an utter fool out of herself. The critics wouldn't care — or even know — that she had a Ph.D. and years of experience doing therapy. If her cameo didn't go well, psychologically speaking one brief appearance on the screen could wipe out years of professional success.

Only when her husband pointed out the inconsistency of teaching others how to take risks then ducking this one herself did Russianoff go right to the phone and call Mazursky to say she'd take the part. Accepting his offer fulfilled a lifelong ambition. As a child Penelope Russianoff had dreamed of becoming a performer and intended to try — until her height topped six feet. After that she limited her performing to speech making, until over four decades later she appeared in *An Unmarried Woman*.

In many ways this experience was a disaster. As Russianoff told the class, "The reviews said I was perfectly awful, awful; 'laughable as an actress,' *Cue* referred to my 'flat, monotonous voice.' I'd always thought everybody liked me. It never occurred to me that people thought I was *awful*.

"It was quite a jolt."

I saw Penelope Russianoff in that movie. To me her performance was awfully good; much closer in its understatement to the manner of most therapists I've known than the overblown Hollywood stereotype (such as Judd Hirsch's acclaimed portrayal of a psychiatrist in *Ordinary People*). And what Russianoff didn't mention was the more favorable reviews she got, of which there were quite a few. As with the rest of us, her memory was best, word-perfect even, for isolated murmurs of criticism.

This is what makes the act of performing in public so daring. As vulnerable as we are on any stage, the least whisper from the rear of the balcony that sounds like less than a rave can send us spinning into despair. One actor told Martha Friedman that even if he got a standing ovation, if one person remained seated in the thirtieth row, that seated body would have his full attention and anxiety. Another traced his stage nerves to a vivid childhood memory of appearing in a Christmas pageant and overhearing his father whisper to the director, "I hope he doesn't spoil it."

"He's now known as a very talented actor," Friedman reported, "but hard to work with. So you get the idea of where stage fright comes from."

One reason that performers and anyone else working in the public eye can be so touchy is that their nerve endings are constantly sanded raw by this fear of being exposed. Since it would be gauche to admit such a fear (to yourself even), instead you pick fights with the phone company; or hassle your agent; or brood distantly among people you'd like to be close to. A lot of the "madness" assumed to underlie genius is little more than this constant fear of humiliation leaking out in more acceptable forms — such as lunacy.

Another popular alternative is consuming copious amounts of alcohol. Richard Burton said that drinking was always his preferred means of dealing with a lifelong certainty that "one of these days someone is going to find me out." Burton's colleague Anthony Hopkins — who compares acting to "being in a public confessional" — says his own drinking problem began as a way of numbing this fear of exposure. From his own perspective as a movie director/producer, medical doctor and novelist, Michael Crichton has an interesting perspective on the renowned capacity for alcohol of those who work in what he calls "self-revealing occupations." "What all these people share in common," says Crichton of such actors, painters, writers, and others, "is a form of work which requires considerable public exposure — or the hope of it, or the threat of it. The pattern of anxiety inherent in such self-exposure may lend itself to treatment with alcohol."

THE COURAGE TO CREATE

Anyone whose creative work must be put on display for comment is in a real bind. On the one hand, to do their very best work, they must *reveal* themselves. Yet if they have any doubts about the self being revealed — and who doesn't? — the risk they're running is catastrophic. This risk is one of having not only a superficial self on display for judgment and possible rejection but an actual self they must dredge up for scrutiny if their work is to be any good.

Malcolm Cowley once answered his own inquiry about the relationship between art and character by concluding that they did correlate, in a rough way, and that a genuine scoundrel could not produce a masterpiece. Why not? As Cowley explained, "The artist, no matter what his sins may be, tries hard to give himself away; the scoundrel tries to conceal his character. In the end, however, he cannot help revealing himself — not in his subject matter, not in his direct statements, but in the shape and color and rhythm of his phrases (or of his brushwork, if he is a painter). False, false, the reader (or viewer) feels instinctively."

When teaching writing I try to have students read their work aloud. This not only bonds the class quickly in a brotherhood of peril, but helps members confront in a low-stakes atmosphere the high-stakes risk of self-exposure. Fear of this risk underlies all manner of writing problems. Among them are vagueness, pretension, writer's block, and what's usually put under the heading of "fear of writing." This actually is a misnomer. Writing itself isn't scary. What's scary is imagining other people's reactions to our words. The better our writing, the more danger we're in. Good writing, like good acting and art of any kind, must reveal something authentic. This risk must be taken. There's no alternative to risking self-exposure in writing of any consequence. "A writer gives himself away all the time anyway," W. H. Auden once pointed out. "He has no *important* secrets."

The more we show, the better our writing, and the greater our risk of being found out and humiliated in public. Not wanting to take this risk inspires some awfully convoluted self-expression: jargon, bureaucratese, what's been called in general "cover-your-ass writing."

I often hear about courses in "effective communication" and the like. But most of us have no problem communicating, if we're willing to risk feeling embarrassed. The risk of embarrassment must be taken to do creative work of any kind. While creativity is generally assumed to have some correlation with talent, the more important correlation is with nerve. Lack of nerve is the brake that keeps even gifted people from making use of their talents. Working artists of all kinds usually know others more talented than they who are delivering mail or selling real estate rather than risking scrutiny of their work by others. Norman Mailer once said that any number of his classmates at Boys' High in Brooklyn wrote better stories than he did. What they lacked was the willingness to dare looking the fool for their efforts. As Mailer explained, "A lot of writers are killed off early. They just can't take the ridicule."

The fear of putting our work on display usually comes under the heading of "What would people think of me?" But it's seldom "people" in general that we're concerned about as much as specific individuals, and sometimes only one. Getting a fix on those people or that person can be an enormous help in reducing the risk of subjecting our work to public scrutiny. Early on in writing workshops, I ask members to focus mentally on the person whose reaction to their work most concerns them. It could be a parent, an in-law, a sibling, child, spouse, lover, or perhaps our ninth-grade English teacher. Whoever it is, that's our censor-in-chief (though it's really not that person at all who inhibits us; it's our fear of what we imagine that person's reaction will be that inhibits our work). I don't ask that this person be named aloud, only that the students confront him or her in the privacy of their thoughts and imagine how they'll deal with his or her response to their writing. In reality this isn't easy. It may not be possible. To some degree we'll always be censored by the opinions of people we care about. Perhaps we ought to be.

One of the great creative opportunities presented by age is that this crippling fear of other people's opinions declines. After publishing eighteen books of nonfiction, at the age of seventy-two management expert Peter Drucker published his first novel. Asked why he had waited so long, Drucker replied, "Because the ultimate test of the writer is the novel and I never had the courage to try it. But once I passed seventy, I was no longer terribly worried about making an ass of myself." Although reviewers were not kind to this maiden effort, Drucker soon was at work on a second novel.

A sociologist who interviewed 143 older musicians, actors, painters, and sculptors found that most said advancing years had added more than subtracted from their creativity. Not the least reason was that concern about social scrutiny was so much less an issue for them than it was when they were younger. In a book on what he calls *The Ulyssean Adult* — those who stay creative into old age or become more so — John A. B. McLeish writes that for many of his subjects, "the later years mean they are freer than they have ever been to adopt unorthodox concepts, and unorthodoxy is one of the recognized parents of creativity. . . . Freer airs blow for many men and women in their later years: the stakes are less, intimidating jailers are gone, or in the steady process of maturing, new reserves of courage together with wisdom and compassion have brought them to the open fields of change and experiment. . . .

"Thus the creative life is not only as possible for men and women in the later years as when they were much younger, but in important respects often more possible."

At the deepest level, it's not just the fear of looking foolish to others that declines with age, but also the fear of looking foolish to ourselves. And in the end, isn't it fear of ourselves that we're really dealing with here? Because the real risk is not of others seeing us naked so much as seeing our naked self reflected in their eyes. It's bad enough if others notice we're wearing a clown suit. But should we catch a glimpse ourselves in the mirror they're holding up, that can *really* be devastating.

As terrifying as the fear of an audience might be, said Cornelia Otis Skinner, an even more fundamental fear was the "fear of oneself" that acting aroused. This fear is experienced in many ways. Frank Langella once observed that he found emotionally demanding parts in serious stage roles to be unusually traumatic because they called on the actor "to go to truths you spent a great deal of time trying to avoid." Susan Sarandon found that portraying a vengeful rape victim in the play *Extremities* left her feeling less jeopardy from the physical hazards of the role (which resulted in back problems, neck problems, bloody noses, a black eye, and one finger in a splint) than from the psychic ones. In the process of portraying violent vengeance eight times a week, explained Sarandon, "you have to reveal a dark side of your nature, which is not a pleasant sensation. . . . I don't think most people would admit you can feel that much hatred."

This could be the most harrowing risk taken by artists of all kinds: pulling curtains on themselves that are easier to open than to close. Among writers, writers of fiction are in particular jeopardy every time they put words on paper. Once this process is set in motion, if it's a good process anyway, the writer cannot always control what comes out. Sometimes the best results are the most surprising ones, and certainly ones with the greatest potential to be embarrassing.

Because the risk of embarrassment — of making an ass out of yourself, of getting egg on your face, of being laughed at and humiliated — is so hard to take, it's also one of the most valuable. Only when we're willing to dare looking foolish for our efforts can we give a speech, pitch a baseball, or stand up for a principle. As philosopher Michael Polanyi has written, "We must commit ourselves to the risk of talking complete nonsense, if we are to say anything at all."

Taking a risk of any kind ultimately makes it necessary to confront the risk of embarrassment. Any time we take a chance we create a new pattern for our lives. Others may think it silly. We may think it silly. This underlying risk can prove more harrowing than the more obvious one we've taken. Nowhere have I found this more true than among those who strike out on their own financially. From the outside their risk appears to be of their livelihood. From the inside it's even worse.

THE ENTREPRENEUR

Among the plastic combs, dyed feathers, and sequined jeans of a boutique show in New York, Valerie's Way stood out like a Degas in Disneyland. "Beautiful," visitors murmured as they walked past this booth. "Gorgeous."

"Thank you," the smiling woman inside this booth murmured back. "Thank you."

Dozens of lace blouses hung around her. Most were of Victorian design, with high necks and long sleeves. Each combined different bits of lace with compatible pieces of velvet or beads or little cloth flowers.

"They're so beautiful," said a young woman with streaked blond hair as she fingered the blouses. "So beautiful. I stop to look often.

"I'd love to buy," she added wistfully.

"Why don't you?" asked the smiling woman inside the booth. "You can, you know." Both women chuckled uneasily before the one outside moved on.

The smiling woman was Valerie Fine.* Of medium height, her brown hair pulled up in a loose bun, Valerie's delicate features offset large green eyes. Over purple pedal pushers and black pumps, she wore a simple version of the blouses being admired, one with just a bit of purple velvet nearly hidden within mounds of fragile lace at the neck.

* A pseudonym.

"Oh, my God, they're beautiful," gasped a young woman who had stopped abruptly before Valerie's booth.

"Thank you," said Valerie.

"Tell me," asked the woman as she glanced cautiously at the blouse's price tags, "are any of these under one hundred fifty dollars?"

"Nooo," said Valerie slowly. "I do have some lesser-priced blouses over there. They're one twenty-five." She gestured to a rack where simpler versions were hung, some sleeveless, few decorated. "Everything on the wall is two fifty each. And I have a few skirts for two hundred."

The would-be customer looked forlorn. "I've never seen such lovely work," she said softly before moving on.

"Thank you," Valerie called after her.

During a lull, Valerie turned to a tall, blonde woman named Denise who was rearranging blouses at the rear. Together the two calculated that they'd made $5000 worth of sales so far — enough to cover expenses, but without much to spare. They were interrupted by an older woman's voice asking, "Do you ship?"

"Do I ship?" replied Valerie sweetly. "Oh, sure. Do you pay?" She laughed. "If you pay, I ship."

Valerie then explained to the woman that all she had to do was look over the samples, remember what she liked, then write or call with descriptions and colors. "If I can't match them exactly," said Valerie, "I'll send you something in the same feeling. But I'll need a deposit."

"How can I be sure you'll ship?" persisted the customer.

"You can't," replied Valerie. "You have to take a chance."

"But you won't take a chance on me."

"I can't," said Valerie with a tight smile. "I've lost too much money."

The owner of a boutique in Los Angeles stopped by to tell Valerie how well her blouses were doing for him. "And you're so wonderful to pay me," Valerie responded warmly. "I can't tell you what a pleasure it is to sell to someone and have them send me a check right away."

This man was followed by a Dallas store manager who ordered two of the less expensive blouses and two skirts. "I wonder if I'm selling these skirts for too little money?" mused Valerie to

Denise after taking this order. "Nobody's batting an eye over the price."

She then advised the woman working with her that if anyone asked, to tell them that the minimum order was three items. "And if they won't take three as a minimum, then keep going down till you get to one."

A young man dressed in black whose hair looked as though it had been cut by a lawn mower passed by. "Nice," he mumbled after glancing over Valerie's wares. "Really nice."

"Thanks," said Valerie.

"You know what I like?" she told Denise as the young man moved on. "Everybody likes lace. Even punk rockers."

A woman in the booth across the way interrupted their conversation to tell Valerie that someone had been sketching her blouses. "Sketching?" asked Valerie with a startled look. "Who?"

"A girl in black. She was standing over there." The woman gestured to one side, and Valerie stormed from her booth to look up and down the aisle. The sketcher had vanished.

"That makes me so mad," Valerie said, biting off her words. "I mean, I'm a mild person, but . . ."

A woman interrupted to ask who owned Valerie's Way.

"It's my business," said Valerie, recovering her composure. "And I have people sewing for me. But the lace is antique."

After the woman moved on, Valerie leaned over and whispered to Denise, "You know, this is the first year I've been able to relate to the fact that this *is* my business."

Valerie Fine traces her business back to the day a boyfriend left her in the midseventies. They'd been close for years, and without him her life seemed to lose focus. Working as a waitress wasn't rewarding. And not much else seemed to be going her way. Then a friend asked Valerie if she would like to join her in the south of France that winter. Valerie hesitated only briefly before saying yes. "That's how I often make decisions," she explains. "Just in a couple of seconds."

Friends play an important role in Valerie Fine's life. One of the reasons she's never left Boston is because a substantial cache of lifelong friends still lives there. Some go back twenty years, one even to kindergarten. "I remember how we met over milk and cookies," she laughs. "We giggled together and felt like sisters. She lives in Brookline now, and comes to help me out sometimes at the store."

When she left Boston for France in the fall of 1975, starting her own business hadn't even occurred to Valerie. She just needed to get away and was willing to quit three waitressing jobs and take her entire savings of $3000 to do so. In Montpellier, Valerie filled her time by haunting the local flea market. What immediately caught her eye there were the mounds of antique lace. Such pieces often sold for mere centimes. Although she knew of no real market for such an item, Valerie had always loved lace. So from love of lace alone she began to fill her apartment with old camisoles, petticoats, and blouses from the flea market.

These purchases were shrinking Valerie's bankroll faster than she'd anticipated. Soon she would have to return to Boston and resume waiting on tables. Although Valerie didn't mind being a waitress, it was hardly a career. And as her thirtieth birthday approached, this concerned her, as did the toll waitressing had taken on her body: the aching back, tired feet, and veins showing through on the legs.

On a whim, Valerie wired a friend in Boston to ask if she'd like to invest $500 in a lace business. A day later her friend wired the money with a message saying to regard it as an investment in friendship. This gesture meant more to Valerie than the money itself. She wanted to start her own business but was scared to do so without someone else's okay. Now Valerie had it, to the tune of $500. Her bankroll forced a decision. Should she sink the money into more lace? Or should she take back only what she'd already bought and hold on to the $500 as a hedge against waiting tables? Valerie decided to buy.

Her accumulated lace filled three large suitcases. Getting these suitcases back to Boston proved to be a problem. The problem was more psychological than physical, because once she'd filled these bags with her future, Valerie had a hard time letting go of them.

"I had this thing that I couldn't leave the suitcases alone," she recalls. "I would drag two along, then go back for the third. Finally I got them on the train. But I was having horrible anxiety attacks. I worried that I wouldn't be able to get them off the train. Or that I'd get off with two and leave the third behind. I remember very little about that trip. I was probably hysterical."

In moments of crisis, Valerie Fine is subject to anxiety attacks. Her heart races, she gets short of breath, dizziness sets in, and she feels on the verge of collapse. Like Camille, Valerie says, she takes to her bed. All she can think while lying there is, "I can't handle this." This thought plagued Valerie for the sleepless twenty hours she spent in a hotel bed near the Paris airport pondering her future without a home, boyfriend, or job and only three suitcases filled with dreams.

Forcing herself from this bed the next morning, Valerie struggled to the airport with her suitcases still clutched tightly by her side. There she walked them to the last possible point before they were taken from her to be loaded on the plane. Then Valerie boarded the plane herself to endure a jittery eight-hour flight back to she wasn't sure what.

Much as she dislikes such anxious episodes, Valerie says the best parts of her life usually grow out of them. She refers to these interludes as ones "when I throw everything up in the air and don't know how they'll land.

"When you're on the verge of losing everything," Valerie explains, "when you're in a point of free-fall, you're free to do anything; go in any direction. If you have something, you can't. I had nothing."

After Valerie arrived in New York, things took a turn for the worse. A friend from Boston who was supposed to meet her at the airport didn't. For lack of a better alternative she called her ex-boyfriend's two sisters. They offered to put Valerie up for a time in their Manhattan apartment. In the cab that took her there, Valerie felt herself slipping into panic. This feeling grew acute after she arrived and the two women asked to see her lace. Suppose something that had shimmered so in Montpellier's softer light looked merely worn and tattered in the harsher glare of New York?

The sisters adored her lace.

Buoyed by this scrap of encouragment, Valerie set about cleaning, pressing, and restoring her stock. With an Art degree from the University of Maryland, she had a strong foundation in color and design to reinforce a natural sense of style that combines flare with understatement. On different occasions Valerie may combine a purple camisole with white duck pants. Or Levi's and lace. One day she'll be completely free of jewelry, on the next a tiny ring will adorn her little toe.

After she'd spent weeks translating this style into blouses of white lace with their bits of color, Valerie's housemates announced that the time had come to stop procrastinating and start selling. They'd even compiled a list of stores she should try. Feeling like "a total schlepp, hair below my waist, the original hippie," Valerie allowed herself to be pushed out the door by her friends with orders not to come back until she'd visited every store on the list.

None bought. At Bendel's, the buyer and manager did finger her blouses and whisper to each other. They told Valerie to try again in a couple of months.

A discouraged Valerie Fine returned to Boston. She hoped that hometown contacts might buy. They didn't. Not even smaller stores in her native city wanted any of Valerie's blouses. On the verge of throwing in the towel, she tried one last boutique run by a woman she knew. This woman examined Valerie's wares noncommittally for a time. Then she said, "I'll buy."

"Which one?" asked a delighted blouse maker.

"All of them," replied the woman.

From this initial success Valerie's business was born. Favorable comment about her designs began to spread around Boston. Valerie tripled her prices. Sales increased. "It was an accident, really," she says of her good fortune. "No one was more shocked than I by what people will pay for this clothing."

Not that Valerie was hesitant to ask for it. "I don't feel funny about taking money," she explains. "My feeling about money is that it's like lettuce or corn. I'll make this for you if you'll pay me ten ears of corn."

Friends began to offer Valerie not only moral but financial support. She turned down one $2000 loan offer from a man who wanted a relationship as interest, but accepted this amount from other friends. Most of the money went for a buying trip to France where she replenished her dwindling stock of lace.

Sample cases tightly in hand, Valerie now returned to Bendel's one year after being told to come back in a couple of months. "Where have you been?" asked the buyer.

"But I thought you weren't interested," said Valerie.

"Silly," responded the buyer. "Of *course* we were interested. We just needed to make sure you weren't a flash in the pan."

After she sold to Bendel's, Valerie found that other major stores in New York wanted to buy from her as well. The increased workload made it necessary to hire seamstresses. Valerie's business was now in a critical phase. Although its prospects warranted expansion, the owner lacked capital. As a young woman without a track record, Valerie knew that conventional sources of financing were not available to her, so she took a partner — an older woman with time and $5000 to invest. The pair spent two unhappy years trying to work together in the midst of arguments, rising tension, and lengthening periods of sullen silence. Valerie wondered if her business would survive the strain. Visions of waiting on tables came back to haunt her.

"But one night I was sewing a lampshade," she recalls, "and I had a revelation that I'd rather waitress or wash dishes than have a lousy partnership. The next day we had a screaming fight." Soon after that the two women went their separate ways. With three sewing machines, a stock of lace, and $2500 from the dissolution of their partnership, she moved into a one-room apartment in Boston's harbor district and waited for panic to set in. In retrospect she realizes that nothing better could have happened to her. "All of my best things seem to happen to me when I'm in that state," Valerie reiterates. "There seems to be something related to those horrible anxieties, to having to fight through them to something better. When a crisis happens, everything changes. You're free to make a choice, to take a risk."

With this impetus Valerie began to develop a vision of the business she owns today: Valerie's Way. In this vision she owned a little shop and showroom. Customers came by to try on blouses. Tea was served. And off to one side Valerie hovered lightly, suggesting, "Try this. Try that."

In a little shop next to a hardware store near Boston's wholesale district her dream began to take shape. This was where I first met Valerie Fine a year after she'd signed the lease. Tiny, with lace garments covering the walls, Valerie's Way was inviting. Wicker chairs were set here and there. Victorian hats punctuated the lace on the walls. Throw rugs covered the scarred hardwood floors. Like the kitchen of an old friend, Valerie's Way was cramped but cozy.

When we met, Valerie's business was humming once again, grossing $100,000 a year. As a by-product of her success, Valerie was faced with new difficulties. Antique clothing had become popular and supply was now a problem. She had to develop sources of lace other than French flea markets. (Valerie can pull a blouse off her rack at random and read it like a map: "This piece I bought in Montpellier. That came from a shop in New York. This one's from a broker in Philadelphia.") Competition appeared. In the ultimate flattery, another woman began "knocking off" Valerie's designs, though with nothing like her flair.

By now Valerie was shipping to a dozen states and several foreign countries. A department store in Germany was marking her blouses up to $700. Unlike the early days when she often had to wait quite a while before getting to see buyers, Valerie now was ushered right into their offices and greeted with smiles and busses on the cheek. Best of all was her improved cash flow. "I love getting the checks," said Valerie. "And they're getting bigger, which is exciting."

To her surprise, Valerie discovered a good head for business beneath her flyaway hair. While she still saw herself as basically a post-hippie dress designer, "I'm real clear about my business," Valerie added. "Business is business. I do a lot of what I do by rote. By what I feel is right. I never really sat down and analyzed things. I just did what felt right. Obviously I'm doing something right." She pondered the sound of those words, then laughed, adding, "I'm not as disorganized as I sound. I do have an accountant and a bookkeeper."

Although her volume and gross were up, the costs of expansion kept Valerie working on a close margin. For a recent buying trip to Europe she'd had to borrow money. Taxes were coming due. Ten employees were now on her payroll: seamstresses, clerks, a manager. Just before departing she told me, "I'll leave here with no money in my bank account, no money in savings and none in checking. If I really focus on it, I guess it's scary."

Valerie Fine originally interested me as an economic risk taker. Unlike many who are apparently in that category, she had no subsidy: no working spouse, money from home, or career to fall back on should she fail. Valerie's risk was compounded by being younger than the average business owner, and a woman as well. During the time I spent with her, businesses were failing at a rate unsurpassed since the Depression. Yet Valerie said that the scariest risks she's taken and dangers she's faced have not been financial. While the risks of failure and loss of money scare her, even scarier has been the prospect that her business would succeed and leave her personal life a shambles. As Valerie explained, when you're in a job — waitressing, say — at least you're with a group of people. Everyone's in the same boat. There's a sense of sisterhood, and brotherhood. Once you're accustomed to that spirit, how do you relate to being out on your own? Why are you out there in the first place? You begin to doubt your motives. Others doubt them for you. Your family may support you, or it may not. In her case a cousin warned Valerie's mother that she had gone off the deep end, selling all her furniture and moving to France to buy old underwear, and ought to be seeing a psychiatrist.

Of even greater concern to her has been the risk of losing friends as a tax on her success. Valerie's found that a lot of old friends who married young and had children are now frustrated with their lot and envious of hers. In more than one case this envy has bent or even broken friendships.

New men in Valerie's life can be even more put off by her success than old friends. Few whom she meets seem able to take her status in stride. Some need to prove they're stronger than she is. Others hope maybe this woman could take care of them. Valerie laughed while telling me this, saying, "For the first time in my life I've begun to consider the possibility of having a househusband." Then she glanced at my notes, adding, "You're not gonna write this, are you?" Then she laughed once more and said, "Oh, what the heck."

During the year we were acquainted, I always enjoyed the many hours we spent discussing Valerie's life, her business, the risks she'd taken and those she'd ducked. Not until late in that year, when I came to seem less of an adventurous risk and more of a dangerous one, was she anything but forthcoming and good-natured in our conversations.

In one of the last such conversations, Valerie wondered if maybe I ought to use a pseudonym in writing about her. I said I could, but that this seemed inconsistent with a portrayal of her as a risk taker. Valerie saw the point immediately, the logic. But in such a case logic is beside the point.

When we first met at Lou's Luncheonette down the block from her store, Valerie regarded talking to me as a lark, an adventure. But the longer we talked the more anxious she grew about the danger involved. This was not helped by my pointing out during one conversation that she wouldn't necessarily like everything I wrote about her. No one ever does. Reading someone else's words about yourself is like hearing your voice on a tape recorder, or seeing your face on television.

This thought visibly unnerved her. Valerie is intensely ambivalent about public exposure. She wants it; this woman is not without ego. At one time she aspired to be a singer until an early turn on stage cured that ambition. She felt far too exposed before an audience. Valerie in general is quite concerned about her public image. Any number of times press photographers have asked to take pictures of her with her lace. She usually consents, and seldom likes the results.

Just before we met, Valerie indulged a dream of achieving recognition by writing *Women's Wear Daily* to suggest herself as the subject for a profile. The fashion daily agreed and interviewed her during a sales trip to New York. Soon after our first conversation the profile appeared. Its lead sentence described what a close grip Valerie keeps on her sample case. The article then went on to depict the success of Valerie's Way at some length. Her product was described with adjectives such as "exquisite," "delicate," and "eye-catching."

Even though she'd initiated this publicity, its tone was positive, and her business picked up in response, Valerie found feeling so exposed was unsettling. "I feel some sort of image of me was projected," she explained. "I feel that something is expected of me." Such as? Valerie pondered the question, laughed, and said, "To be really together."

She'd first seen the article while riding in a taxicab after seeing a buyer from Lord & Taylor. First Valerie skimmed the piece. Then she sat back and tried to absorb it, to put the publicity in context. "I sort of saw myself in New York in a taxicab alone, reading this article in *Women's Wear Daily*, smoking a cigarette (I usually don't smoke). But the big thing was *alone*.

"In a certain way what I'm doing is setting me more and more apart. I met a doctor two months ago. I really liked him. Later I called him for some addresses of people he knew in Paris. And he said, 'Were you in *Women's Wear Daily*?' I guess that bothered me. I was excited that he saw the article. But what's he gonna expect of me now? How can I be enough?"

This article became the fulcrum, the focus of Valerie Fine's changing status and her mixed feelings about that change. In practical terms it brought her more business and better prices. Doors opened to her that before had been closed. People she hadn't heard from for some time got in touch with her. ("Now that you're famous," one letter opened). In response, Valerie began to have a vision of herself as successful on a grander scale than she'd ever dreamed. For a time she scurried about looking for a bigger store. Then she pulled back, asking herself, "Why not stay small? Just have a nice little business?" But Valerie realized she couldn't. She couldn't imagine not doing the most that was possible with her business and her life. One friend told Valerie she *had* to expand; it would be too boring not to.

As Valerie's Way grew, its owner began to choose her words more carefully when we talked. The carefree woman I'd first met now reflected before speaking, seemed to want to be more precise, more collected and analytic. After observing how she responded to an article about herself in a newspaper, Valerie began to wonder how she was going to cope with my portrayal of her in a book. Late in our relationship she admitted, "I'm getting more and more terrified about this project. My fear is escalating. Particularly as I get more public."

As she realized, Valerie Fine's sense of risk had changed along with her status. In particular, the success of her business had created stakes where none had existed before. Now she had something to lose: a thriving enterprise with several employees, stock, an expensive lease, and financial obligations. Although its owner says she could lock the door to Valerie's Way tomorrow and walk away without looking back, Valerie also admits that she's come to like being able to stay at the St. Moritz in New York and eat at the Four Seasons.

On reflection I realized that disguising Valerie's identity was perfectly consistent with the type of risk taker she is, and is not. Valerie herself has very mixed feelings on this score. On the one hand, because of her love of adventure and ability to emerge stronger from the heat of a crisis, she was more willing than most people I spoke with to claim the mantle of a "risk taker." Valerie said that in her family she is the goad to be daring — the one urging her brother to quit a hated job, and telling her mother to risk a trip alone to Europe. "Just do it!" she tells them. "There's ecstasy on the other side of a crisis." But even as she respected her daring, Valerie was painfully aware of her inhibitions. "Maybe the people who take risks have so many other fears," she said during one of our conversations, "that the risk the world sees them taking is not the biggest risk they could take."

One day in New York we had lunch with a sometimes comedienne, a married mother of three. This woman spent most of the meal admiring the risks Valerie had taken to achieve financial independence. Yet to Valerie — who gave up her dream of performing because of crippling stage fright — the risk was all on the other side of the table. "To me," Valerie said afterward, "she's taking a much bigger risk than I am by putting herself in front of an audience and making herself so vulnerable."

Four years after Valerie's Way began, its owner moved her business from its cramped quarters in the wholesale district to a larger, classier, and more expensive store on Boston's tony Newbury Street. Overnight Valerie's sales improved, as did the nature of her clientele. What before had been mostly jobbers, buyers, and the odd shopper wandering in off the street now gave way to chic Beacon Hill and Lexington residents who didn't flinch at the $500+ retail tags hanging on her wares.

I visited Valerie's new store once. This store was easier to get to than the old one, more spacious, and had a soft beige carpet underfoot. But I didn't feel comfortable there. I felt like a guest who'd been moved from a friend's disheveled, inviting old kitchen into their forbidding, newly decorated parlor.

Never before had I understood so clearly what Valerie kept saying: that by winning her financial gamble — the lesser one — she might isolate herself and lose more important personal risks. In facing this dilemma she is not alone. Anyone who chooses to work on their own quickly discovers that the risk of destitution is not necessarily the biggest risk they're taking.

ON YOUR OWN

After her career as a corporate psychologist was successfully launched, a friend of mine named Lorraine left the Manhattan insurance firm where she worked to become a self-employed consultant, lecturer, and writer. On her first day without an office to go to, Lorraine wrote me a letter because she no longer had use of a WATS telephone line. So far, Lorraine wrote, her first day of self-employment had been terrible. She'd checked for the mail fifteen times before lunch — which she ate at 11:00. The second day Lorraine wrote me another letter, shorter this time, saying her mood had improved somewhat. On the third morning she called with an inquiry. "You've been working on your own for eleven years, right?" asked Lorraine.

That's right, I replied.

"Well, I have an important question. Do you get dressed in the morning or what?"

Lorraine's question rather took me aback. In fact I was dressed even as we spoke. Usually I am. Getting dressed for work wasn't an issue that seemed to merit reflection. But after thinking it over, I could see how important this issue was. The real reason for such a basically unnecessary act is to keep morale up: to remind the world, and especially yourself, that you're a workaday grown-up like any other. There's always a fear lurking in the back of your mind that one day you'll decide to work in a bathrobe, the next day in pajamas, and on the third day just not bother to get out of bed at all.

Such risks confront anyone working on his or her own. There are many others. Few have to do with money. To the world at large your key risk is financial. Certainly that's an awesome risk. But the danger of destitution is tangible; it's one you can anticipate and prepare for with savings, loans, and reducing your standard of living. If worse comes to worse, bankruptcy doesn't carry the stigma that it used to. Harder to anticipate and prepare for are the less tangible risks of feeling isolated; of feeling like you're making a fool out of yourself; and — if you have Level I tendencies — of coping with the boredom of success.

Most of those who strike out on their own do have Level I tendencies. They almost have to. Without a taste for excitement, the risk of self-employment would be debilitating. Approached as an adventure, giving up a paycheck doesn't feel like such a big risk. For those who have such tendencies, coping with the monotony of work with guaranteed wages would be the bigger risk.

For years, ever since I "went free-lance," others have commented on my guts in doing so. Such comments usually come from people stuck in jobs from which they'd love to flee. Yet for me and most free-lancers I know, leaving a steady job never felt that gutsy. In fact, if any of the job applications I filled out before doing so had been successful, I might be an assistant to some associate vice-president today. Since they weren't, I was forced off the precipice into the abyss of self-employment. To my surprise, this life turned out to be rather appealing. Its most memorable period was at the outset. For most of the first three years on our own we lived on beans, fear, and hope. Free-lancing was my skydiving. This isn't an experience I'd care to repeat, yet it was intense. Every day tingled. All the stages of looming disaster became familiar to me: tension, fear, and terror followed by excitement, a sense of challenge, and motivation to get cracking. Concentration was never a problem. Like any disaster survivor, I look back on that experience with a mixture of relief that it's over and regret that my life today isn't as intense.

In general I find that this spirit characterizes those working on their own. A sense of excitement and adventure actually lowers your sense of risk. It almost has to. Otherwise this risk can't be taken. When actor Harold Gould (who later played Valerie Harper's father on "Rhoda") left a secure job teaching drama in college to become a full-time actor at the age of thirty-seven, he found his colleagues back at the University of California, Riverside, in awe of his daring. "When I meet the old guys from Riverside," he later commented, "They say, 'Boy, you really did the courageous thing.' I never saw it that way. It was an adventure. All the unpredictability of show business was so exciting after tramping from class to class revising your notes."

Contrast this approach with that of a friend of mine. In his late thirties Jeff quit his job as a microbiologist to join me in the ranks of free-lance writers. From my perspective Jeff's first year looked promising — more promising than mine was, certainly. In just a few months' time he sold articles to a number of publications, including two of national standing. The next thing I knew, Jeff was back at work as a microbiologist. What happened to his dream of a writing career, I asked? Jeff replied that he simply had not met his projections. What he had done was to plot a growth curve in advance, which he expected to meet or exceed in his first year. Not having risen far enough on this curve, Jeff prudently threw in his hand.

Prudent as it might have been, this is not the best way to strike out for the territories. A certain blindness to the odds against you is more useful. This isn't to say that those who take such a chance and stay with it are imprudent, or fearless. One secretary who quit her job to pursue a lifelong dream of writing television scripts says she spent the first two weeks bursting into uncontrollable tears and checking to see if her old position had been filled yet. I can always recognize an actual freelance (as opposed to one getting money from home) by the field of panic crackling in their vicinity. Also the trembling hands, fluttering eyelids, and involuntary twitching of facial muscles.

But the self-employed learn to live with fear, learn even to welcome it as a source of energy and concentration. "When you have two dollars in your checking account," fledgling publisher Mary Ellen Pinkham once observed, "and fifty thousand books in your basement, you learn how to sell books." But destitution as such, as frightening as it is, isn't necessarily the leading source of fear on your own. Consider the case of best-selling author Peggy Anderson. Although she spent years eating peanut butter and biking about Philadelphia before the success of *Nurse* allowed her to eat out and buy a Honda Accord, Peggy says that even when most desperate, she knew that her mother would come to her financial rescue if necessary. This never became necessary, but simply knowing that her mother's bank account was there if needed made Peggy feel undeserving of the regular praise she got for her courage in choosing to live without a paycheck.

More wearing than the dangers of destitution in her case were those of isolation. The trauma and sheer loneliness of working on her own drove Peggy to borrow an empty desk in a busy office to do her final month of work on *Nurse*. Like so many who strike out on their own, Peggy Anderson has found that the more exciting risks (including financial) are at the first level, the more daunting ones at the second. These are the risks I call the three "shuns" of self-employment: isola*tion*, humilia*tion*, and frustra*tion*. The last speaks for itself. No one expects an independent life to be smooth. But the first two risks are far harder to anticipate.

Out on your own, you quickly feel isolated in any number of ways. There's the loss of Xerox privileges, and the company of those waiting on line. A coffee cart no longer summons you to the hallway with its Pavlovian bell. You don't run into friends in the elevator, or at lunch, or much of anywhere that you don't arrange in advance. Even an office you don't care for at least has familiar faces. Bitching about what's wrong on the job is stimulating. The brotherhood of fellow bitchers can be intense. Discovering how much you miss such company is a major, unanticipated risk of striking out on your own.

Since so many of us do build our social lives around the workplace, finding out who (if anyone) is left in your life once you leave that setting can be harrowing. In *Megatrends*, John Naisbitt suggests that it is social isolation more than technological limitations that will keep us from working at home in "electronic cottages." One woman who tried ended up putting a mirror over her desk for the company. Even as I'm writing, a friend is about to give up the flourishing public relations firm she's run from her home for three years for no other reason than loneliness. Another friend once took six months off from successful careers in government and television to write a book (which was also successful). Although he enjoyed the writing process itself, this man has often told me it's not an experience he'd repeat. As he explains with a half-smile, "I just don't enjoy my own company that much."

Beyond the company guaranteed by a job, only after you've left one do you realize how much your identity was tied to whoever employed you. The first business letters written on blank paper rather than letterhead do not feel properly dressed. Neither do the calls you now make without a title or employer with which to introduce yourself. Taking the risk of contacting others on your own behalf makes you realize how drastically the stakes of that gamble are lowered by doing so on behalf of someone else.

What you're confronting now is the profound, underlying risk of humiliation. Having presumed to be one who could make the break and work on your own, your bluff has been called. Now you must confront in your own eyes and those of others whether you're actually capable of doing so. The eyes of greatest concern are those observing you intently from the office you left behind.

In the second chapter I described the case of Timothy Prentice, who left a secure job as head of an architecture firm to become a sculptor at the age of forty. According to Prentice, the risk for which he's usually congratulated — that of daring to live without secure income — was not the one that most concerned him. The danger that kept him up nights, said Prentice, was of making a fool of himself in the eyes of his fellow architects. To his colleagues, Prentice explained, disappearing from the ranks of architecture is tantamount to disappearing, period. "The first couple of years," he said, "I worried a lot about the perception, the opinion of my peers. Like: 'Who the hell is he to think he's a sculptor?'" Prentice even went so far as to use the term "fear of my peers" to describe the danger he felt.

Any self-employed person quickly realizes that his or her relations with other-employed colleagues become a bit *strained*. This is because you now personify their ambivalence about quitting. Only after striking out on your own do you realize how many of those back at the office wish they could too. You discover this when so many of them tell you. Now you're their surrogate risk taker. But the flattery implied or even stated is usually laced with defensiveness ("I would've done what you're doing, except that . . ."). And implicit in this ambivalence is a prayer that your failure will confirm their wisdom in not leaving steady work.

"When you take career risks," says my friend Lorraine, the corporate psychologist, "other people often *need* you to fail to justify their own fears and inertia." In her own case Lorraine quickly discovered how many people, some much older than she, now dealt with her across a chasm of envy. "It was as though I'd stolen their dreams," she explains, "all the years they'd been telling themselves that they'd try it, and they clearly weren't and I was."

One woman who began an interior decorating business in her early forties found that it wasn't just old colleagues and friends but her very family who weren't sure they wanted her to succeed. "I come from a long line of losers," she explained. "I'm breaking that pattern. My mother and I have always been real close. Now there's a distance."

One of the riskiest consequences of going it alone and the hardest to anticipate is the toll it takes on relationships from the past. This is a complicated, subtle problem and seldom one with a clear finger of blame to point. On the one hand, successful enterprise starters are inevitably confronted by old friends who charge them with going high hat, getting stuck up, never having time for old friends, etc., etc. — often with cause. On the other hand, the success of one who's gone it alone is a powerful beacon illuminating the timidity of friends who can't take this plunge and hate themselves for it. The person who makes a go of it becomes a guilt-laden reminder to those who never tried.

Throughout the decade since he left regular employment, Washington newsletter editor Robert Ellis Smith has found himself the subject of ambivalent envy on the part of colleagues who feel mired in jobs they loathe. Many of them are neighbors employed by the Federal government, as Smith once was. "They come home," explained the forty-three-year-old editor, "their guts all twisted about some memo they didn't get out. They feel as if they have to eat crow all day in the office while I work at home. To them my life looks idyllic."

Understandably so. From an office over his garage on Capitol

Hill, the graying, affable editor puts out the *Privacy Journal* once a month. This has earned him an ample if not spectacular income since he founded it a decade ago. More important to Smith is that self-employment gives him the time and flexibility to be involved in local politics, coach soccer for his two boys, and manage a restaurant on Block Island during the summer. As Smith concedes, in many ways his life *is* idyllic.

But when his employed friends compliment him on the risk he's taken to create that life, Smith always feels sheepish, because he knows how casual his decision to become an entrepreneur really was. The real story, Smith admits, is that in 1974 an American Civil Liberties Union grant he'd been working on ran out. For the first time in the twelve years since graduating from Harvard, he was faced with the need to look for work. Until then, Harvard's old-boy network had been a dependable source of reporting jobs on newspapers, directing the ACLU's privacy project, and serving as the Assistant Director of the Office for Civil Rights in the Department of Health, Education and Welfare. Not relishing the idea of looking for a job, Smith procrastinated by spending $1000 — a fifth of his savings — to print and mail a sample newsletter on privacy like the one he'd put out for the ACLU. Only when subscription orders actually came back did Smith realize that he'd made a year's commitment. His *Privacy Journal* still felt interim, however, something with which to bide his time until a real job came along. After ten years he still feels that way. One of these days a job will turn up. When others praise him for daring to strike out on his own, Smith often jokes that it's easier than looking for work. "But it's sort of true," he admits. "It is easier than looking for a job."

If anything, adds Smith, he admires the courage of those who still slog it out in the bowels of the bureaucracy.

After he's been on his own for five years, Smith was sounded out about joining a computer trade association as their Washington representative. He was tempted. Perhaps this was the job he'd been waiting for. The work sounded challenging, and he had no objection to a regular paycheck. Then Smith was told how many people within the organization would have to interview him and approve his being hired. At that point he let the offer slide. "It all came back to me," explains Smith, "having to clear everything with so many people as I had to at HEW — all the time that's taken up in a bureaucracy with personality conflicts, personnel problems, bureaucratic politicking, protecting your turf, cajoling, getting other people to go along with what you want them to do."

Although Smith continues to think of his self-employed status as temporary, that experience made him wonder. "I don't think I'm suited to being somebody else's employee," he says. "I've always been a thorn in the side of whoever had the misfortune of supervising me. I've always been a loner. I think I was destined for this all along."

Robert Smith's attitude is characteristic of entrepreneurs in general. From the outside this breed looks real nervy: Sergeant York at the cash register. Certainly they've always looked that way to me. Me and my typewriter is one thing. But me and a payroll to meet is something else. The very idea makes my eyelids twitch. Where do entrepreneurs find the nerve not only to strike out on their own but to create an enterprise as well?

A number of studies have been made of entrepreneurs in recent years. From them a picture emerges of the type of person best suited to starting a business. At the heart of this portrait is a stubborn, independent, and often abrasive quality that impels the entrepreneur to work for himself because he can't work for, or with, others. One student of the breed has suggested that the following traits are useful if one is thinking of going into business for one's self: "Stubbornness to the point of bullheadedness, independence, sullenness, argumentativeness, peevishness, periods of elation and despair, anxiety and insecurity."

By reporting this I'm not trying to debunk or romanticize entrepreneurial tendencies. (I wish I had more of them.) What I am trying to do is emphasize that starting your own enterprise calls for certain *qualities*. If you've ever seriously thought of doing so, it might help to be aware of what those qualities are. If you haven't and feel guilty about it, this could prove a relief.

At a workshop in New York for women who were interested in starting a business, the psychologist-businesswoman running the workshop laid down a hard line from the outset. For your business to succeed, said Judith Haynes, it must become an obsession. If you're single, forget about time to date. If you're married, starting a business will test your marriage. There are few days off, no benefits, no corporate backup or safety net of any kind. Sleepless nights will be the norm, not the exception. "If you can be scared off by what I have to say," concluded Haynes, "you have no business being in business."

For starters, most new businesses fail within five years; some say three. For women, the usual obstacles are exaggerated by discrimination. The government, banks, and financial institutions in general are geared to helping big corporations run by men, not small businesses started by women. You'll hear Horatio and Hortense Alger stories. Ignore them. Failure is more likely than success. Furthermore, even if your business succeeds, it is unlikely that you'll ever make more money than you would by working for someone else — although you will work longer hours. You must be very clear about your intentions. If your goal is more time and money, *don't* start a business. Do this only if you *must*.

Among the women attending the New York workshop was a dark-haired nurse in her early thirties who was struggling to take over a camping equipment business she and her husband had started before he went to work for someone else. The nurse said that her biggest problem was being firm with those who were giving her bad service. Even when she was tough, the woman found that she went to pieces afterward. In one dispute in particular, her landlady had been demanding $75 for gas, which the nurse was holding back because promised repairs hadn't been made on a heater. "I know in the end I'll have to say, 'Call my attorney,' " she concluded, "but I can't do that."

"Why not?" asked Haynes.

"Because I want her to like me. I don't want her to be mad at me. If I let her take advantage of me, she won't be mad at me."

"But will she like you?"

"No. But I can't stand all the yelling and confrontation."

"So why not just let your husband handle it?"

"Because it feels important for me to do it. Anyway, this is much more exciting than nursing. It's such a change. But it's so much harder for me than for my husband. I get hysterical."

This exchange characterized the two sessions of this workshop I attended. Far more issues of the spirit arose than those of the pocketbook. Haynes thought that if anything, such obstacles were harder for women to surmount than the financial ones thrown in their path. Women, she told her students, are raised to be "people pleasers." Or to wield power behind the scenes. The need to use power directly in their own business calls for renouncing any claim to being a fluttery Southern belle or seductive femme fatale. "It requires an enormous amount of courage to give up being a sweet young thing," she said, "to go ahead and assert yourself. It's so much easier to let your husband handle it. When you go out in the business world, it's very frightening not to be able to say, 'Okay, Frank. Take care of it.' It's very frightening to have to take care of things yourself."

The thought that any one of us could start our own enterprise is an important part of the American dream. In most cases this dream will never be fulfilled. Nearly three-quarters of those who filled out my questionnaire endorsed "start my own business" as an ending to the sentence beginning "Sometimes I've thought I'd like to ____." But on a separate question, only 9 percent said that with a strings-free gift of $10,000 they would actually start a business. In 1980, 8.5 percent of all Americans were self-employed, down from 18 percent in 1950, and 80 percent in 1800.

Obviously there's some conflict between fantasy and reality when it comes to starting businesses. One reason is that we're usually focused on the wrong risk when considering the dangers of such a move. When we think about striking out on our own, most of us pale at the thought of getting along without regular income and decide we'd rather not. We're Level II types unable to take the Level I risk of cutting loose to chart our own path. But those who do and stay with it usually find that the more daunting risk of *running* a business — as opposed to starting one — occurs at the second level.

Give any business founder five minutes and he'll have half a dozen stories to tell about bill collectors pounding on the door, creditors whistling through the keyholes, and having to eat peanut butter sandwiches in the dark because the electricity's been turned off. But these are old war stories. They're how the entrepreneur wins his stripes. Color comes to his face as he tells such stories, and excitement rings in his voice.

Far from being intimidated by the trauma of starting a business, the entrepreneur thrives on it. It's not that business founders don't feel traumatized. One man I spoke to together with his wife had sunk all of their savings and taken on considerable debt to start a computer software business. When I showed him my questionnaire he went right for a question about symptoms of fear. "Heart palpitations?" the man read aloud. "Yes. Sleepless nights? Yes. Sweaty palms? Yes." Finally he looked up and asked, "Is there any place to check, 'All of the above'?"

It's not fearlessness that distinguishes entrepreneurs from the rest of us; it's the way they cope with fear. During the start-up phase especially, a period of "almost unbearable uncertainty," write Orvis Collins and David Moore about a group of male midwestern business founders they studied, "entrepreneurs, as men of action, show at their best. They are men who appear to perform with peak effectiveness in a crisis."

With their ability to tolerate fear and even depend on it for energy, entrepreneurs respond to adversity in a predictable fashion. To them being knocked off balance provides a wonderful opportunity to land on their feet in a new and better place. Surveys of those who have founded their own business consistently find that the most common motivation for doing so is being laid off, fired, demoted, transferred, or blocked from promotion while working for someone else.

Rather than deal with the trauma of being fired or frustrated by seeking a more secure job, they respond by creating a countertrauma. "The antidote to insecurity," write Collins and Moore of their group, "is, in a sense, more insecurity. . . .[The entrepreneur's] mode of coping with insecurity and danger is never to return — in more than a tentative way — to organization security, but to go deeper into dangerous territory. Eventually, in his seeking for a world which he can control and which is secure, he begins a new enterprise."

This is partly a matter of choice. But it's also because the typical entrepreneur has so little notion of how to wait for advancement within an organization and less interest in learning. This seems to be part of their heritage. In comparison with corporate executives, entrepreneurs have been found to recall their childhoods as turbulent, characterized by conflict with authority figures and punctuated by attempts to flee constricting structures. Doug Kreeger, for example, who went on to found a highly successful camping equipment business in New York, was given the nickname "Runaway Kreeger" by his elementary school teachers because of his tendency to bolt from the classroom. In a typical pattern, his work history before Kreeger & Sons got underway consisted of several jobs briefly held.

One way of characterizing such a person is as someone for whom the risks of steady employment are intolerable. This may sound contradictory, but only if the concept of vocational risk is limited to loss of tenure, income, and benefits. To entrepreneurs there are worse risks than those. To them the peril of boredom from settling into routine work with predictable income feels far more ominous than the exciting dangers of striking out on your own. Like risk, security is in the fears of the beholder. As the founder of a manufacturing company once put it, "I could never stand the *insecurity* of working for other people" (emphasis added).

A key difference between those who are able to work on their own and those who aren't is whether money symbolizes security or a straitjacket. In case after case it's not even going broke as such that keeps people mired in frustrating jobs but the fear of giving up any fraction of their standard of living. On the surface this is expressed as a reluctance to sacrifice eating in four-star restaurants and taking winter trips to Aspen. But at a deeper level it expresses a simple fear of risking any part of a life to which they have become accustomed. By contrast, as compared with their primary goal of looking for action and building new structures, entrepreneurs are remarkably oblivious to the danger this poses to their standard of living. Perhaps they have to be. "Possessions are the really dangerous risks, I'm convinced," the owner of an independent movie theater once observed. "They distract you, and in a new business, one of the few resources at your command is concentration."

As such, income is a perilous goal for the business founder. Trying to make too much of a profit too fast bleeds an enterprise of capital. One investor of "venture capital" in new businesses says he's always impressed by entrepreneurs who work in small offices, drive cheap cars, and let him pay for lunch. Those with big offices who pick him up in a limousine and insist on picking up the lunch check get crossed right off his list.

One of the major misconceptions about entrepreneurs is that money is what motivates them. On the contrary, says former National Association of Manufacturers vice-president Richard Cornuelle of the entrepreneurs he's observed over a quarter century's time, "They seem to care so little about money that they lose less sleep over it than ordinary people when they take risks with it."

A survey of 109 men who had left steady jobs in St. Louis to start businesses found that compared with a group of employed men they were significantly more dissatisfied about every aspect of salaried work except one: the salary itself. Unlike the lack of challenge, lack of opportunity for advancement, and problems with bosses and coworkers, pay was the only major part of their former jobs that these entrepreneurs did not complain about.

During several decades spent studying entrepreneurial motives, Harvard psychologist David McClelland has found them clustered around the need for visible *achievement*. Money has a different meaning to such a person than an employed one. Economic incentives not only don't motivate entrepreneurial types, McClelland has found, but may actually hurt their performance. This is because, in his words, "the money makes them nervous. It is the challenge of the job itself that rewards the achiever people."

It's not that such people don't want to get rich. On the contrary. But as with gamblers and criminals (to whom they've been compared), wealth per se has little meaning to the entrepreneur. As Ted Turner puts it, "Money is how you keep score."

Turner is a classic entrepreneur on a grand scale. Between his cable television empire, professional sport teams, and sailboat racing, the Atlantan's life is dedicated to looking for action. Turner once claimed that his main reason for starting Cable News Network was "a sense of adventure." His wife has speculated that her husband must have been a hyperactive child, since he's such a hyperactive adult.

In a recurring entrepreneurial pattern, Turner seems driven by a need to do better than the father with whom he constantly fought. And like so many empire builders, Ted Turner seems far more excited by starting new businesses than running existing ones. Some financial analysts think that the reason his total empire has had such trouble getting into the black is because its founder finds this boring.

To more timorous eyes, Turner appears to be not only an outlandish risk taker but a fearless one. *Time* magazine has called him both. Turner's own perspective is different. When he took over the Atlanta Braves and made one of the first big-ticket free-agent deals, I watched a television interviewer ask the team's owner if he wasn't a bit scared. Turner replied that he'd been scared every day of his life.

When my colleague Julia Klein went to Atlanta to profile Turner for a magazine, I asked if she would ask the founder of Cable News Network whether he considered himself a risk taker. Turner's response was quick and unequivocal: he did not. Only the fact that he and his company were doing what no one else had ever done and spending large sums of money in the process gave him that image. But because he felt confident and had done his homework, Turner said he felt on solid ground. "I'm basically conservative," he told Klein. "I try not to exceed the speed limit, and when I raced it was in a strong boat."

A final, characteristic trait of Turner's is his attitude toward failure. Those who play poker with him say the man's renowned prowess at this game is due to his indifference toward losing. While learning to sail as a child, Turner earned the nickname "Turnover Ted, the Capsize Kid." As he later observed (about sailboat races), "It's great to win and it's not as much fun to lose, but it's not that big a deal."

This attitude actually typifies entrepreneurs. It almost has to. One way they're able to take risks that the rest of us can't is that they reduce their stakes drastically by being relatively oblivious to the prospect of failure. Among a group of entrepreneurs he studied in Austin, Texas, management professor Albert Shapero found that not only had many of them failed at one or more businesses, but that three-quarters of them said if their current business failed they'd probably start another. From the outside it's easy to wonder, "Won't they ever learn?" But this is a decidedly non-entrepreneurial attitude. As Shapero pointed out, "In order to see starting a company as a credible act, it may . . . be necessary to be blind to some of the risks." Of the forty business founders in his survey, two-thirds said they saw their risk as minimal. Since the vast majority of new businesses do fail, including many prior ventures of the men being studied, Shapero concluded that "the results do make us wonder whether an entrepreneur perceives the same risks that a rational outsider would."

Like Philippe Petit, a business founder may *know* objectively that whoever gets on the wire may fall off. He just doesn't believe it could happen to him. Otherwise he'd never get on in the first place. This trait, which might be called "informed ignorance," is one of the entrepreneur's most treasured assets. As David McClelland points out, successful businessmen are not merely reckless and filled with derring-do; rather, they accumulate the best information available, then move ahead based on their faith in themselves. In fact, adds McClelland, such men and women are at their very best in situations that demand action before all the facts are in. In time the facts themselves may change under the influence of entrepreneurial zeal.

This is what Gene Gossfield discovered. At the age of fifty-two, after two decades as a marketing executive for a siding company, Gossfield started a restaurant with his wife. Other than doing some financial projection and taking a course on restaurant management, they did virtually no preplanning. Yet their restaurant — Under the Blue Moon — has been such a success in eight years' time that imitators now surround them in Philadelphia's Chestnut Hill neighborhood. Rather than seeing it as foolhardiness, Gossfield looks back on their ignorance as integral to "the enthusiasm, the innocence, the wild excitement we had at the beginning." Not only did their naiveté allow them to buck odds a better informed person might have avoided, says the restaurant owner, but it had the practical effect of attracting as early customers a loyal band of "semiowners" who developed a stake in helping this unlikely venture succeed.

I often hear those who muse about starting a new business talk about the exhaustive planning needed to "minimize" their risk. One academic student of the breed has gone so far as to suggest that "the successful entrepreneur is that individual who can correctly interpret the risk situation and then determine policies which will minimize the risks involved." That doesn't characterize any business founder I've ever met. It's not that entrepreneurs don't plan and try to hold down their risks. They do. But anyone whose primary goal is risk minimization seldom starts a business in the first place. It's too scary, even when the facts are friendly.

Earlier I mentioned a husband-wife team who were experiencing all of the fear responses to their new computer software business. In describing the potential benefits they saw from the use of computers by entrepreneurs, analyzing and managing risks was high on the list. Someone thinking about starting a business, they pointed out, could factor the variables into a program, then use this program to forecast what they were up against. Did you do this, I asked? The two looked at each other. Then, after a long pause, both grinned sheepishly and said simultaneously, "No."

Repeatedly those who found successful businesses later say that had they known what they were getting into, they wouldn't have. But that's just the point. In my experience even people who are intelligent, prudent, and orderly in other aspects of their lives can be awfully fuzzy about the details and risks of a new venture they really want to start. Once under way, they are protected by a combination of informed ignorance and a love of the adventure involved in pushing off from shore.

In fact, to a classic entrepreneur the *real* risk doesn't come until later, long after a new business is rolling. Any number of business founders whom I consulted told me that they found the risks of expansion far more harrowing than those of starting up.

The founder of a successful cookie company bearing her name told me that at the outset this felt more like a game than a gamble — she and her husband making cookies for sale in their kitchen. Only when they had made enough of a profit to purchase expensive equipment and begin to widen distribution did she begin to feel in danger. Now it had become, in her words, "serious — continually a risk."

To expand a successful business, bigger loans must be taken out, with more collateral. Inventory grows. More space must be leased, often at higher rates. New insurance policies are required. More employees join the payroll. Their lives become partly your responsibility. All of a sudden one's stakes have skyrocketed. The sense of risk grows with the business.

Steve Poses, a former antiwar activist who led the renaissance of Philadelphia's restaurants with his *nouvelle cuisine* at The Frog, now owns several spinoffs. Poses says unequivocally that expanding his business felt far riskier than starting it. Only in retrospect can he see how naive it was to think that he could start a new restaurant with $35,000 and a lot of chutzpah. Protected as he was by ignorance, Poses says that getting The Frog underway felt like "falling off a log." Running a chain of restaurants feels like anything but.

Of course only someone with more Level I than II characteristics could say such a thing. To those who prefer their risk at the first level, business success poses all manner of danger. For one thing it means that the buzz, the rush of getting an enterprise off the ground, has ended. Steadier management skills are now called for. This period often calls for shedding partners and backers who helped you get started but now stand in your way. It can involve giving up old friends who found you better company when struggling. In general it means redefining your life around being a success rather than a failure or a question mark. For a boredom-phobic person this prospect is not necessarily welcome. As Atari's founder, Nolan Bushnell, complained before he left that company to start a new one, "Being successful is kind of dull."

So to a Level I type, starting a business can feel less risky than running one. Winning the gamble of founding a business means you're no longer a buccaneer, but a businessman or businesswoman. Perhaps coping with the dangers of that identity is where their real challenge lies.

For Level I and II types alike, striking out economically is one of the most challenging risks that can be taken. For this reason it's also one of the most valuable.

To security-oriented Level II types, setting out on this uncharted path involves important lessons about developing nerve, confronting fear, and learning to live on less. To Level I types, for whom financial insecurity is a thrill, every bit as valuable if more ambiguous lessons can be learned from confronting the risks of success, boredom, and commitment, which are inherent in any ongoing enterprise.

This is the way Merilyn Jackson looks back on her own seven years as a business owner. Today an attractive and blunt-spoken brunette of thirty-nine, Merilyn quit her job as assistant to the personnel director of a Philadelphia hospital more than a decade ago to buy a cheese store up the street from Under the Blue Moon. This called for far longer hours of work (in addition to raising two children) and many more headaches than being an administrative assistant. But her work resulted in three profitable first years. Then, as the economy turned down and wholesale prices shot up, her profit margin was reduced to a sliver. At the same time, Merilyn's equipment was deteriorating. She had no capital to replace or restore it. Without collateral or a track record she couldn't get financing. Finally, seven years after buying it, Merilyn sold her store at a loss. Her years of 80-hour weeks and sleepless nights were over.

Does she regret the experience?

"I loved it," says Merilyn. "I really loved it. I worked harder than I ever thought I'd have to work in my life and loved every part of it."

As she explains, even though her business failed, Merilyn feels like a better person for having owned it. Prior to running her own business Merilyn had never had much self-discipline. During years of nine-to-five jobs, she'd proved herself competent but disorganized and was often late for work. On the eve of becoming responsible for the success or failure of a business, Merilyn stayed up late many a night weeping. The consequences of her disheveled work habits were about to fall on her own shoulders. Merilyn wondered if there would come a day when she wouldn't even open the doors to her store because she just couldn't be bothered.

To her surprise, Merilyn found that the pressures of being her own boss forced her to concentrate, to become better organized and more self-disciplined all around in ways that persist to this day (she now works as a free-lance pastry chef). And even more important than improved work habits, says Merilyn, is the lesson owning a business taught her about commitment. A veteran of two failed marriages, she realized that commitment was not her strong suit. As Merilyn puts it, "I was never really committed to anything in my life, except my children. Commitment is not something I'm good at. My pattern in the past has been that when things got rough, when I had a failure, I ran. Owning my own business taught me the elements of commitment — that commitment has in it 'for better or for worse,' not just 'for better.' It taught me that commitment means sticking through the worst times. I think that was an important lesson for me to learn."

And in a way, she feels that this lesson was more surely learned because her business failed. As Merilyn puts it, "If I had had only a good business, never any problems from the word go, how would we know I was really committed?"

ULTIMATE RISK

In what seems like another life, I used to take part in "encounter groups." Such attempts at total honesty were very exciting. As during high school, or a tornado watch, they usually crackled with the promise of danger. Encounter groups were always stimulating, and I learned quite a bit from taking part in them.

One of the main things I learned was how difficult it can be to pin down what risk taking means in such a context. Many of those who took part in these groups were passionate advocates of "taking risks" with each other. Yet my impression was that those who sat tight, didn't say much, and looked scared were taking the biggest risk just by being there. By contrast the most fervent apostles of taking chances struck me as change-obsessed, stimulation-seeking, and even action-addicted people who moved restlessly from one group to the next. My favorite was the middle-aged plumber who came from Phoenix to attend a group my wife Muriel and I were leading in San Diego. "These encounter groups are great," the plumber told us. "I get to as many as I can. I used to go to Vegas and gamble. Now I go to groups."

Thankfully, the worst excesses of this movement have gone the way of Jerry Rubin's headband. Its spirit lives on in the words of descendants such as Wayne Dyer and Leo Buscaglia.

Among contemporary self-helpers, Leo Buscaglia has particular reverence for "taking risks." As Buscaglia writes in *Living, Loving and Learning*, "Let's talk about risk because risk is so nice. Once you begin to become hooked on risk, your whole life changes." A closer examination of his work reveals that what he basically means by this is being more open to others. As an illustration, Buscaglia refers often to the hugs he gives and gets even from those he's just met. "Don't tell me that it ever gets *boring* to hug!" says Buscaglia.

Boredom is a particular concern of Buscaglia's. "If you're bored," he advises, "if you're afraid, if you don't like the scene that you're in, get the hell out! . . .

"If you don't like the scene you're in, if you're unhappy, if you're lonely, if you don't feel that things are happening, change your scene. Paint a new backdrop. Surround yourself with new actors."

By his own description, Leo Buscaglia's life — or as he refers to it, "all my running all over the country and all the crazy things I do" — resembles that of a band on tour. He especially likes airports and loves riding on airplanes because on them, "you meet old friends you've never seen, you make new friends because people know they may never see you again; it's like true confessions." During speeches Buscaglia often reminds his listeners that he needs them, and that without the people he meets in a busy schedule of appearances his life would not be complete.

In theory such openness to the many need not be inconsistent with commitment to a few. Certainly Buscaglia sees no such inconsistency. Nearly as often as he pleads with us to take more risks he exhorts us to be more intimate, more involved, and more committed to lasting relationships. To illustrate what he means by commitment, Buscaglia refers often to the half-century marriage of his parents. Yet Buscaglia himself — who seems to be in his mid-fifties (he won't reveal his age) — has no such commitment. As he has explained of his lifelong bachelor status, "Even the most saintly woman wouldn't put up with my life-style." On a loftier plane, Buscaglia once told an interviewer that to him intimacy does not mean exclusivity. "If you remember in my *Love* book," he explained, "I said love is never exclusive, it's always *inclusive* and that I will recognize that I have become a lover when I can say that I love all things." Buscaglia did emphasize that he had a number of intimate friends of long standing, ones he treasured "even if they're on the other side of the world."

So in the case of Leo Buscaglia a picture emerges of a warm, dynamic, and broadly loving man whose love seems best expressed in brief encounters on the run. He puts openness to such encounters under the heading of "risk," the kind we all ought to be taking. This concept of risk is based on change, movement, and the struggle against boredom. "Boredom arises from routine," he explains. "Joy, wonder, rapture arise from surprise. Routine leads to boredom, and if you are bored, you are *boring.* "

The antidote to boredom is, of course, change. As Buscaglia puts it, "To experiment with your own life is exhilarating. . . .

"But I warn you that if you decide to take full responsibility for your life, it's not going to be easy, and you're going to have to risk again. Risk — the key to change."

And there we have it. Risk means change, taking off, new faces, a better scene, fresh embraces, exhilaration, and ecstasy — all enlisted in the war against boredom.

The irony is that for many of his listeners, those with less hectic lives and stronger commitments, the Buscaglia approach *would* be risky. So much is at stake. But for one such as Buscaglia himself, what could be safer? If you find it exhilarating, what's daring about embracing strangers? Where's the danger in being open with hordes of people in auditoriums and airports? For the Leo Buscaglias of this world there's little risk in dashing about having intense minirelationships. That's thrilling. For them a bigger risk might be to limit their intimacy to one or a handful of people and confront the perils of boredom.

My impression of the most fervent apostles of "risk taking" in general is that they're excitement-oriented, easily bored, and best able to achieve intimacy when they know it will end. They are loners whose action-packed lives keep them on the move at many levels. Wayne Dyer, for example, like Leo Buscaglia, is a popular apostle of "going for it" much as he does in his hectic, appearance-filled life. Of his two unsuccessful attempts at marriage, the forty-three-year-old psychologist has explained, "I have too much to do. I am too committed to my work. Sustaining a one-to-one relationship just wasn't possible. . . . I find that I just have more and more that I want to do. I'm full of zeal."

Without wishing to comment on Dyer's marriages as such, or Buscaglia's lack of them, one might ask whether the high-decibel "risk taking" they propose doesn't make lasting relationships unlikely. For them this may be appropriate. But if "change" is so high on your list of values, what's risky about ending old relationships and starting new ones?

Psychologist Bernie Zilbergeld (author of *The Shrinking of America*) calls this approach to risk taking the psychological equivalent of a one-night stand. As he explains:

> Hugging is easy, loving is easy, expression of warm feelings is easy . . . when there is no past and no future, when we don't have to worry about the fact that you want children and I don't or that we have fundamental differences about raising the children we do have, or that we don't agree on where and when to vacation, how often to have sex, who should control our finances, and all the other issues that can make intimacy feel more like war than love.
>
> It is easy to love everyone when you don't have to be with anyone longer than a few minutes or hours. It is easier to hug a stranger, even taking into account the possibility of getting slapped for it, than to hug your spouse after he or she has criticized your personality or sexual prowess. It's easy to tell others how to have relationships and to raise children when you yourself do not have to deal with the demands, frustrations, and hassles of real relationships and children. . . .
>
> Most of us want to have a past and a future with the people we hug, but that past and future often get in the way of wanting to hug them.

The problem with the Dyer-Buscaglia approach is not that it lacks merit. Buscaglia in particular seems to be a warm and exuberant man well worth spending the evening with in an auditorium. But their vague and promiscuous exhortations to "take more risks" with each other are at best simplistic, at worst irresponsible. Any psychiatrist will tell you that his waiting room is divided between those who don't take enough risks in their emotional life, who guard themselves too closely, and others who take too many, who never know when to stop. Tracts proposing that we all take more risks with each other are the equivalent of a psychiatrist stepping out into his waiting room and giving everyone a little pep talk on the need to be bolder. In essence this is what the evangelists of risk are doing. Without regard for individual differences or for what may be at stake, they advise one and all to take more risks. Invariably this translates into seeking change and gambling with relationships.

Reduced to its essence, what such psychological "risk taking" refers to is constant movement, cutting your losses, keeping stakes low, and seeking "change." How-to missives invariably use the term "risk taker" synonymously with "change seeker." The assumption usually is that risk involves movement, movement stimulates growth, growth is better than stagnation, and stagnation is inevitable when you stay put. Therefore: take a risk; make a move.

This concept of the risk taker as psychological pioneer is reiterated constantly in American media. A typical women's magazine article, called "Taking a Chance on Change," counsels readers on how to get over their fear of change. According to the author, this fear is "always stifling and always self-destructive. Being its victim means hiding, retreating, saying no to life." Various case studies are offered of daring women who gathered up their courage to risk leaving relationships, moving homes, and changing jobs. By contrast, one case is studied of a woman who had worked for eight years at a New York bank and twice refused transfers to London. This woman's reasoning was presented as a rationalization for her suffocating fear of change. " 'You see,' she said, 'here I'm somebody. People know me. I know my way around. What I have may not be exciting, but it's something — and I don't want to lose it.' " By favorable contrast we are offered the case of Nora, who has accepted two transfers in four years. "Women like Nora," the article concludes, "who muster the courage to pack up and try a new place generally find that, in the end, the huge effort pays off."

I've dwelled on this article not because it's so unusual but because it's so typical in equating risk with movement, novelty, and change. Faced with the choice between moving on and staying put, any American with gumption knows which choice involves the most risk. Where's the risk in staying put?

In a treatise titled "How Taking Risks Can Enrich a Marriage," a pair of marriage counselors made this point for a reader of *McCall's*. This woman's husband had been offered a promotion. Taking it would mean leaving a community that included relatives and friends of long standing. What should they do? The counselors suggested that this couple consider the possibility that their life might be stuck in a rut. Such a rut, or "fixed pattern," as the counselors called it, "may represent security and stability to you and your husband, but it also may represent rigidity, since new experiences are a source of personal growth." For this reason, they asked the couple to reexamine whether the old relationships they valued so much might have become a source of too much emotional comfort. They were advised to reflect on "whether your long-established friendships are still truly stimulating." Perhaps, it was suggested, some new faces might prove more so.

The problem with such typical advice is that it wraps active, dramatic, and exciting moves in the holy garb of "risk taking." For someone who is genuinely afraid of a necessary change, it would be. But more often equating risk with change merely camouflages the pot stirring and stimulation seeking going on.

A study of those who scored high on a psychological "change-seeker" index (which tests one's interest in personal growth) found that such a score was also a good predictor of "stimulus-seeking" behavior in general. Those most interested in personal growth proved to be highly interested in a wide range of novelty such as gambling, use of drugs, and frequent change of sexual partners.

In *Machisma*, Grace Lichenstein devotes one section to examining the lives of a group she calls sexual risk takers. These women changed partners frequently and aggressively sought sexual satisfaction in ways that would have been scandalous even a couple of decades ago. "The biggest sexual risk takers," writes Lichtenstein, "are women who consciously divide love and sex." How so? What's the risk? Such a sexual style is no longer uncommon, risqué, or even based on terribly high stakes in an age of effective birth control and legalized abortion. And while her subjects themselves claimed to be trying men on in search of a "perfect fit," as one admitted, "The best sexual nights I've had have been with somebody I've met that afternoon. It becomes an all-night, torrid affair, awake until dawn. But very often I'm not interested in that person again. Unfortunately, it seems that once I achieve the conquest, a lot of the glitter is gone from the relationship."

In the course of this project, I don't know how many times I was told about a person who was "a real sexual risk taker." Usually this turned out to be someone who did it with a lot of people in a number of positions. This always sounded like fun. Certainly the "risk takers" themselves seemed to think so. But other than contracting herpes, it never was clear what risk they were taking.

Sexual or otherwise, relationships are rich with the potential for pot stirring, sensation seeking, action addiction, and sundry adventures. Just as there are those who seek unusually strong jolts to the organism by seeking thrills, others get a similar jolt from turbulent relationships. We've all known people (perhaps even ourselves) who go out of their way to pick fights, provoke confrontations, get caught cheating — so they can come alive in the process of "working things out." At best they marry each other and lurch happily from crisis to crisis. From the outside such relationships usually look outrageous. How can they put up with each other? we wonder. But as with any other source of strong stimulation, bad can be better than good when it comes to our emotional lives. "Although most people assume that we love the people we do in *spite* of the suffering they cause us," point out psychologists Elaine and William Walster, "it may be that, in part, we love them *because* of the suffering they cause. Under the right conditions, anxiety and fear, insecurity, loneliness, frustration, jealousy, anger, and mixed emotions are all capable of fueling passion. Passion demands physical arousal and unpleasant experiences are just as arousing as pleasant ones."

This is why so many of us end up in relationships with cads. Not because we're self-destructive; just because we're bored. Decent people have an unfortunate tendency to be predictably decent, hence boring. To someone in need of stimulation, a stormy relationship can be just the thing.

One man I've known for years never seems so frustrated with a relationship as when everything is going smoothly. Only when involved with building a new relationship or repairing an old one does color rise to his cheeks and a sparkle enter his eyes. This approach is taken not only to romance but to friendships of all kinds. His favorite ones involve lots of "working things out." Nothing seems to bore him so much as time spent together without problems to work on. I spend as little time as possible with this man. What to me feels relaxed to him is tedious; what's exciting to him is exhausting to me.

One risk in human relationships that seldom earns this title is the risk of doing nothing. Of letting things run their course. Of not trying to confront every problem and control all outcomes. Forgoing the lesser risk of confrontation and change can leave you open to the deeper risks of commitment and community.

Just as physical derring-do is overrated as risk taking, so are subtle psychological steps underrated. Among these might be included staying rather than leaving; letting intimacy develop slowly rather than pressing for it fast; coming to terms with yourself as you are, rather than looking for ways to change; and letting things progress naturally, rather than initiating some course of action that you hope you can control. To excitement-oriented people in an action-based society such risks can be greater than making a move. The danger of coping with the routine that is part of any ongoing relationship presents a far greater challenge to a Level I type than escaping such routine by stirring up some action.

In a book on boredom, philosopher Sam Keen suggests that seeking stimulation can be a means of avoiding intimacy. In Keen's conception, an exaggerated fear of boredom is precisely what keeps us from the profound personal adventures that lie beyond monotony, especially the adventure of actually knowing another person, and of being known. Writes Keen:

> The first law of intimacy is: if a relationship is to deepen into intimacy it must go beyond romance or politeness, pass through disillusionment and monotony, and emerge on the far side of the boredom barrier. . . . We must become bored with the romance of personality before we begin to reveal ourselves. A life of continued stimulation and surface excitement prevents the adventure of profound intimacy.
>
> With this law in mind it becomes clear that many styles of relationship prevent boredom at the price of avoiding intimacy.

And this is not just a matter of romantic intimacy, Keen adds. Even friendships include the danger of being known intimately by another person. "Each step requires a further risk . . . ," he writes. "It's both dangerous and exciting because there is no place to hide. Friends see through all the sham."

The irony is that second only to "risk" and "change" on today's scale of values are "intimacy" and "community." Yet on the terms usually proposed, one set of values negates the other. Constantly pursuing change ensures that we never have to stay in one place long enough to become known very deeply. By staying on the move we become a moving target. Nobody can ever quite pin us down, except perhaps as a "risk taker." Staying put may risk sticking you in a rut. But part of that risk is the danger of becoming known to others who are stuck with you. Once they do know you, and on more than a surface level, you're confronted with the further risk of discovering whether you're still acceptable: likable, lovable, forgivable. These are frightening issues, involving profound danger. Everything is on the table. The stake is yourself. Not wanting to risk that self is what leads us to seek the lesser risk of change.

By seeking change through perpetual motion we actually make that goal less attainable. For all their novelty, new faces are easier to manipulate than ones that know us better and want something deeper, something less predictable in a relationship. This is what Rollo May refers to when he writes of "the courage to invest one's self over a period of time in a relationship that will demand an increasing openness." As May points out:

> Intimacy requires courage because risk is inescapable. We cannot know at the outset how the relationship will affect us. . . .
>
> A common practice in our day is to avoid working up the courage required for authentic intimacy by shifting the issue to the body, making it a matter of simple physical courage. It is easier in our society to be naked physically than to be naked psychologically or spiritually — easier to share our body than to share our fantasies, hopes, fears and aspirations, which are felt to be more personal. . . . For curious reasons we are shy about sharing the things that matter most. Hence people short circuit the more "dangerous" building of a relationship by leaping immediately into bed.

Here is a classic illustration of our concept of risk falling behind the times. For most of history, the dangers of making love were greater than those of making a commitment. Ending a relationship was far riskier than starting one. Marriage was considered inevitable, till death, and even the risk of choosing a partner was taken out of our hands by arranged betrothal. Elaborate social and religious conventions reinforced this commitment. Leaving a marriage might also make it necessary to leave one's church, one's community, even one's family. For women in particular, risking divorce also meant risking destitution. With so much at stake, leaving a marriage was a catastrophic gamble, much greater, certainly, than entering one.

By now, however, especially in this society, the relative risks of beginning or ending a marriage have changed hands. Today starting a marriage typically feels riskier than ending one, to Level I types in particular. On my questionnaire 80 of the 512 people who filled it out mentioned marriage or remarriage as the biggest risk they had ever taken or could imagine taking. By contrast, only 8 listed divorce as the biggest risk they had taken, and 10 more as the biggest risk they could imagine taking. This isn't altogether a valid comparison, since 35 percent of the respondents had never been married, but the contrast is suggestive.

One hardly wants to argue that ending a marriage isn't a gamble, and at times necessary. But as the active, exciting alternative, the one promising movement and change, ending a relationship has received more credit than it's due as "risk taking." More basic in many cases is the fact that leaving a partner is more stimulating than staying with one. Breaking up a relationship is nothing if not exciting, it does take moxie, and like any catastrophe has bittersweet appeal. No treatise on marriage and divorce would go so far as to suggest ending a relationship for the sake of adventure, but that message can be construed.

In a manual for women who are leaving their marriages, for example, the point is made that this is not the best alternative for everyone. If fulfillment can be found in marriage, more's the better. But the book goes on to paint a picture of the divorce process that portrays not only the anxiety but the exhilaration involved in terms any skydiver would understand. "There is joy in freedom," this manual advises, and painful as it may be, the period of breaking the marital bond can be one of both "high tension" and "drama."

While scary, the author continues, "The unknown is also an adventure, and you can react to this situation in that way. It is a rare chance to explore parts of yourself and the world that you have never known. Fear can also be excitement, the kind of thrill that any scientist or explorer feels when he or she is on the verge of discovery. The mystery of the unknown is seen as a challenge."

Here is the crux of the problem. Ending a relationship *can* be challenging, dramatic, and exciting. To suggest otherwise is frivolous. Even when their elation alternates with despair, newly divorced people can be exciting company; usually more so than when they were married. Their turmoil leads to openness and a need to share with others. If we're starved for adventure, ending a relationship is an obvious alternative. And calling this "risk taking" adds a patina of mettle-testing to the process.

In a sense divorce has become a modern rite: an opportunity to see what we're made of. In southern California they joke about not taking anyone seriously until after their first divorce — except they're not altogether joking. Some go so far as to formalize the ritual of divorce with announcements, ceremonies, and hors d'oeuvres. A marriage counselor says that among her major challenges is getting across to couples in trouble that "divorce is not a necessary ritual, that individuation and maturity can be achieved without shedding the spouse."

One reason that divorce has taken on such adventurous, character-building overtones is that it's so often portrayed this way. In movies such as *Kramer vs. Kramer, Ordinary People, Shoot the Moon,* and *An Unmarried Woman,* the rather tedious married couples we meet at the outset blossom and become interesting — noble even — as their marriages crumble. Noting a similar trend in fiction, critic Anatole Broyard has found it almost obligatory among contemporary authors that "if a husband and wife are mentioned as hanging around in a novel, they must be divorced before the end of the book." Broyard continues:

> Perhaps every marriage is a bad novel unless it breaks up. There's no real ending, for example, without a divorce. In fact, there's no beginning either, since the characters are already married, the initial drama is over when we meet them. In marriages in novels,

there's just a middle, a sort of middling feeling, like middle-aged spread. . . .

One of the most serious conjugal problems is dialogue. Husbands and wives, in the very nature of things, are thrown together in circumstances which render good dialogue almost impossible. It is only in the first stages of erotic derangement that men and women manage to say interesting things. Also, there's a built-in paradox here: the better the dialogue, the more destructive it seems. Once husbands and wives start getting off good lines, you know that they haven't got far to go.

Adventurous as it may be, in the current state of affairs getting divorced can involve less risk than staying married. Among the unmarried the risk that a marriage won't work out is the one most often discussed. An unmarried friend in her mid-twenties tells me that her principal fear about making such a commitment is that she will make the wrong choice and have to bail out. She also tells me — only semifacetiously — that the average length of relationships in her circle is three weeks. Is this a fear of failure, or a fear of success? Is the greater danger that a marriage will be tumultuous and end up in divorce court, or lasting and end in monotony?

Lasting relationships pose profound dangers of becoming tedious and ordinary. Riskier yet is the danger that despite your best efforts, someone else will get to know you intimately. What then? The fear that someday we'll be seen through and found out is hardly limited to those onstage. The danger of rejection by someone who knows us well is profound. If we are known only on a superficial level, we can take solace in the assurance that any rejection will not be of our real selves.

The freedom to take or avoid the risk of letting a genuine self be known is a relatively modern phenomenon. When life was lived on a more intimate scale, being known to others was as inevitable as breathing. Others watched you from birth and knew far more about you than ever needed to be said. Taking a partner was simply an extension of that process, one more person who knew you well.

But as life is lived on a grander, more anonymous, and mobile scale, the degree to which we allow others to know us is our choice to make. Choosing to let others see more than a carefully burnished facade is profoundly dangerous. Suppose they don't like what they see?

The risk of self-revelation was noted as the biggest imaginable by a number of people who filled out my questionnaire. "Public confession of my innermost feelings" was what a thirty-one-year-old doctor said was the biggest gamble he could take. Wrote a forty-two-year-old lawyer: "Publicly telling every occurrence in my life." Even a nun of seventy called "making known my innermost convictions" her biggest conceivable risk.

This being the case, allowing someone to enter our lives who might get a glimpse of us is risky in the extreme. Now that marriages are seldom arranged, it's up to us alone to find that Certain Someone. Not that help isn't available. A Christian Youth Leaders' seminar recently dealt with the problem of "narrowing the risk in mate selection." Or for $29.95 a computer program is for sale called "Lovers or Strangers." According to its advertising, this will help prospective partners answer questions such as, "Were you made for each other? Are the two of you destined for romance? Spend an evening with Lovers or Strangers and find out. Lovers or Strangers can tell you how compatible you are in love, sex, money, work, play and more. . . . Requires Apple II Plus, 48K, DOS 3.3, and a willing partner."

To help us assess, manage, and reduce the downside risks of intimacy, we not only have seminars and software but radio call-in date making, computer match-ups, and the ultimate in reduced-risk courtship: videotape dating. One user of such visual prescreening of suitors called her goal "the very elimination of anxiety when the doorbell rings."

With such a sense of peril, is it any wonder that the inability to make a commitment has been called "the social fact of the age"?

The dangers of commitment to another person are diverse. There's the danger of discovering soon afterward that you made the wrong choice. Or worse yet, discovering *long* afterward that you made the wrong choice. There's the risk of having to discover whether you can love someone day after day. Or scarier yet finding out if you're lovable day after day. And for some men especially there is profound danger in giving up the control over their own lives that a successful marriage requires. As psychologist and Vietnam veteran Arthur Egendorf concluded after getting married at thirty-five, "Establishing a committed relationship takes more courage than walking into a bullet."

If finding and committing ourselves to a partner feels this dangerous, where does one put the risk of starting a family?

We've never fully confronted how much the improvement of birth control and legalization of abortion have shifted our sense of risk from having sex to having children. When the latter was more a matter of custom than choice, there was far less emotional risk involved in starting a family. This just tended to follow inevitably from getting married and making love. Now that having children is a discretionary item, it's also become a major gamble, with the highest of stakes. Yet because it's so seldom called that, we don't appreciate the daring involved in becoming parents — least of all in ourselves. To the contrary, starting a family is supposed to sound the death knell of risk taking. The search for romance and derring-do is replaced by watching "Love Boat" and buying Pablum. Few would go so far as to argue that having children isn't a risk. It just seems like such a *boring* one. As a thirty-seven-year-old nonmother once explained, her lack of enthusiasm about having children was based on "the awful *dailiness* of being a parent."

The most typical assessment of family life and boldness is that the two are antithetical. Whatever its rewards, starting a family stereotypically is supposed to make you settle down, stop taking chances, and become one more face at PTA meetings. As the new father tells me in a television commercial, he's glad he moved his money to an insured money market account, "Because now, more than ever, I can't afford to take chances."

This assessment of what parenting does to daring tends to be accepted by parents and others alike — the former defensively, the latter scornfully. The first child makes you one second slower, says race drivers, the second two. They also talk of losing good drivers to the "yellow fever" that accompanies parenthood. According to Saint-Exupéry, few of us even hear the call to adventure because "domestic security has succeeded in crushing out that part in us that is capable of heeding the call. We scarcely quiver; we beat our wings once or twice and fall back into our barnyard."

In a more or less tongue-in-cheek portrayal of the various ploys used by his colleagues to justify a loss of nerve, one mountain climber included what he called "The 'Responsible Family Man' Ploy":

> How often has the marriage altar (halter?) proved the graveyard of a mountaineer's ambitions? Climbing weekends becomes less and less frequent and, despite well-meant advice from climbing friends on the benefits of "the Pill," it is only a year before the union is blessed with child. In many cases this is the natural end of things, but a few diehards still put in an annual appearance — pale shrunken ghosts, who glance nervously over their shoulders before they speak.
>
> "Don't seem to get away much nowadays," they mutter despondently. "Can't take the same risks — unfair on the kids. . . ."
>
> Some aging climbers, no longer able to make the grade on the crags, have been known to contemplate matrimony as the only honorable way out.

What has to confound any parents about such judgments is the assumption that starting a family represents the end of daring. Only according to the most limited stereotype of risk taking could starting a family be considered the act of a timid soul.

Consider the absurdity of this stereotype. A man or a woman gets married and has children. Because of the love he or she ideally feels for this family, the risk of losing them or being lost to them feels profound. Astronomical stakes now exist where none did before. That person may not only lose interest in dramatic physical adventures because the stakes have risen so much, but may find such risks less interesting than those of raising a family. Yet because the latter risks do not lend themselves to dramatic retelling, we choose to say they consign us to the category of "settling down," rather than filling up our glass of daring. In fact, having children hardly means your risk-taking days are over. The experience does demand that you redefine your concept of risk.

In *Singled Out*, his generally humane essay on life after divorce, Richard Schickel endorses the contention of an unnamed Frenchman that "the sickness of the family is the fear of risk. Its credo is the economy of self, out of which comes the prohibition of all intense activity." There's truth to this argument in the sense that family life does tend to clip the highs and cushion the lows of singledom. But I can't imagine any parent seriously arguing that raising children lacks intensity of feeling: certainly not one who's ever had to take a child to the emergency room.

Many resist having children for fear of giving up their "freedom." Yet nothing severs the tie to your own parents more surely than starting a family of your own. Having children means forgoing your own claim to be a child. Paradoxically, one reason not to take this risk can be a fear of independence.

A similar point can be made about change. Unlike the psychological makeover promised by this year's nostrum, nothing changes you more surely than becoming a parent. Taking responsibility for another life forces you to reconsider your very reason for being. In the process, depths of caring, vulnerability and courage can be discovered that one never knew existed. As screenwriter Robert Towne reflected at forty-five after three years of parenthood, "I was terrified at the idea of becoming a father. . . . I associated it with conservatism, with decay, with growing old and dying — and actually I have found it the single most liberating experience of my life. . . . I'm less frightened than I was before because of this little creature."

One of the most startling revelations of having children is discovering how much even close friends who are already parents held back from you about both the danger and exhilaration involved. Parents turn out to be something of a secret society. Those who take the risk of having children ought to brag about it more. By being so closemouthed about not just the satisfaction but the excitement, the elation, and the perils of raising children, parents allow themselves to be assigned to this psychological purgatory of "settling down."

To keep up their end of the debate better, parents ought to make a more positive, vigorous, and aggressive portrayal not only of the satisfaction but of the risk involved in raising children, and the adventure. This portrayal would be based on the notion that far from reducing one's capacity to take risks, parenthood goes a long way toward fulfilling that quota, and makes other forms of risk taking seem tame by contrast.

Recall the case of Kay Collins. After giving birth to Molly, Kay stopped riding on motorcycles. This was partly due to new fears, but more importantly because that type of risk taking just seemed superficial now. At Michael Tindall's trial for drug smuggling, his father testified that only after becoming a father himself did his son begin to lose his compulsive need for action. "It's like the poison drained right out of him," said the elder Tindall.

When I first started thinking about writing a book on risk, my wife and I were new to parenting. In trying to compile major risks one might take — the top ten of risk taking, as it were — I was able to anticipate many: looking foolish, leaving a job, getting married, even having children. But as a new parent I overlooked altogether what might be the hardest risk of all to take — the risk of letting your children take chances.

Once the enormity of this risk began to dawn on me as our child grew older, I started asking parents of longer standing how it felt to let their children take chances. It quickly became obvious how awesome this danger felt. One mother told me she didn't get a good night's sleep the whole year her son was in Vietnam. Her son never could understand this. Now that his own daughter is a teenager, he can't sleep on nights when she's out.

Since his twenty-one-year-old son joined him on the car-racing circuit, driver Mario Andretti acts much more anxious about his boy's safety than he ever has about his own. Congressman Jack Kemp, the ex-quarterback and fervent apostle of "risk taking," says he felt far more nervous while watching his son play professional football than he did while playing himself. Kemp's Republican colleague Senator Howard Baker found his twenty-six-year-old daughter's decision to run for Congress "terrifying," something I doubt he would say about his own entry into politics.

A thirty-four-year-old policewoman, the veteran of ten years as one of New York's finest, says of her attitude toward this career: "I love the job and I have no fears for myself. But I wouldn't, as a mother, want my [fourteen-year-old] daughter to be a cop. I'd be afraid of her doing it. It's too dangerous. I'd advise other women to do it, but not my own daughter."

So if genuine risk is defined as acting in the face of your strongest fears, letting your children take chances could be the ultimate. Put somewhat differently, if losing a child is the ultimate loss, then allowing your children to expose themselves to danger might be thought of as the ultimate risk.

This is why I'm so wary of those who exhort us to take more risks with each other. How can they know what's at stake? I think we're beyond the point where such "risk taking" can be proposed as uncritically as it once was, when "change" had a lock on the risk-taking market. But Leo Buscaglia still fills auditoriums. And I'm sure Wayne Dyer has more to tell us about risks we ought to be taking.

The point we have yet to reach is one where frenetic psychological risk taking is not only looked on more skeptically, but the risks of commitment — to raising a family especially — are better appreciated.

Only if risk is limited to movement, change, and excitement can it be considered to decline as families grow. One could just as plausibly argue that the love and support of a family makes you *better* able to take risks if you include those such as looking foolish, starting an enterprise, changing careers, running for office, being open to others, and letting yourself be known to them. Any one of these risks and many others can be more, not less, possible with the support of a family. Having the primary relationships of your life settled may free you to unsettle other parts. Indeed, there are those who use their families as a goad to take more, not fewer, risks.

TWELVE

THE FAMILY MAN

At midday on a summer Sunday the air was alternately heated by a bright sun and cooled by breezes coming off San Diego's Mission Bay. The Bay itself was filled with multicolored sailboats tilting gracefully to one side. In a grassy section not far from the water a jazz band played. Leading this band was a graying man in glasses who held his slide trombone in one hand and beat time with the other as he wound up the scat section of a Dixieland song: "Yadda, yadda, ding, ding, ding."

"Sing it, Pops!" called out the pony-tailed boy beside him after taking a trumpet away from his mouth.

Before the musicians, a crowd milled about eating fried chicken and potato salad from paper plates. A few listened languidly as the bandleader addressed them.

"We're the Coulson Family Jazz Band, from La Jolla," he said, panting slightly. "The kind of jazz we play is early jazz. The reason we call it early jazz is that we started to be a jazz band when the children were quite small and they couldn't stay up late . . . and so, when we practiced, we had to practice early." Beside him a young woman with a four-string banjo, whose orangish hair was cut in a spiky punk look, laughed sarcastically. The man grinned, then continued, "So we call it, you know, early jazz." He then turned to the band and called out, "Okay, what's next? Let's do 'Tiger Rag.' Ah-one, and ah-two, and ah one-two-three . . ."

As the band moved swiftly through this old standard, the supporting instruments died down at times so that the pony-tailed boy could blare forth with an assertive trumpet, his cheeks taut and dark eyes nearly shut behind thick glasses. At times the bandleader stopped to watch this performance, then led the crowd in applause, saying, "Tom Coulson, ladies and gentlemen!"

After "Tiger Rag," the bandleader described their origins for a few seated picnickers. Eight years before, their family was living on a sheep ranch in northern California. They were beyond the reach of a television signal. To pass time they made music. For a Grange talent show, the family worked up an arrangement of "Tin Roof Blues." Ever since then, and for the last few years in earnest, he and his wife and seven children had been the Coulson Family Jazz Band.

As this story was being told a slight brunette joined the band on a seat behind the drums. Painted on the bass drum was a caricature of this woman holding drumsticks aloft with a deranged grin. Beneath this cartoon was lettered MOM. As she took her seat the bandleader nodded toward this woman and said, "That's Jeannie, our drummer. We're a Catholic family, you know, and she's in charge of rhythm. (The banjo player groaned.) She's probably the only Dixieland drummer who is directly responsible for the birth of seven members of the band.

"Now we're gonna do a number that features Nancy — she's somewhere behind that tuba — and her sister Monica, who plays the rare Brazilian rosewood clarinet, and David on the rare left-handed soprano washboard, Gail on the banjo, and Daniel on trombone. Ah one, and a two, and ah . . ."

I first met this band's leader in San Diego during the early seventies. Bill Coulson's reputation at the time was as an aggressive, bold, and charismatic leader of encounter groups. Although soft-spoken, he had a remarkable ability to command the attention of crowds with eloquent calls to "build community" and "take risks." But just as his group-leading career seemed about to take off, Coulson abruptly disappeared from that scene. At times his face could be seen hovering around the edges of a summer workshop for group leaders, which he still codirected, then it would quickly vanish. Rumors circulated that Bill Coulson's life had taken a boring turn: that he had decided to "spend more time with his family."

For an apostle of risk taking, this seemed like an admission of defeat. It looked like Bill Coulson couldn't take his own advice; that his nerve had failed and he'd thrown in his hand on the verge of winning a big pot. As if to confirm this perception, Coulson soon left the heady breezes of southern California altogether to live with his family on an isolated sheep ranch north of San Francisco.

It was only years later that Bill Coulson told me the whole story. To him, the debate between adventure and commitment was part of his upbringing. Although devout Catholics, both of his parents had show-business aspirations. Before leaving the stage to raise three children his mother was a vaudeville dancer. At forty, Bill's father abruptly decided he'd rather try for a career in radio out west than continue selling soap in Chicago. In a memoir about his father, Bill described what happened next:

> He didn't wait around. Within a few months he had distributed his soap samples, sold our house, bought a truck and had us on our way to southern California.
>
> How would it be to knock on the door of a Hollywood studio and ask for a movie-star job? It was as bad with radio announcing. In desperation my father told a small station that if they would let him talk, he would do it for free. And he would sell ads for them too. Within a year he was manager of the station. . . . He brought a microphone into our kitchen for "Breakfast with the Coulsons." Sponsors paid for this, if you can imagine; I could blow my nose on the air and sponsors gave us money. "Blow it good, son, for the folks in Radioland. Folks, you can get these same tissues at A and J Market. . . ."
>
> I took some kidding from classmates, but it was a small price to pay for a father who was happy.
>
> The whole experience left me with a somewhat distorted sense of values. My father's success has made me believe that a person could have what he wanted, if he didn't worry about how silly it looked. Though this does not exactly lead to a stable life it's a heck of a lot of fun.

At Arizona State University Bill Coulson's main interests were jazz and Catholicism. He met Jeannie when she took a Newman Club leaflet from the earnest young man in glasses who was handing them out at a basketball game. Although herself an all-purpose Protestant from Kansas, by the time she and Bill married two years later, in 1955, Jeannie had become an enthusiastic Catholic convert.

Jeannie Coulson is a soft-spoken, pretty woman with a shy smile little different from the one she flashed when being crowned as her high school's homecoming queen. At a glance she would seem quite conventional — if one didn't know that she began playing drums in public at thirty-eight, and that before entering ASU in 1951, she and a girlfriend hitchhiked from Kansas to Oregon. Four years later, with her degree in Education and his in English, she and Bill began working for a large oil company in Los Angeles. Jeannie worked in accounting, Bill as a management trainee. Employees were not allowed off the company premises for lunch. They also were advised not to hold hands in the courtyard. Both were miserable.

When the opportunity arose to become "vested" in the company's pension plan, the Coulsons decided to quit while the quitting was good. Jeannie got pregnant. Bill enrolled in graduate school. Eventually he completed doctorates in Philosophy from Notre Dame and Counseling Psychology from Berkeley. By the time Bill completed the latter degree in 1965, their family included six children. They were living in a Quonset hut and eating lots of hamburger. Only after Bill joined La Jolla's Western Behavioral Sciences Institute in 1967 did their financial plight ease.

Their plight eased enough, in fact, for Bill to indulge a longtime dream and buy an airplane. This was an aging twin-engine Mooney. It has just enough room for all nine Coulsons with one-year-old Nancy — their seventh and last child — tucked into the tail. The Coulsons' trips in this plane are an exciting family memory. In particular they remember a turbulent trip over the Rocky Mountains with Bill flying in and out of little holes in the clouds. David, the oldest child, threw up over the Grand Canyon. Eventually they had to make an unscheduled landing in a small Colorado town and hole up in a small hotel.

Bill Coulson got what he calls his first indication that he wasn't cut out to be a private pilot while flying alone to Pasadena. After ascending through a break in the clouds, Bill found none ahead of him through which to descend. His mouth went dry. "I wasn't thinking of getting killed," he recalls, "but of crashing and getting my name in the paper. It would have been embarrassing for everyone to see what a fool I am."

Bill radioed the Navy's air controllers for help. They directed him to a little town called Ramona, south of Palm Springs. As he passed over a Navy airfield on the way, the controllers tried to shine lights through the clouds so Coulson could get his bearings. He couldn't see a thing. His gas was running out. The walls of his mouth felt like tissue paper.

Despite a Vietnam-era disdain for the military, Bill found himself feeling very respectful of Navy controllers. He asked their permission to go up 2000 feet. They gave it. Finally Bill spotted Ramona lit up like a Christmas tree beneath him, with a parallel row of lights marking off its airport. He landed safely and spent the night in a ranger's shack. The next day Bill flew back to La Jolla and drove to Pasadena.

Combined with a subsequent forced landing during a thunderstorm, which damaged his plane's propeller, this incident forced Bill Coulson to reconsider his pilot's credentials. "I have a reckless streak in me," he explains. "I finally realized that it would be a shame to wipe out this family because of my need for adventure."

So Coulson sold the plane (though not before trying to trade it for a tugboat, his kids insist). By now he was heavily engaged in the exciting work of leading encounter groups. Bill's growing reputation led to speaking and group-leading invitations from around the country. He loved doing this. His family hated having him do it. Jeannie Coulson recalls the period during the late sixties and early seventies as the hardest for their family. Now she and the children had to share Bill with what one of them called "Dad's people." Bill himself felt torn between his love of the limelight and that for his family. As he later wrote about this dilemma, "If one encounters strangers on a woodsy weekend, then it bothers the people left at home. . . . Eventually all such experiences bother the participants themselves, for they cannot carry them on. Either the experiences are too intensely stimulating to maintain, or participants realize the artificiality of relating [in such an exciting way] to those people with whom they do not live."

Once he realized this, Coulson quit leading groups virtually overnight. He renewed his Catholic faith. And at the urging of his children, Bill turned down invitations to work out of town.

At Jeannie's initiative, the Coulson family began to meet as a group themselves. The family was transformed by the results of these meetings. When asked what they wanted more of in their family life, the children said they wanted their father around more. They also wanted some excitement. Putting the two together, Bill, Jeannie, and the seven children began a series of odysseys, or "family adventures," as they called them. These included a cross-country trip in an old Chrysler station wagon; a month in Europe, which Bill bartered in exchange for writing reports on family travel for an airline and a travel agents' publication; a year on the sheep ranch near Mendocino; and three years back in Tempe, Arizona, where Bill and Jeannie had met.

In the town where he played professionally during college, Bill renewed his love affair with the slide trombone. Before long he'd joined a jazz combo and begun to work in pit bands. More and more nights he was gone playing gigs. And once again Bill was faced with a dilemma: whether to continue doing work he found exciting but that took him away from his family, or to cut back on that work and perhaps give it up altogether, "for their sake."

Bill resolved this dilemma by inviting his family to become a working band. This was easier said than done. Although most of the kids could play an instrument, none was a drummer. So Jeannie learned to play drums. Expanding their repertoire beyond "Tin Roof Blues" called for constant rehearsal. These sessions strained the attention span, patience, and social life of the children. Bill and Jeannie solved this problem in two ways. First, they used outright bribery. Each younger Coulson was offered a dollar for every song mastered. Second was the threat of humiliation. Bill booked them to play for a meeting of his father's Rotary Club at the Disneyland Hotel. They had only two weeks to prepare. This turned the tide. The fear of embarrassing themselves kept the family at their instruments nightly for most of that two weeks. "As we have learned many times since," explains Bill, "we can work very hard if we become convinced we are going to have to pay for it in public if we don't. . . . Once we set a date and announce it publicly, we cancel other plans, pull together, and go to work."

When the Coulsons moved back to La Jolla in 1977, their repertoire consisted of nearly half an hour's songs. Soon after appearing "at Disneyland" (as they told people), the Coulson Family Jazz Band was hired to play for forty-five minutes before home games of San Diego's professional tennis team. Then they were booked into the actual Disneyland. The old "Gong Show" had them on. The band began to play regularly for San Diego Charger football games. And when the Kennedy Center invited them to play for a conference in Washington, the National Park Service asked them to stay over the Fourth of July weekend to play on the White House lawn.

Not the least part of the band's success was financial. Although hardly strapped, the Coulsons were not particularly well off. The cars they drove always looked one gasket away from the scrap heap. Their kitchen was usually littered with cents-off coupons. With the band now playing for union scale, the Coulsons' budget began to balance more easily. Each child got part of the take as well. But to Bill and Jeannie the band's greatest contribution has been to their sense of family. As Jeannie puts it, "Music pulls us together. A family has to protect itself. There are so many distractions and activities that separate family members. When we're rehearsing for an important performance we can even turn off the tv without getting mad."

As befits a man with two doctorates, Bill sees broader significance to his family's band. Coulson theorizes that when kids enter adolescence, whatever is going on outside the family is usually far more exciting than what's going on inside the family. Once teenagers realize this, their parents can nag, cajole, beseech, and try to make the kids feel guilty about not staying home more. Or, they can go into competition. They can try to create adventures within the family that are as exciting as those outside. He's even coined a phrase for such counter-attractions: Exciting Family Challenges, or EFC's.

In their own case, of course, the band is their EFC. But Coulson suggests that any family can become a band in the broadest sense of the word. "It needn't be a musical group," he wrote in a treatise on the subject. "A band is any group of people pulling together for a common purpose, as in 'a marauding band.' Think of it as a verb. Families disband. They divorce. Maybe they can band."

The kids' perspective on their band is a little more mundane. Mostly they enjoy making music, and money. The younger Coulsons agree that the band has been good for their family. But whether it's an "EFC" or makes any broader point is something they leave up to their father. "I really like the man," says twenty-three-year-old Gail, "but I don't agree with much of his philosophy. Fortunately most of the time his philosophy doesn't get in the way of his actions."

In general the Coulson children have a more diverse perspective on their family than its leadership does. They titter about their father's "wild ideas" but are glad he has them. The band especially has been a popular family project. But the way it should be run is subject to controversy. Some of its members are more polished and ambitious than others. As a result, the former sometimes berate the latter for their casual approach toward performing. Then the latter will twit the former for taking it all so seriously. At time such debates have broken out while they're onstage. A continuing quarrel between two of the children led to one being ordered out of the car and told to walk home after a concert. So the excitement of this family adventure has many dimensions, not all of which are positive. But could it be otherwise? Any venture risks failure. And if nothing else, this is a venturesome family. Perhaps because of their daring, for better and for worse, the Coulson family has an unusual closeness. They seem genuinely to enjoy each other's company.

Late one night, eight of the nine Coulsons gathered to review the status of their band, and their banding. The way they arranged themselves in their living room was a virtual map of the family. Wearing a golf cap and white sport shirt over Levi's, Bill sat alone in an easy chair at one end of the group. In white slacks with a red knit top, Jeannie shared a sofa with seventeen-year-old Monica, a pretty blonde in her senior year of high school. Nancy, fourteen, who has dark hair, a huge smile, and once won a role as Beverly Sills's daughter in an opera, lay on the floor at her mother's feet. At times the two tangled their feet. Next to Nancy's sprawled the long body of Daniel, nineteen, his blond head at a right angle to her dark one. Off to one side were the two oldest children: David, twenty-five, nearly as blond as Daniel and with a wider smile; and Gail, twenty-three, of the punk-cut orangish hair. Tom, twenty, their pony-tailed lead trumpet, sat by himself in a dining-room chair.

An early topic of discussion was the picnic they had played a few days before. Someone had requested "You Made Me Love You." Daniel didn't want them to play it. Although amiable to a fault, Daniel wants to make a living from his trombone. Sloppiness offends him. Rather than stumble through songs they haven't mastered, Daniel thinks the band ought to stick to tried and true material. His father disagrees. As the band's leader, Bill insisted that they play "You Made Me Love You" the best they could. "I'm always willing to do anything anybody who pays us wants us to do," he told the family meeting. "We're just there to entertain. We're not very sophisticated. But Dan thinks sometimes I have too reckless a streak. Isn't that right, Daniel?"

"Yeah," murmured Daniel without looking at his father. "Yes. That's true."

"But I say 'trust me,' " continued Bill. "I've been very successful."

"And I say we look foolish a lot too," said Daniel.

"You see, Dad," interjected Tom from his chair, "you can't say you've been very successful *because* of the stupid things you've done. You're very successful in *spite* of the stupid things you've done."

After a moment's hesitation, a ripple of laughter swept through the room. Tom is their musical point man, the performer who even more than his father will step out front with a blaring horn for daring solos. But Tom, too, takes a professional approach to his music. Like Daniel, he'd begun to play with other bands. This makes Tom impatient with what he sometimes feels is goofing off in the family version.

Bill suggested that being embarrassed was a risk you had to take to perform in public. He thought it also made for more adventure. When they were in San Francisco, for example, Bill insisted that they all go down to Fisherman's Wharf to play on the street for change. In the eleven minutes that his kids put up with this, Bill recalled that they made $20. Jeannie thought it was more like $4. Her husband revised his version to $11 in 20 minutes. "Anyway," he concluded, "we did all right. If we had stayed there all day, we really would have done all right. You guys were really wantin' to get out of there."

"But it's really humiliating," said Nancy about playing on the street, as they sometimes do before and after local sporting events. "I feel like I'm just an *entertainer*."

"Like tap dancing in the street," agreed Tom.

"Or shining shoes," added Monica.

"I feel especially humiliated when people like Melissa and my friend Carol come and they see me," continued Nancy.

Even Bill had to admit feeling embarrassed the time they were playing outside San Diego's Sports Arena and someone dropped a dollar bill in his cup of beer. This made him wonder if people got the impression that they were destitute and reduced to begging on the street.

Bill then observed that it seemed like most of the risks they took as a family centered around the band. "I think just having us all together out in public is a risk," suggested Daniel to scattered chuckles.

"Do you think that sometimes we take the risk of appearing ratty to people as a group?" Bill asked.

"Yeah," said Monica, "I think the other people in the family appear ratty."

"A lot of times," suggested Tom after the laughter died down, "people will say to me, 'your family sure seems weird.' But they don't mean it like criticism. It's almost like admiration. They just think a lot of things about us are unusual that don't strike me as unusual until they point it out."

Monica found the same thing. She said that her friends from high school really liked to come over and be around their family. Daniel concurred. "They think it's neat that we talk to each other at least," he said of visiting friends.

"What do they think when they come over and we start fighting?" asked Bill.

"They like it," replied Dan with a grin.

"They start placing bets," said David.

"I think it just proves we're human," Dan added.

Bill then asked his children if any of them felt more cautious than others, and who they considered the biggest risk takers among them.

"I feel cautious," said Nancy. She thought that with her punk look and style Gail was their biggest risk taker. Gail denied being a risk taker, and pointed the finger at David, who was trying to make it as a cartoonist in New York. David in turn thought that Lainey, the absent Coulson, had taken the biggest risk by moving out of the family altogether to start one of her own on the sheep ranch up north. (Lainey, twenty-two, married at seventeen, and was raising one child with another on the way.) "No one else has really done that," David pointed out about Lainey's independent path.

Bill wondered if anyone present thought that there might be some disadvantage to the family's closeness, not enough incentive to strike out on their own. Nancy thought not. As the youngest Coulson pointed out, she auditioned for every dancing role she could, partly because she knew her family stood behind her. Tom agreed. "Maybe by growing up in a family like this," he said, "you don't look at things as a risk like other people might. Not as many things seem risky to you because they seem more, you know, the norm."

Gail was the only Coulson to speculate that with less support at home she might have had to take more initiative in her own life. A talented artist, Gail recently had been making her living by working part-time in a museum shop and singing with the band. She wondered if this alternative wasn't too easy to fall back on. Still, Gail liked being part of the band, especially because now that she had her own apartment, it gave her an opportunity to "be with my brothers and sisters, which is something I wouldn't make much occasion for otherwise. I'm really grateful for that because otherwise it would be too easy to wander off. And I really like them." Even with her reservations, the second Coulson child added that being part of her family and its band "does make me feel better about taking chances. I know I've done it before — taken the chance — and it hasn't changed the way they feel about me."

Gail then called across the room to her father. "Dad, I was gonna ask you a question about taking risks. When you give a speech or try something like getting a new shtick, or in the band when you try a song and feel miserable, how do you feel when your risk doesn't pan out?"

"Well," replied Bill, "I think lately it makes me feel like I'm doing the right thing. Because I think that you can't really grow and become successful at what you're doing unless you fall on your face now and then. So if I fall on my face, I say, okay, I must be doing the right thing."

As he said this, Bill's voice lost some of its declaratory timbre and became softer, almost gentle in tone. "I guess also because I have a lot of security in the family," he continued, "if I make a goof and it's obvious, I don't get too embarrassed about it anymore and don't even need to console myself with the philosophy about — you know — 'risk taking.' I just figure, well, what the heck? People are gonna like us anyway. We like each other. So it doesn't matter. If I get in trouble with anybody else, it doesn't matter that much as long as I'm not in trouble with you."

"What kind of risk would you like to take that you don't?" Gail asked.

"Me?" replied her father. He hesitated. "I think I'd like to sing more," Bill finally said. "I'd like to sing *out*. When I do sing I think I sort of hide my voice a little bit. And I think I'd like to sing out. Sometimes when Gail sings and everybody's applauding, I get to say, 'Gail-e-ree, dynamite!' Like a circus barker. I really like to do that."

"I notice you sing loudest when you're singing harmonies," Tom observed. "Background things."

"But I'm afraid to sing right into the mike — out!" continued Bill. "When I was in college, every now and then a band leader in a new combo would ask me, 'Do you sing?' And I'd always say no. And I always wanted to say yes. But I never had the nerve."

Gail asked her father what risks he wasn't taking in his professional life. Bill thought for a time, then replied that subjecting himself to professional criticism was a risk he felt he was ducking. At one time Bill Coulson published a fair amount of writing on psychology, including a book called *Groups, Gimmicks and Instant Gurus*. Some reviews of this book were friendlier than others. One in the *New York Review of Books* was quite un-friendly. The experience left lasting scars. "I think that kind of scared me." Bill told his children of this decade-old memory. "I just didn't want to *risk* that anymore. So I quit writing."

Bill Coulson hoped that as his family moved out into their own lives, he would be forced to resume his public life and risk invit-ing criticism. "I look at our family as kind of a mutual support organization in the future," he told them, "where we keep in touch and will be doing interesting things and let one another know what they are. And I think that if I fall on my face some-where, I can write the kids and tell them about it and they'll be interested."

"You'll write to me?" said Nancy, who wants to go East to dance. "In New York?"

Jeannie continued her husband's line of thought. What she especially liked about her own family was the way they stood behind each other, no matter what. "I think that if we fail we're a pretty tolerant group of the others," she said. "If we ever do anything wrong, the family gives each other a lot of support in spite of all the criticism that anyone is talking too much or play-ing the trumpet wrong or whatever."

Despite being a sometime hitchhiker, Jeannie told her family that she'd always felt shy. Giving speeches in class was a special torment. But she found herself able to do what scared her none-theless. "Sometimes I think I have more nerve than is good for me," she said. "Like playing the drums. I've had to play them even though I play badly — and it's not good for me or fit for anybody else."

"Who says you play badly?" asked Dan.

"Well," added Tom, "I think it's good that Momma gets to play the drums even though she's scared to.

"You know," Tom continued, "I think it would be great if our family sounded top-notch. But it's not that important to me. I mean, the family's important enough in other ways that I guess I kind of decided that it doesn't matter how it sounds as a band because there's more to it than being a band.

"Though I still do feel that as long as we're out there playing, we might as well sound as good as possible."

The hour was growing late. The Coulsons' family meeting

hadn't even begun until nearly 10:00 P.M., the only time everyone was free. In its coming-to-a-close mood, members of the family began reminiscing about past adventures. Like David throwing up over the Grand Canyon. Or the many times they got lost in France because no one spoke French. They seemed to have particularly fond memories of crossing the country in 1970. "In an overloaded Chrysler," Jeannie explained to a visitor. "And we had about five flat tires because it was so overloaded." Her children howled at the memory.

"The rims got *wrecked*," added Bill to more laughter.

As members of this family got up to move in their separate directions, their mood was relaxed, even elated. It had been some time since they'd had such a gathering. Gail still lay on the floor on her stomach. She called David over and told him that she had a kink in her back. Would he work it out for her? David did so, moving his hands slowly up and down his sister's spine. "Is that better?" he finally asked. Gail nodded.

"Thanks a lot," she murmured.

"Sure," said David, getting up to leave.

IN CONCLUSION . . .

THIRTEEN

THE AMERICAN
WAY OF RISK

Every article in Quest *is chosen on the premise that in some way it reflects the courage to take risks.*
— THE EDITOR

Unlike most subscription offers, there is absolutely no risk involved in trying out Quest.
— THE PUBLISHER

I've always thought that our ads had more to tell us about who we are than any other medium. With all that time, research and money at stake advertisers can't afford to have illusions about who Americans are, and what we're up to. In recent years our ads seem to be telling us that we're in the midst of a renaissance of adventure. In miniversions of "That's Incredible," they portray us climbing rocks for Right Guard (and Hawk Cologne, Burlington Fabrics, Getty Oil, and Camel Cigarettes), rafting white water for Pepsi (and Schlitz, Old Milwaukee, the Army, the post office, and Ivory Soap), hang gliding off cliffs for Blue Strato after-shave (as well as Wrigley's Gum), and skydiving for Lowenbräu beer. Not only in ads but in fact, *Newsweek,* the *New York Times, U.S. News and World Report,* and other publications have speculated, Americans are seeking adventure in greater numbers than ever before. But such reports are shy on statistics because statistics are hard to come by when it comes to adventurous leisure activities.

For over a decade, one man has made a valiant effort to record participation and fatality rates for such activities. This man is Vincent Zemaitis, an actuary for the Metropolitan Life Insurance Company. Through constant phone calls to those involved and compilation of what news reports and government statistics are available, for well over a decade Zemaitis has tried to stay abreast of our interest in adventurous pursuits ranging from aerobatics through mountaineering to snowmobiling. During this time he's found that Americans are participating in thrill sports at about the same rate as they always have: well under 2 percent of us, and the fatality rate from such participation has stayed consistently between 1 and 2000 deaths a year.

So obviously our reporters and advertisers have not given us a snapshot of reality when they portray Americans as more thrill seeking than ever. What they *have* done is portray our aspirations very clearly—the advertisers especially. In recent years their research has told them unequivocally that to important market segments (younger ones especially), goals such as "adventure" and "excitement" rate very high. At the same time, their research confirms how "risk averse" Americans actually are, particularly when it comes to trying new products.

This tension between dreams and reality taxes the ingenuity of copywriters. On the one hand they don't want to make customers feel hypocritical by implying that they're more daring than they actually are. On the other hand they do want to agree with them that they're well within that spirit. This calls for deft copywriting.

Some confront the problem head-on. "Are you the outdoorsy, All-American type?" asks Altman's Department Store next to a picture of its outdoor wear. "*Sure you are.* Everybody is. . . . And who cares if your only contact with the *great outdoors* is a Saturday stroll in Central Park. It's your attitude that counts."

Others are more subtle. "Discover the Wolverine woman in you," suggests an ad for hiking boots. "Is there a secret person in you waiting to get out? A part that responds to the call of the wild? Rugged outdoor fashion is the way to express it."

This is what's known as "image-enhancement" advertising. At the moment, the risk-taker image is among the most popular being sold. Even products with no conceivable relationship to adventurousness are being peddled in a context of risk and daring. And this is not just to the Pepsi generation. In keeping with the demographic times, Levi's already has a radio spot aimed at baby boomers with thickening waists, one of whom is wearing their fuller-cut jeans as he pants his way to the top of some steep rocks calling out, "More slack on the rope . . . more slack!"

Then there's Saab. "When you experience the goose-bumping acceleration of a Saab," the Swedish carmaker promises, "you have room to share it with a wife and two kids and a year's supply of groceries." Not to be left behind, Volvo says its Turbo model "can make even a trip to the corner grocery an adventure."

The most vivid illustration of advertising's response to the dreams of its changing market came when white-haired Robert Young and his soporific prescriptions of Sanka for jangled nerves was unceremoniously replaced with a late-thirtyish group of kayakers, horse jumpers, rock climbers, lumberjacks, and skywriters who suggest that Sanka is the coffee risk takers drink.

As veteran ad researcher Art Kover points out, this approach can only succeed with products in which the customer perceives no real peril. With an obviously dangerous product such as a lawn mower or chain saw, you want to play down its riskiness in advertising. "You'd scare them off," says Kover of the potential customers for such products. But where a product poses no perceived danger to the user, then you're free to try to "associate the product with a risk-taking image at no real risk."

The actual intent of such advertising is to minimize our risk in purchasing products. If the greatest danger we feel when making purchases is to our self-image (as market researchers say), then buying a product that associates us with an adventurous, daring way of life reduces our actual risk of losing face in the marketplace. Therefore, the more a product can make us look like risk takers, the safer it is to buy. A conservative strategy confirms our identity as risk takers.

This is the American Way of Risk. It is paradoxical, ingenious, and rooted in the fact that we exalt high-sensation, Level I risks, which few of us take but many of us wish we would. We want to be seen as an unusually bold people; we just don't want to engage in the activities we think of as bold. Rather than revise our concepts of boldness to conform better to reality, we conjure images of risk, auras of daring, the look of a risk taker that conform to our notion of who risk takers are without requiring that we actually take any risks.

"You learn to take a calculated risk," explained an executive to corporate consultant Rosabeth Moss Kanter, "to be ninety percent sure. That's the game to play. The thing to do is to make it *look* like a risk but to have it in your back pocket. You need the attention that comes from taking a risk but the security of knowing you can't fail."

In theory Americans are daring people — those who left the deadheads behind as they sailed away in the *Mayflower* to conquer a wilderness. Valid as it may once have been, this image of ourselves is long out of date. From those who sailed from foreign shores not always sure they'd get here (or even where "here" was) we've evolved into a people restlessly roaming the interstate highways searching for a motel where the best surprise is no surprise.

When they visit this country, the descendants of those left behind in the Old World often comment on this passion for predictability: the carefully planned vacations, recipes followed to the quarter teaspoon, and no-risk guarantees in abundance. With 5 percent of the world's population, we currently own nearly half of its insurance policies.

By romanticizing our dangerous heritage, we overlook the even more basic need this engendered to tame and make secure our perilous surroundings. What we've retained is a myth about ourselves as the ones who crossed an ocean, cleared a land, braved winters, coped with new diseases, confronted peculiar animals, and continued on into the wilderness. Understandably this heritage has led to a concept of risk that emphasizes physical danger, change, and movement. But now that our ventures are rarely into the unknown, we're left with movement alone as the essence of our notion of risk. Shorn of actual daring, this notion is one that is based on taking action, making a break, *doing something* — preferably something dramatic. As a result we're prone to call all manner of restlessness "risk taking."

As a much-transferred businessman told psychiatrist Robert

Coles, "I could stay in one place. I could dig in. I've tried doing that. But I get bored. So does my wife. So do our kids. We like to travel. I get tired of the same old people. I don't know why; I just do. There's no place that's ever claimed me one hundred percent. . . . I never get tired of exploring. My kids don't either. One of them wants to be an astronaut. The other wants to be a scuba diver. Two explorers!"

The risks Americans most honor with that title usually involve a going to rather than a staying put, a headed there in preference to staying here, and change over stasis. In a nation of migrants, perhaps equating movement and change with risk is inevitable. The American worship of change (in the abstract, anyway) is nearly a secular religion and is considered the essence of risk. Risk takers are go-getters; stay-at-homes get stuck in the mud.

This prevalent attitude is Level I in the extreme. It's a concept of risk best suited to a seventeen-year-old boy, presumably single, who is constantly in motion, looking for action and sometimes even in danger (which he seldom realizes). This, as we most often use the term, is real "risk taking." "The risk taker," suggests psychologist Rosiland Forbes, "is the person who creates action where there would otherwise be none." Such a concept of risk leaves most of us in the coward category. Being suited primarily to adolescent males, it discourages the rest of us from ever seeing ourselves as risk takers. In a society whose average age is now thirty and rising, it is a recipe for self-contempt.

The seventeen-year-old-boy concept of risk sets an unattainable standard for even adolescent males to reach. Yet being Americans, we don't want to see ourselves as spineless wimps. So rather than work up our nerve actually to take more Level I risks or change our concept of risk to include more from the second level, what we have done is to devise pseudorisks that we hope will give us all the excitement of real ones with no actual danger. Having made life as predictable as we can, we then zealously seek out opportunities for "risk" and "adventure" in complete safety. This doesn't set us apart from universal human aspirations. A prayer for safe adventure is hardly unique to Americans. What does set us apart is the energy, imagination, and resources we've devoted to pursuing our paradoxical ends. In the process we substitute excitement, stimulation, and sensation for the taking of actual risks.

A simulated war game, called the National Survival Game, has recently become popular in the United States. In this contest, separate teams hunt and shoot each other with paint pellets. In addition to marking you "dead," these pellets sting a little. Players wear goggles to protect their eyes, and sign waivers in case of injury. "The most Exciting Game You'll Ever Play!" reads an ad for the National Survival Game. *"Take the challenge! Get into the action! Join the excitement!!* of the most *stimulating new sport* in the country!"

Since some early problems with liability insurance were ironed out, this game has been played by nearly 10,000 Americans of all ages, mostly men. As one participant explained of his fondness for the National Survival Game: "It brings out all the primeval things. You are the hunter and the hunted. . . . It's a physical and mental release. You let all your anxieties go. It gets the blood boiling. It lets you live out a fantasy of being Mike Mercenary in Angola."

There's pressure throughout American society to make the dangerous seem safe and the safe dangerous. In his book *Mountains Without Handrails*, environmental lawyer Joseph Sax describes the way a U.S. Forest Service manual responds to our twin demands. In "primitive" sites especially, the manual advises, their challenge is to regulate camping by means that are "obvious enough to afford a sense of security but subtle enough to leave the taste of adventure." Sax emphasizes that this approach does not mean that the Forest Service is engaged in flimflam. Rather, they are simply responding to their constituents' wishes. As Sax points out, "They sense quite accurately a desire for 'controls,' 'regimentation,' and 'security,' and at the same time a demand for a 'taste of adventure,' 'solitude,' and a 'testing of skills.' "

This is the American way of risk. It's risk taking with a no-risk guarantee. The more predictable an experience becomes in fact, the riskier it has to appear. The actual perils of live television give way to the taped thrills of daredevil shows. The safer cars grow, the more they promise that "we build excitement!" "Step on the exhilarator!" "Come alive!"

Among the more popular forms of "adventure" available to Americans in recent years are ones that recreate daring chapters from our history books. "Wagons Ho," for example, advertises their recreational wagon-train trip as an "authentic adventure." When I wrote for further information, Wagons Ho's response began "Dear Pioneer," and complimented me as most likely being "a pioneer at heart."

In today's America, dozens of groups regularly refight the Battle of Yorktown, stage frontier shoot-outs, and recreate any number of Civil War battles with a careful eye for detail. Every July the American Mountain Men rendezvous for a week in Wyoming, where they are forbidden to wear or use anything common after 1840. "I knew the Indians and the buffalo wouldn't be there anymore," said one thirty-two-year-old at the rendezvous. "But I wondered, if I got the same tools, wore the same clothes, and got on a horse, whether I could approximate what the mountain men felt."

The irony is that such pseudoadventures themselves are based on a misreading of those they're recreating. Contemporary historians have clarified our portrait of early American to show that it was neither as dangerous as we imagine overall, nor dangerous in the ways we imagine. Recalculation of the mortality rates on wagon trains, for example, has consistently revised it downward (to an estimated 4 percent). Such research has also found that wagon trainers were far more likely to be killed by accidents with the firearms they brought to protect themselves from Indians than by Indians themselves. Even their commitment to being pioneers has come into question. One random sample of westward migrants from towns in New England and New York found that 70 percent of those who braved the wilds of the West returned to the comforts of the East within a period of years. Nor was the West they braved all that wild. During interviews with dozens of those who helped settle Oklahoma territory late last century, historian W. Eugene Hollon found that what most remembered was "the wretched loneliness and almost total lack of excitement in their lives." In general, says the historian, violence was relatively rare in the newly settled West. "Most frontier people were friendly, hard working, and fair-minded," he points out. "But these simple virtues, along with the hardship and general boredom, do not make good materials for exciting narrative."

A lot of what we "know" about our past is a product of legends concocted to quench the American thirst for vicarious adventure. This thirst grew especially strong as the nineteenth century drew to a close. Genteel novels about domestic life now stood aside to make way for the muscular pulp of Jack London and Frank Norris as well as such classics as *The Red Badge of Courage* and *The Virginian*. Fanciful reenactments of Custer's Last Stand were popular stage attractions at the turn of the century, as were depictions of Davy Crockett at the Alamo. The nineties' biggest dramatic hit was a play called *Blue Jeans*. This play featured a working buzz saw from which the hero was rescued nightly as his gizzard was about to be rent. Once *Blue Jeans* lost its power to shock, the thunder of actual chariots took over, racing across a treadmill in a staged version of *Ben Hur*. And Buffalo Bill Cody — claiming "God is my property man" — tamed the West nightly with his Congress of Rough Riders of the World. At times Cody would invite prominent members of the audience to join him in his coach onstage to make their adventure a bit less vicarious.

For those who wished to participate as well as watch, bicycling became a national craze. As the century ended, an estimated 10 million Americans owned bicycles, a tenfold increase in just seven years' time. Bicycling was such an important expression of our turn-of-the-century exuberance that pictures of men and women astride their two-wheelers became common in advertisements for everything from pianos to cigars. Hiking, boating, and camping also grew fashionable for both sexes as part of a broader concern for "health." As she emerged from her Victorian parlor, America's "New Woman" invaded male preserves with a vengeance. "Oh, to be a wild Kossack!" wrote a turn-of-the-century feminist. "Fight hard and drink hard and ride hard. . . . Oh, for a horse between the knees, my blood boils, I want to fight, strain, wrestle, strike."

As all of this suggests, the late nineteenth century was a time with interesting parallels to our own. Just as we're now struggling with the transformation from our industrial to a technological economy, this was a time when economic upheaval accompanied the transition from an agricultural society to one organized around factories. After arriving late to our shores, the industrial revolution was rapidly consolidated in increasingly large factories and offices. Time clocks were introduced. So was "scientific management." The expansion, consolidation, and merger of existing corporations rivaled the creation of new ones. Farms declined. Cities exploded. Insurance became the universal protector that it remains today.

As American life grew better organized, complaints began to arise that something was missing. The term "boredom" entered our vernacular. So did "thrill." "Neurasthenia" — the era's most popular neurosis — sent listless Americans to their beds by the thousands. The doctor who coined this term listed neurasthenia's symptoms as "desire for stimulants and narcotics . . . fear of responsibility, of open places or closed places, fear of society, fear of being alone, fear of fears, fear of contamination, fear of everything, deficient mental control, lack of decision in trifling matters, hopelessness."

Then as now, a widespread response to social torpor was the call to live more adventurously or, in Theodore Roosevelt's term, "strenuously." But when it came to going beyond camping or bicycling, most turn-of-the-century Americans put limits on their strenuosity. More to their taste was Coney Island's Switchback Railway, the forerunner of today's roller coasters, which was modeled after a mining train and introduced in 1884. This ride was such a hit that higher, longer, and curvier roller coasters were soon developed, along with "loop-the-loop" and "cyclone" rides, in a golden era of amusement parks. At the Chicago World's Fair in 1893, even the rousing martial strains of John Philip Sousa and scandalous dancing of the cakewalk were overshadowed by the fair's hit: a 250-foot-in-diameter "pleasure wheel" invented by George Ferris.

As the century ended, actual opportunities for children to be independent and take initiative were declining. Ex-country kids no longer had to learn how to hunt, split wood, or keep an eye out for snakes. But *The American Boy's Handy Book* by Daniel

Beard gave millions of urban children the opportunity to study such skills. And teenagers in the city who until recently had dominated volunteer fire squads were transferred onto football teams, decked out in scout uniforms, and set to reading the novels of Horatio Alger and Ned Buntline. Tales about medieval knights took on special significance. The Princely Knights of Character Castle, a group founded in 1895 for twelve-to-eighteen-year-old boys, included ranks such as "herald" and "keeper of the dungeon." Even college men could keep their medieval flame alive by joining the Knights of King Arthur, then reading 8000 pages of heroic literature to earn promotion from the rank of "page" to "esquire."

As Joseph Kett has explored at length in his book *Rites of Passage*, "adolescence" came into its own during the late nineteenth century — as a word, a concept, and a means of keeping our children in line. Consistent with the changing needs of the economy, creating a protected stage of life between childhood and adulthood limited the actual opportunities for initiative by young employees-to-be and replaced them with the cults of adventure in which "rhetorical glorifications of strenuosity and will power coexisted with the thrusting of youth into positions of extreme dependence." Adds Kett:

> It is possible that increased regulation of the child's total environment might have produced psychologically more dependent and less mature young people. . . . One could argue, for example, that such young people, denied conventional outlets for their desire for autonomy, took refuge in the fantasy world of 19th-century adventure literature, in the stories filled with sentiment, seduction, violence, pirates, Indians, desperadoes, and young stalwarts who brazenly cut loose from family ties and made their own way.

This era also witnessed the birth of our "playground movement." In theory, such settings were to be ones where children could be active, playful, and free. In fact, as Kett observes (with reference to the founders of this movement):

> Joseph Lee, for all his praise of spontaneous play, made effort upon effort to ensure that the games played in playgrounds would be carefully regulated. Henry S. Curtis claimed that he was converted to the principle of organized play when he realized, while

watching some boys at play, that no one was trying to win and, even worse, no one seemed to care what the score was. Edward J. Ward reduced it all to an aphorism: "a playground is not a playground without supervision."

Such settings proved far more attractive to producers than to consumers. "An administrator's heaven and a child's hell," commented a British architect after touring the fruits of our playground movement over half a century after it began. Of the asphalt and wire-mesh settings she'd visited during two weeks in this country during 1965, Lady Allen of Hurtwood observed, "Your people seem terrified of risks. They are dogged by fear of insurance claims resulting from accidents in public playgrounds. I've never seen anything like it."

In England, Lady Allen was part of an "adventure playground" movement. This began in response to the painful realization by European play supervisors that once World War II ended, their charges clearly preferred bombed-out rubble to well-tended play areas. In order to compete, some of them began to make their settings as rubblelike as possible. By scattering old boards about, as well as bricks, tires, rope — whatever junk they could find — these play leaders gave birth to the first adventure playgrounds.

Such playgrounds continue to have their greatest success in Western Europe and the British Isles. They can be surprisingly anarchic. When she visited an adventure playground in Belfast, San Diego State recreation professor Mary Duncan was startled to see children climbing an adjacent building as their play leader stood casually by. Duncan kept waiting for him to blow his whistle and order them down. He never did. When she finally asked if he wasn't worried about the children's safety, the supervisor said he wasn't, really. In the first place it was their prerogative to choose such activity more than it was his to stop it. But more important, as he pointed out to Duncan, the children were actually rather cautious in their approach to the wall they were climbing. He pointed to a preschooler, for example, and predicted accurately that the boy would climb to a low window ledge but no higher. "The children choose their own level of risk," their supervisor explained. "They know their own limits."

Only a handful of adventure playgrounds have ever gotten off the ground in this country. One of them is in Irvine, California. Set in a man-made ravine and surrounded by a high stockade fence, Irvine's version consists of two dusty acres that have been deliberately left barren. Outside the single entrance to this setting is a hand-lettered sign that reads, "ADVENTURE PLAYGROUND, Summer Hours, 10:00 'til 5:00, Tuesday through Saturday." Just inside the fence a second hand-painted sign adds:

OUR RULES

1. NO BARE FEET
2. NO THROWING ROCKS OR DIRT CLODS
3. (*blank*)
4. BE KIND TO OTHERS & NATURE
5. NO WRECKING FORTS
6. RETURN TOOLS

Set on the cracked, dry mud beyond this sign the summer day I visited were half a dozen crude structures like the backyard forts that kids build, or used to build anyway. Posted on one of these structures was a sign in a child's hand reading PLAY AT YOUR OWN RISK. Each of the forts was surrounded by a clump of children who were sawing, pounding, and yelling at each other.

"Someone go get a shovel," said a blonde girl of about eight to the others around her.

"You can't go in the shed alone," protested one of her companions.

"I did," said the blonde, "and I didn't get in trouble,"

"Bees were chasing us," a third girl explained from the crowd. "We couldn't go."

But go they did. While her helpers were gone, the blonde, whose name was Jackie, took time off to tell me how her summer had been going. "I come here on Friday," she said, ticking the day off on one finger. "Monday I have tennis, Tuesday racquetball. Wednesday I have a day off — no, Wednesday I have Ranger Rick. Thursday I have tennis — I play tennis with my mom; she teaches me. On Friday, camping club, here."

At this point Jackie's companions returned. One of them was

pulling a shovel behind her. She handed the shovel over to Jackie. Jackie began using this to stab at the dry ground.

"Can I help?" asked the girl who had brought the shovel to her.

"Not right now," replied Jackie.

At the next fort, two eleven-year-olds named Dick and Wally, deeply tanned beneath sun-bleached hair, sat before a structure they'd spent the morning building. Both looked pleased. Their fort consisted of four pieces of splintery plywood nailed precariously together. Within these walls an old flowered bed sheet served as carpeting. Outside was a couch pillow on which the two boys sat.

"At first I thought it would be dumb," said Dick of the adventure playground. "It looks kind of wrecked. Then we got building."

Do you know of anything like it, I asked?

"Just parks where they've already built stuff," said Wally.

"Not where they let you build," added Dick. "There used to be a field by my house. But they put up a house on it. Before that there used to be a lot of forts there."

As they talked with me, Dick's mother joined us. "Did you claim it?" asked the fortyish woman as the two boys showed her their fort proudly.

"We did!" they exclaimed together. Dick then led his mother toward the playground headquarters, explaining as they went, "You have to sign a paper that says if we move or break a tool or something . . ."

The headquarters consisted of a small wooden shack with a wooden sign in front reading GENERAL STORE STAFF. Along with well-used hammers, saws, and miscellaneous debris on the floor of this structure was a tattered document titled "U.S. Adventure Playground Report." This report indicated that there are seventeen such playgrounds in this country. One in Santa Cruz, California, was shut down after two seasons because of neighbors' complaints about its disheveled appearance. Despite their excellent safety record, fear of legal liability is the principal reason that there aren't more adventure playgrounds in the United States. Yet as the report pointed out, in fact "the adventure playground offers children the illusion of danger. It is a contrived, controlled form of risk. Really more exciting than dangerous."

According to old-timers, the highlight of Irvine's adventure playground was when a drain clogged during the rainy season and produced a lake that couldn't be emptied for six months. Kids flocked to this unintended attraction to float boats and splash about in the muddy water. When the drain finally was cleared, a lot of the playground's clientele disappeared along with the lake.

In order to get insurance, explained Founding Director Tom Maloney, Irvine's adventure playground could not include either a pond or a cable slide as do some others. In general, said Maloney, a slim, moustached man in his midtwenties, they had to stick to "the illusion of risk" in order to be acceptable to the residents of Irvine. Irvine is an upscale, planned community where everything from the color of homes to the height of shrubbery is rigidly controlled. The $33,000 stockade fence that sealed its adventure playground from view was essential to winning community approval.

Despite such limitations, Maloney felt that Irvine's adventure playground was basically successful. If not the equal of a good empty lot, at least it was better than an antiseptic playground with fixed equipment. The result might be a bit contrived, he conceded. But in a setting such as Irvine, what's the alternative?

I had gone to Irvine's adventure playground in search of an antidote to the American way of risk. What I found was the perfect illustration: an utterly controlled, thoroughly supervised, and altogether predictable setting papered over with a patina of "adventure." The atmosphere was closer to a theme park than an empty lot, its philosophy more indebted to Walt Disney than Huckleberry Finn.

Perhaps this was inevitable in a setting so close to Disneyland in so many ways. Walt Disney was way ahead of the crowd in sensing that while they wanted an adventurous life, even more than that Americans wanted a tidy one. When he opened the original theme park in 1957, amusement parks had fallen on hard times. This was not because they were unsafe; it was because they were disheveled. Only when we could be sure of not encountering even a gum wrapper beneath our feet were we willing to brave the waters of a Jungle Cruise, the elephants on a Safari Game Hunt, or rides into the Magic Kingdom.

To the public such attractions are the highest expression of Walt Disney's genius. Among his colleagues the real brilliance of Disneyland's creator was in grasping how much control Americans would tolerate, even expect, as a prelude to their adventure. Achieving this measure of control was not just a matter of Walt Disney's megalomania. This was the kind of amusement park we wanted; one in which even the ground before our feet is continually swept free of visual danger.

For settings in which you're supposed to let loose, theme parks are an anal-compulsive's dream come true. Their fetish about litter is symbolic. Between a theme park and a carnival, say, there's no real difference in safety. (If anything, the carnival's rides are safer because they're checked out so regularly while being taken apart and reassembled.) The real difference is in the constant reassurance, for which we pay a premium, that our adventure will go according to plan. From the moment an attendant waves you insistently into a parking space, reminders are constant that nothing has been left to chance. From guards with walkie-talkies through the ubiquitous sweepers to grounds designed like a board game, there is never any question that everything's in hand.

The risk of visiting an amusement park wasn't always considered so ersatz. In a landmark decision made over half a century ago (*Murphy* v. *Steeplechase Amusement Co, Inc.*, 1929), Chief Justice Benjamin Cardozo of the New York Court of Appeals ruled against the plaintiff, a young man who had broken his kneecap on a Coney Island ride called The Flopper. This ride consisted of a belt moving upward on an inclined plane, which often forced patrons off their feet against padded floors and walls. "A fall was foreseen as one of the risks of the adventure," wrote Cardozo for the majority. "There would have been no point to the whole thing, no adventure about it, if the risk had not been there. The very name, above the gate, 'the Flopper,' was warning to the timid. . . .

"The antics of the clown are not the paces of the cloistered cleric. The rough and boisterous joke, the horseplay of the crowd evokes its own guffaws, but they are not the pleasures of tranquillity. The plaintiff was not seeking a retreat for meditation. Visitors were tumbling about the belt to the merriment of onlookers when he made his choice to join them. He took the chance of a like fate, with whatever damage to his body might ensue from such a fall. The timorous may stay at home."

Today, of course, the timorous are invited to come out and play. Their conflicting demands for order and excitement tax the imagination of amusement-ride designers. The problem is that there are just so many ways the body can be safely twisted, turned, and thrown about. Ride designers are running out of ways to repackage such movements and make them seem fresh. Furthermore, insurance premiums are skyrocketing. Seers say that the real breakthrough will come from the manipulation of our senses alone. Simulation is the model here. Inspiration for the adventures of our future are more likely to come from flight simulators than roller coasters.

Early versions of such entertainment are already being built. Among them is the SR-2 Adventure Capsule. This was developed by Doron Precision Systems of Binghamton, New York, a company that spun off from America's leading builder of flight simulators. The SR-2 Adventure Capsule has twelve seats, is the size of a minibus, and looks like a small space shuttle. After its door is rolled shut, customers are plunged into one of twelve "experiences" projected onto a small, wide screen before them. As film rolls, stereo sound effects replicate screaming roller-coaster rides, the screeching tires of speeding cars, or the buzzing propellers of a barnstorming biplane as the capsule itself is rocked gently up and down and from side to side in harmony with the adventure being projected.

Among the "experiences" SR-2 offers is one they claim is based on actual footage shot from an F-4 fighter plane while bombing and strafing a deserted beach in the Mekong Delta during the Vietnam war. As their promotional literature promises, "Riders feel the thrill of a navy fighter pilot being catapulted into real action."

"A lot of adults and young people can't have that experience," a Doron executive told me after we screened this one. "With our device they can."

Based on participating in three SR-2 experiences, I can confirm that one at least (involving a car actually roaring around Paris's streets at more than 100 miles an hour early one morning) left me a bit dizzy and wobbly-kneed. Simulation works. Better yet, as far as Doron is concerned (and tells prospective SR-2 customers in a sales letter), "It's *safe*, rated as a twelve-seat theater by a major insurance company. That means low insurance payments for you, and a wider age-range appeal among your guests."

Perhaps this is our inevitable trend: from loosely controlled to highly controlled pseudorisk in amusement parks, then on to total simulation. Theme-park operators have already found that among their main attractions are computerized games little different from those outside their gates. In intent, such games are the fulfillment of the American Way of Risk: a stimulating, exciting, even heart-thumping form of excitement with no danger, stakes, or risk of any kind except the loss of quarters. The game makers know what they're selling. "Sweaty palms are guaranteed," advertises one. "You're liable to get dizzy," warns another.

The boys and men who dominate arcades sound like mountain climbers as they describe the arousal, excitement, and intensity of playing their games. Sociologist Sherry Turkle, who's studied users, talks of electronic games' ability to restore a sense of *control* to adolescent boys in particular, to whom so much else in their lives feels out of control. By providing "microworlds" to which we can escape and exert ourselves in safety, she thinks, video games "serve the same function as cars, motorbikes, even baseball."

But do they? Motor vehicles and sports at least include some actual stakes and consequences. Computer games don't. Nor are they intended to. "The armchair adventures of the personal-computer user can be every bit as exciting as the real thing," promises a review of such software, "without the personal risk."

An introduction to the popular Adventure genre of games in a children's magazine has this to say about them: "To be adventurous is to take a chance on something you are not sure will work out your way. An adventure game works the same way. . . . An adventure game takes you places you can never really go and lets you do things you will never actually get to do. And best of all, if you get 'killed' you don't stay dead."

I don't know which is the more discouraging part of that statement: the assurance that contrived risks are like real ones, or the assumption that actual adventure is beyond the reach of any game player. Especially as their technology is improved (with laser disks, three dimensions, surround sound, tactile-sensation controls, etc.) such games will offer us the fulfillment of our prayer for no-risk risks that "feel" almost like the real thing. From the comfort of our favorite chair, without even having to risk a walk out the door, we'll be able to simulate heart-thumping, palm-sweating, goose-bumpy adventure. Flying rocket-ships. Racing cars. Holding up banks. Making love. Just let your imagination roam.

The scarier real life gets, and the more it feels beyond our control, the more tempting simulated reality becomes as a safe form of risk-taking that is under our control. The games that do this have been the subjects of heated controversy. Parents and others are concerned that the kids playing them may be searing their brains, eyes, and budgets on these electronic Svengalis. Or that they're learning how to become little Attila the Huns at a quarter a lesson. My concern is closer to the opposite: that by feeding our hunger for risk with little appetizers of pseudorisk, they'll leave users frustrated, passive, unable to distinguish real from simulated danger — and what's worse, uninterested in trying.

The real danger of computer games is that the world they teach about is ordered, controllable, and ultimately predictable. (After all, *somebody* wrote the program.) But isn't that a lot of their appeal? And isn't our love affair with computers in general a prayer that life be more programmable? As one computer game designer says about why he likes his work, "You can create a universe, a whole world that's predictable, a world that operates by *your* laws."

For all the commotion, I wonder if many parents aren't inwardly pleased that their children are learning lessons and taking chances in this orderly way. We want our kids to be both daring and under control. That's the American way. Simulation seems to offer the perfect resolution of this dilemma. It provides maximum excitement with minimum consequences. And as a bonus, the game players don't get dirty.

I don't mean to brush this issue aside with a sneer and a chuckle. Like any parent I want my child to learn about taking chances without being in any real danger of harm. No parent wants to feel that his or her children are in actual jeopardy, even when they're having an adventure. Yet we would like to see them put to some tests. If a child can be tested — even scared — without being in actual danger, then what's the problem?

The problem is that no simulation of risk can provide its benefits. The one thing simulated adventure can't offer is what makes an adventure real: stakes. In place of stakes simulation offers sensation. By learning to associate daring with excitement without danger of loss, our children are being taught potentially hazardous lessons about risk and consequences.

Mountaineer Robin Campbell once observed about the hazards of overly controlled climbing experiences for children, "If there is some likelihood that such children will continue to climb as a result of this process of education, then such training constitutes a recipe for disaster, since experience will have taught the child that his fears can be safely ignored."

Adds his colleague Tom Price: "I think there is no question that much of what we describe as adventure is not adventure at all, and it is my view that if this is the case we should stop calling it adventure. Young people find adult thought processes confusing enough as it is and we only add to the confusion when we describe walking on an empty, rounded hill, laden with emergency equipment, as an adventure (whereas, for example, making gunpowder, or cycling two feet behind a bus to take advantage of its slipstream, is condemned as irresponsible.) We pay lip service to adventure, but what we mostly teach is prudence, and the importance of being comprehensively insured. As a middle-aged family man I find nothing wrong with this, but why can't we acknowledge it?"

This is the real question. The issue is not one of risk versus safety so much as authenticity versus sham. No matter how much our mind and our senses may be fooled in the short run by the excitement of safe "adventures," in the long run systems

269

subjected to them are in for a letdown. Up to a point the body can be fooled. But simulated risk never includes catharsis. Its excitement is rooted in novelty. Computer games grow boring and must be replaced every six months to a year. Theme parks must offer bigger and better attractions every summer to turn a profit. Physiologically, spiritually, and in every other way, simulated danger is self-contained, a ship without a destination, a story without a conclusion. There's no lasting satisfaction in "taking a risk" you knew you couldn't lose. How could there be? No courage was called for. Nothing was at stake. No goal is attained by such "risk taking" other than stimulation, and therefore nothing is actually learned about danger and risk, stakes and consequences.

The greater danger of simulated adventure is not the reckless risk taking it encourages but the ignorant kind — not risks taken in hopes of avoiding the consequences but risks taken without realizing that there were consequences. The better we get at mimicking reality, the more danger there will be of life being compared to a good simulation rather than vice versa. From there it's just one small step to beginning to perceive real danger as no different from pseudodanger.

This is not just a hypothetical problem. Amusement-park operators are painfully aware that when a fatality occurs on one of their rides, once it reopens the lines waiting to have a go at that ride will be longer than ever. Those on line don't imagine they'll be the ride's next victim. But knowing someone has actually died on the ride they're about to brave adds depth to the excitement.

Similarly, those responsible for supervising national parks will often find that their most dangerous spots — where backwoods bears are least predictable, or rushing water most treacherous — are the ones that attract the greatest number of excitement-seeking visitors who have no notion of the actual danger they're encountering (and stand fully prepared to sue for not being forewarned should they fall victim to such danger). Since the movie *Deliverance* appeared, at least nineteen drownings have taken place among those attempting to recreate its challenge of Georgia's treacherous Chattooga River.

After interviewing white-water-raft tourists on some western rivers, two recreation specialists reported, "We found that the outcome sought most strongly and most consistently was that of 'action/excitement,' the desire for thrills, for a real 'adventure.' " The authors of this study went on to suggest that the "uncertainty of the outcome," the anticipation of danger, was what motivated that desire. But is it? I've taken such raft trips. Like most of those who embark on such an adventure I expected to be thrilled and chilled (literally, it turns out; those trips get wet) but to make it back alive. It never seriously occurred to me that I wouldn't. I doubt that it does to most white-water tourists. Certainly there's no warning of such a danger. To the contrary, as a women's magazine once concluded in a picture spread promoting river rafting as a good way to meet men, "The week-long trip is thrilling, romantic — and safe!"

According to a manual on river running, "Whitewater boating is dangerous. Every year people are killed on rivers, not necessarily because they are stupid or ill-equipped but because they lack definite survival skills. . . . Romantic photos and appealing adventure tales usually lure neophytes into the sport, where they wallow along, untrained and unsupported. . . .

"Whitewater river running involves risk."

The lethal danger of pseudorisks is that they become the model for real ones. The co-owner of a New Jersey skydiving center touts his introductory course as "really like a $125 amusement ride." (An average of fifty people a year die skydiving in this country alone.) Outward Bound, which has lost over a dozen participants during its survival courses, barely mentions the hazards as it continues to portray itself as akin to an encounter group in the wilderness. And for his part, one rock climber says about a sport that claims an average of over forty American lives a year, "You have all kinds of narrow squeaks, and yet nothing serious happens. You get all the thrilling sensations without much real risk."

Is it any wonder that we're confused about the meaning of risk? Having grown so deft at simulating risk in the midst of safety and imagining we're safe in settings of danger, how do we know a real risk when it sets our heart to thumping?

In recent years a film called *Scared Straight*, based on harangues by convicts about prison's horrors, has been shown to incipient delinquents in hopes of dissuading them from a life of crime. In fact, there seems to be a slight rise in the delinquency rate among those who have seen it. Presumably this is because the film adds to an aura of excitement surrounding the risk of crime but not to the idea that this risk can be lost. Sociologist James Finckenauer has found that *Scared Straight* is especially misleading to middle-class viewers he's studied because they have so little context in which to place its portrayal of prison life. To them, Finckenauer suggests, watching this film "may be akin to attending a horror movie. They may be frightened while they are there and for a short time thereafter, but their own reality can quickly overcome what may soon be seen as a fictional experience."

By now we've had a couple of generations of Americans whose main sources of information about risk are vicarious. At the extreme they include John Hinckley, who according to the testimony of a psychiatrist at his trial was surprised to see his shooting victims bleeding on the ground because "he hadn't intended to hurt anyone." Or Patty Hearst and her SLA captors, who sat in a Disneyland hotel watching their colleagues being consumed by fire on live television while they frantically switched channels looking for a better version.

As she faced forty years in prison for illegal antiwar activities, Weatherman Susan Stern later recalled her feeling of disbelief. After she felt the "tight cold click of handcuffs," Stern recalled, she at first didn't know whether to panic or giggle. Then she wondered, "When was somebody going to scream cut, retake, and let us out of those fucking handcuffs?"

The implicit lesson of televised, simulated, and artificial risks of all kinds is that there is no danger of actual loss involved in taking a chance. Fear does not anticipate danger. Having separated fear from danger and made it into a leisure activity, we learn to treat being scared as a green light of excitement, not a yellow light of caution. But no matter how much they make our palms sweat and hearts flutter, no-risk risks neither teach nor test anything of consequence. If theme parks, computer games, and "That's Incredible!" are our primary source of information about risks, where do we ever learn that they can be lost? Or better yet, that actual risks with real stakes can be *won*, with much greater satisfaction than winning the simulated variety?

GENUINE RISK

When London was bombed during War II, there was widespread concern that the psychological reactions of residents would be severe. Just the opposite proved true: admissions to mental hospitals dropped, as did the rate of suicide. One British psychologist polled fifty colleagues and found that even patients who suffered from poor mental health before the raids seemed to improve during them. This was particularly true of those who were given useful, if dangerous, tasks such as fighting fires or rescuing air-raid victims.

Something we keep having to rediscover is not only how capable human beings are of coping with adversity of all kinds, but how much they can flourish from its challenge. When mental-health programs are organized to help disaster victims, or veterans of hostage episodes, their organizers sometimes seem disappointed by how little demand there is for such services. But if it's true that human beings were selected in part for their ability to cope with danger, this shouldn't be surprising at all. As disaster expert Verta Taylor has written, "What our research into collective stress situations indicates is that mental health is a dynamic state. It is not gained at one time for all time. . . . Rather it is reenergized by doing and acting and responding to challenges. . . . Perhaps the experience of coping and mastering the many personal crises associated with disasters might even enhance a person's psychological well-being."

It's always a little startling to hear those who have been

through — or even who are in the midst of — life-threatening illnesses say they feel the better for it. Most commonly they report that seeing the end of their life makes them want to live what part they have left more fully. Even a friend of mine who is suffering from the so-far incurable disease AIDS tells me the experience has been "life enhancing" because it has stripped away petty concerns — his looks, money, little arguments — and forced him to take risks he can no longer postpone.

For reasons ranging from the biochemical through the spiritual to the sexual, taking risks can enhance all our lives — even when the outcome is not as we'd hoped. The greatest regrets I heard during interviews for this book were not from those who had taken a risk and lost. Invariably they felt proud for having dared, and even educated in defeat. The real regret, bordering on mourning, came from those who hadn't taken chances they'd wanted to take and now felt it was too late. One woman in her seventies suggested sardonically that her book on this subject would be titled *The Risks I Never Took*.

The case is for taking risks. But such risks must be authentic, genuinely daring to the risk taker. The most common traps we fall into when considering risks to take are assuming that risks are always dangerous; that risk taking has to be exciting; that our concept of risk is static; and that one person's risk is like another's.

A lot of problems are created when Level I and II types try to impose their radically different views of the world on each other. When they're married, for example, and devote futile energy to trying to get each other either to "settle down" or "be more daring." Or when a Level I entrepreneur tries to borrow money from a Level II bank loan officer (which is one reason that so little of the financing for such new ventures comes from conventional sources). Or when a therapist with low needs for stimulation tries to "cure" a client whose need for arousal is constant.

In general, society is set up better to meet the needs of Level II than Level I types. Yet — as we saw in the previous chapter on the American way of risk — a strong current of envy flows from Level II's to Level I's with their calls to be bold and take chances.

Such envy leaves us prone to risks urged by others, which

might be a risk to them but not to us. Because risk is such a subjective concept, and varies so much with time and circumstances, only the risk taker can determine what's genuinely risky. In such a determination, *authenticity* is a far better criterion than objective danger. Someone who crosses the street despite being afraid of getting hit by a car is taking a bigger risk than someone else who leaps from an airplane with a parachute, sure of floating safely to the ground. If risk involves challenging fear, then the street crosser has done so more bravely than the skydiver.

We often hear about the need to conquer fear so that we can take more risks. But even if this were possible, it wouldn't be risks we'd be taking. The more useful approach is learning how to act in the face of our fears. This could also be the best way to conquer them.

PUTTING FEAR TO WORK

One of the more successful forms of phobia treatment in recent years has been one called "flooding." This involves putting clients nose-to-nose with feared objects — airplanes, elevators, spiders — in graduated doses rather than first trying to reduce their fear in more conventional therapeutic approaches. This might be seen as benign counterphobia. One thing we can learn from skydivers and mountain climbers, without carrying it to their extreme, is that fear confronted not only loses its power to control our lives, but can become an exhilarating source of energy.

This is why so many successful performers not only anticipate but welcome stage fright. "I like 'nervous' in the performance," Luciano Pavarotti has said, adding, "I think the best way to be successful is to be constantly scared." Seymour Bernstein, the author of a standard text for pianists, even sees a connection between anxiousness and quality of performance. Citing stage fright victims such as Artur Rubinstein and Gregor Piatigorsky, Bernstein suggests that "the wondrous playing of such artists derives more from their ability to channel their nervous energy than from the measures they take to allay its effects."

As a group, athletes probably have the highest regard for fear of them all. Fear to them is a source of motivation, of concentration and caution. "The prizefighter's best friend," is what former boxing champion José Torres calls a reasonable degree of fear. "They manipulate fear," says Torres about champion boxers. "They use fear as the best and only developer of their superlative sense of anticipation. They convert panic and anxiety — two of the negative components of fear — into alertness and meticulous vigilance. Once mastered, fear becomes the trusted and devoted watchful eye of champions."

There are basically three approaches to fear: to avoid and deny feeling it whenever possible; to confront fear directly and put its energy to work; or to embrace fear for the sake of excitement and self-mastery. On a continuum, fear paralyzes at one end, and becomes addictive when converted to excitement at the other. Neither extreme is terribly healthy. The fear avoider and the fear seeker actually have a lot in common: both their lives revolve around feeling afraid. One scurries for cover, the other challenges fear to a fistfight.

Between these two extremes there's a point of convergence where fear is met, confronted, and used as a source of both caution and energy. This is the point of useful risk taking. Ski instructors, for example, say that the key to making progress on the slopes is pushing beyond one's "comfort zone" into unmastered territory — but not so far as to terrify oneself off the slopes altogether. Similarly, it's been found that up to a point, performance — including test taking — is improved when others are present due to the arousal of their "audience effect."

When teaching writing I always try to send students into settings that are just a bit unsettling, a little frightening, to throw them off stride, enhance alertness, maybe squirt an extra endorphin or two and infuse their words with the intensity that commands a reader's attention. Typically they return from such ventures to write their best work. Most recently a twenty-one-year-old woman took her first trip ever to Philadelphia (thirty miles away) and came back to read us a crisp account of her unnerving encounter in a public rest room with the bag ladies she'd been hearing about but never before seen.

Taking risks involves confronting fear. This is the essence of genuine risk taking. Sometimes all that's required to take a risk is a simple change of perspective: treating a bit of hesitation and nervousness as an invitation to move ahead rather than a warning to step aside. If it is true that we're built for danger, when all else fails we can even justify taking a risk as good for the nervous system. Sol Roy Rosenthal, the research physician who thinks we're genetically programmed for risk taking, thinks further that in the absence of natural challenges we must create opportunities for "risk exercise" by regularly engaging in activities that frighten us.

The problem is that our fears, hence our sense of risk, change over time. In order to take actual risks we must stay aware of what's actually risky to us at any given moment. This calls for ongoing assessment of our need to take risks, and the way that need is expressed.

PERSONAL RISK ASSESSMENT

Because it varies so much with time and circumstances, our concept of risk must be kept current. Fears change and our perception of risk follows along. Something like the fear of flying is typically a "late-onset" phobia (the average age is twenty-seven). One woman I know used to fly her own plane until her first pregnancy, after which she developed an acute fear of flying in anyone's. Even ex-stewardesses sometimes show up in courses for airplane-phobes — usually after marrying and having children.

During the Vietnam war, psychiatrist Peter Bourne saw cases of severe combat fatigue resulting from the conflict felt by career noncommissioned officers who had won medals and reputations for valor as young enlistees in the Korean War, but now had families back home at stake. In a broader sense we all suffer some such confusion with age: feeling less daring, not liking feeling less daring, but not wanting to jeopardize personal and professional stakes that didn't used to exist. This doesn't necessarily mean that we take fewer risks over time. It does mean that the risks we take and avoid change with age, and ought to. If our risks shift from the first to the second level and become lower in their stimulation quotient, this hardly means we're no longer risk takers. If anything, the risks we take with age are bigger, deeper, and more daring. And bigger risks make smaller ones feel trivial by comparison. Before starting her own business, for example, Valerie Fine used to go on extended anorexic dieting binges, which she found quite exciting. These stopped immediately after she started Valerie's Way.

Our perception of risk can change not only over the course of a lifetime but during the course of a day. A dimension of "body clocks" too little appreciated is the influence circadian rhythms can have not only on our alertness but on our courage. Research with animals has found that fear is easiest to instill and hardest to extinguish during certain times of the day that seem to parallel the levels of stress-released chemicals. "If human beings have a similar 'clock' of vulnerability," writes Gay Gaer Luce in *Body Time*, "then blood levels of steroids might guide us in the scheduling of unpleasant or painful medical procedures, not to mention the timing of examinations and other events that might be considered an ordeal."

When I took my first trip ever to a theme park as part of the research for this project, I was far more willing to brave the roller coaster and loop-the-loop before lunch than afterward. During the afternoon even a modest Ferris wheel ride looked overwhelming. In general I find myself braver during the morning than after lunch, and wimpiest of all at night. This is a fairly typical pattern. The reason so much insurance is sold at night is that our need for it feels so much greater at this time. As Claude Monet once said of courage, "In the night I am constantly haunted by what I am trying to realize. I rise broken with fatigue each morning. But the coming of the dawn gives me courage."

To reiterate: because our perception of risk does vary so much with time and circumstances, there's a need to reassess constantly what risk means to us. Yesterday's risk is today's routine and vice versa. To mourn a more reckless and adventurous style based on low stakes and little sense of consequences is a real waste of time. Rather than curse ourselves for cowardice, the more useful approach is first to appreciate the risks we *are* taking, then seek out others we'd like to take as well.

Staying current with our need for risk calls for continual updating of a) risks we're taking now and want to continue taking;

b) risks we're taking now but might well forgo; c) risks we aren't taking and are just as happy to leave untaken; and, d) risks we're not taking now but might like to take.

The latter, of course, is the category most of us are most concerned about.

A BALANCED DIET OF RISK

Having conducted an assessment of our need for risk, we can cast our net widely for ways to satisfy this need, paying particular attention to our taste for more or less stimulation. When it comes to something like choosing a line of work, this factor is too seldom taken into account. While it stands to reason that those who need a lot of excitement would become the commodities traders and firefighters of the world, it doesn't always work that way. For reasons of opportunity, financial security, and mere chance, those who prefer a lot of stimulation often end up doing boring work just as (less often) those who don't like excitement take jobs that are constantly arousing. Only recently has serious attention been given to the price paid for not correlating temperament with work. One study of 400 Lockheed employees in California found that when aggressive "Type A" personalities were put in routinized jobs, their blood pressure went up. When "Type B" people were put in overly stressful work, they suffered similarly. In a rare, practical recognition of such a problem, the president of a New York ad agency recently advised prospective employees, "Some people *need* tension and crisis. They won't like it here."

It's well known that weekend thrill seekers come disproportionately from the ranks of those who find their work boring. As we've seen, to those who are susceptible, boredom can be at least as harrowing as stress, and in many of the same ways. Yet most "stress-reduction" programs assume that antidotes are best based on relaxation techniques, alpha feedback, or even tranquilizers. For some these may be the best alternatives. Others might need more challenging work, riskier hobbies, or a house to rehabilitate in a changing neighborhood.

Psychiatrist Robert Seidenberg once diagnosed a housewife's

seeming symptoms of stress, which included difficulty sleeping, tight stomach, and acute anxiety, as in fact being due to the "trauma of eventlessness" in her understimulated life. The "cure" Seidenberg prescribed was that she look for stimulating work. Once the woman took a part-time job canvassing for a research corporation in dicier neighborhoods than her own, these symptoms vanished. "Plagued by anxiety in supermarkets and beauty salons," reported her psychiatrist, "she suffered no fear in this 'outside' work, only exhilaration, giving evidence once again that the overriding danger to her existence lay in the 'safety' of the housewife's role."

Assessing the need for excitement in job placement has particular relevance for ex-convicts. This seldom is done, even though placing those with a high need for arousal in routine work virtually guarantees their return to crime for respite. Lucky is the former criminal who like Merle Haggard finds straight work of comparable stimulation. Or the ex-prostitute who became a carnival barker. Or the call girl studying to become an emergency-room nurse.

On the assumption that alternative forms of excitement may quench a thirst now fulfilled by crime, some programs such as the rock-climbing group I joined have offered thieves and junkies alternative forms of excitement. Among them have been mountaineering, skydiving, scuba diving, or even "wagon trains" crossing the country. In theory this approach makes perfect sense; substitute good excitement for bad. Early surveys of such programs found that they effectively curbed rates of return to prison. But further research found that the rise in self-esteem and self-confidence that typically followed completion of such a program eventually gave way to reversion to criminal patterns.

The problem is that taking criminals and addicts off the street, shipping them out to the woods for excitement, then returning them to the street where memories of the woods quickly fade can't have a lasting impact. The problem with "survival" programs in general is that the wisdom they impart is so far removed in time and place. As recreation, learning how to cope with the wilderness can be terrific. I've taken part in such programs and enjoyed them immensely. But when it comes to taking risks, the lessons they teach are museum pieces. Worst of all, they imply that risk taking is an expensive proposition that occurs in distant and exotic locales. In theory, rappeling down cliffs or kayaking oceans teaches lessons that carry over into "real life." In fact, such lessons quickly fade. And what's left is the message that risk is a recreational activity.

While it may include such activities, the better risk diet is one based on experiences closer to home. These might include, but are hardly limited to, physically dangerous activities. More essential is that stakes be genuine and consequences real. If the loss of face worries them more than the loss of their life, adolescents might be better challenged to perform in public than to take a survival course. Alternatively, allowing teenagers to join volunteer fire squads — as some communities do — involves risk with a purpose. When it comes to their need for challenging rites of passage, I suspect we have at least as much to learn from West Point and the Marines as from Summerhill. (No matter how they feel later about the Marines' mission, it's rare to come across an ex-leatherneck who isn't proud of passing that test of endurance.) Daring our children to take the consequences of their actions has far more to teach about risk taking than any trip to the woods. Too much protecting of kids from failure takes place under the heading of compassion. Learning to cope with failure is the essence of learning to take risks.

The continually requoted suggestion of poet John Berryman that these are times when courage can't be tested is shortsighted. While it may be true that finding adventure takes more imagination than it used to, adventure is there to be found. Today's adventures, for example, might require substituting time for space. In a study of those who come out once the sun has gone down, sociologist Murray Melbin found that today's "night people" use the darkness much as pioneers used the frontier: as a source of challenge, alertness, and freedom. At night today as in unsettled lands last century there is relative freedom from bureaucracies, greater tolerance of eccentric or even deviant behavior, and a strong sense of camaraderie. As one young man explained to Melbin, "At four A.M., if someone sees you walking the streets at the same time he does, he must think, 'Gee, this guy must be part of the brethren, because no one else is awake at this time.' "

281

A similar perspective applied to regular blood donors has found them enjoying Level I stages of excitement: tension beforehand, calm during the giving of blood, and profound relief afterward mixed with elation. We should have more such opportunities for useful thrill seeking. Going further, one psychiatrist has suggested that as an alternative to suicide, we encourage those who wish to risk their lives to donate parts of their bodies to those in need: a single kidney, one cornea, some bone marrow. Such an alternative may sound absurd. But then what would we call attempting suicide to fight depression?

Making actual stakes and real consequences paramount when it comes to taking risks can lead us up many an odd avenue. I've gotten to the point where I'd almost rather that my son learn to shoot real guns than play with toy ones. At least the former provide lessons about danger and consequences. The latter imply that guns are a harmless diversion. For the same reason, although when we began heating our home with wood I was apprehensive about the risk a living-room stove posed to our boy, now I'm grateful for that risk; throughout the winter, not only filling the stove with wood and lighting fires, but sawing, chopping, and splitting that wood gives us regular opportunities to have conversations about visible danger and risk.

Creating balanced diets of risk for ourselves and our families needn't mean that every entry be a dangerous main course. To the contrary, such menus ought to include appetizers and dessert as well. Putting more risk in our lives might mean merely giving up a wristwatch to create the challenge of finding out what time it is. Or it could mean allowing ourselves to follow a recipe only once (as recommended by some cooking teachers). Or taking back roads instead of main routes, and not using a map. Or doing a jigsaw puzzle without looking at the picture.

Obviously creating diets of risk depends on what one perceives as risky. Here are some suggestions for risks worth taking depending on whether your tendencies are more at the first or second level.

LEVEL I RISKS FOR LEVEL II PEOPLE

1. Run for office.
2. Buy stocks.

3. Plant seedlings before advised it's safe.
4. Do your own plumbing.
5. Don't follow the recipe.
6. Prepare a soufflé for company.
7. Make love in a phone booth.
8. Buy a used car.
9. Get a pet snake.
10. Take a trip without reservations.
11. Eat at a Thai restaurant.
12. Cut down a dying tree.
13. Walk instead of driving when storm clouds are brewing.
14. Learn to tap-dance; perform.
15. Change jobs.

LEVEL II RISKS FOR LEVEL I PEOPLE

1. Don't change jobs.
2. Start an enterprise; keep it going.
3. Have a child.
4. Get married; don't get divorced.
5. Cosign for a friend's loan.
6. Join a religious order.
7. Read Proust.
8. Follow the recipe.
9. Let things happen.
10. Compliment someone.
11. Have an actual conversation; listen as well as talk.
12. Assume a thirty-year mortgage.
13. Write a multigenerational novel.
14. Learn computer programming.
15. Contemplate.

To keep their life lively, one San Diego couple in their midforties treat each other to what they call "weekly adventures." As the husband explains, "In the spirit of compromise, couples often end up doing their third- or fourth-choice thing on weekends. They usually don't even suggest what they would like to do most, perhaps because it would be too self-revealing. Or they did a long time ago and were rebuffed. So weekends are spent jockeying around the eternal question which Marty first proposed:

'What'ya wanna do?' Rather than be only *partially* satisfied *all* of the time, we decided that each of us could be completely satisfied half the time. And it turns out that the percentage is actually much higher. Because knowing that your partner is truly expressing his or her 'wants' is rather delightful. The spirit is contagious. There is a charge of genuine excitement. Often we don't tell each other what we have planned for the day or night, and simply drive off into the unknown. It may be a good play or a concert, a special restaurant, a day in the park with a picnic basket, something erotic, or exotic. There is no reason two alive, normally vibrant adults have to settle for dullness together. It may take a little thinking or planning to break out, but really not that much. All that most people need is a slightly different angle on reality. And to keep shifting that angle."

Of course this couple's approach is based on not having children at home. But as the Coulsons suggest, even those who have children can create adventures that take place within the family. A doctor I know took his wife and two children with him during a year of service as a physician on an island off Alaska as a means of encouraging family unity. A father and his son shared a dog-sled expedition in the Yukon for the same reason. One couple went so far as to take their television-addicted six-year-old son on the entire 2,106 miles of the Appalachian Trail. Their risks on the trail turned out to be more spiritual than physical. In particular the parents found themselves nose-to-nose with the fear of letting their boy take chances: exploring the underbrush on his own, or picking himself up when he fell. Although hesitant at first, it was the son who insisted that the trip be completed when his mother's will waned. Along the way he learned not only how to cook but to wash his own clothes. When columnist Red Smith asked the boy what he'd learned as their trek neared its end, he replied, "That when I can't do something all I have to do is try harder."

What's most appealing about such examples is that they combine risks at both levels: short-term excitement enjoyed among those with long-term commitments. This might be thought of as the most balanced of risk diets. Physical danger may or may not be part of such diets. What's more important is a spirit of being venturesome.

ON BEING VENTURESOME

While I've tried to avoid generalizations about "risk takers" because this is such a relative term, I have observed traits in common among those who might at least be called "venturesome" — the ones who dare to engage in activities at which they might fail. Like Ted Turner, they seem intent on winning but not overly afraid of losing, a potent combination. As sport psychologist Bruce Ogilvie observes, "The great athletes that I have interviewed do not dwell upon their losses but concentrate upon that part of their performance that limited their excellence."

If anything, losing a risk can drive more than discourage the venturesome. Failure, tragedy, fear — all become grist for their mill, the coal of their furnace, a source of energy and test of mettle. Aspiring comedienne Loretta Colla told me that far from feeling dissuaded she felt she'd gained strength even from horrifying nights onstage. As she explained, "I mean, once you've told me to 'get da fuck offa da stage,' what more can you say to me?"

After being stolen blind by an ex-convict named Chris whom they'd taken into their home, a Canadian Quaker later wrote that while it seemed that they'd been unable to help this man, he had certainly helped them. As she explained, "For us it led to a radiant spiritual growth that continues to this day.

"What we did in our relations with Chris was very contrary to the principles of security: we risked our worldly goods very heavily to invest in the dreams and life of a fellow human being we cared about. To do that we had to go *beyond* security, and risk hurt and pain and loss. But *not* to do it would have been a greater risk: the risk of cutting ourselves off from a call to care, of damming up some of the great fountain of love that God puts in each of our hearts."

That sentiment (if not the theology) is utterly typical of the venturesome; the thought that even when its apparent results are catastrophic, they're glad of risks they've taken because the alternative would have been worse. Far from being deterred by the loss of a risk, many seem to regard this as encouraging evidence that they're not being too cautious. Woody Allen has always taken this approach to his regular failures mingled with many successes as a moviemaker. "Failure," he once said, "is a sure sign that you're not playing it safe, that you're still experimenting, still taking creative risks. . . . If you're succeeding too much, you're doing something wrong."

Which isn't to say that the venturesome take chances willy-nilly without concern for the consequences. To the contrary, I found it typical among those taking less charted paths to first engage in a period of reflection and planning. After earning her M.B.A., for example, one twenty-seven-year-old woman told me that she chose to work for a fledgling genetic-engineering company rather than a larger, better established corporation only after making up a meticulous "grid" decision chart that set out in detail the pros and cons of all of her alternatives. Comedienne Abby Stein, who was raised in relative poverty, only worked up the nerve to leave a secure job in the garment industry and begin telling jokes full-time after writing out a list of the worst possible things that could happen to her (the worst being "become a shopping-bag lady"). Realizing that none sounded catastrophic (becoming a shopping-bag lady might even be a source of good material), she took the plunge.

Among 1200 of those he calls "top performers" in business, education, sports, medicine, and the arts whom he's interviewed, psychologist Charles Garfield has found it common that they mentally construct or even write out "catastrophic-expectation reports" before embarking on a risky course of action. This is part of a broader process of mental rehearsal, or what he calls creating "movies of the mind." By anticipating the worst possible scenario in detail, they can decide in advance whether the consequences of failure are tolerable. Those who do no such preparation, Garfield has found, tend to be more inhibited about taking chances due to vague forebodings of doom.

Simply determining what's *actually* at stake in taking a risk can be an enormous help in working up the nerve to do so. As we've seen, what initially appears to be at stake — even to ourselves — is seldom what we're actually risking. Realizing that, say, it's our pride more than our money, or our feelings more than our body that we're concerned about can make risks easier to take. What's really being risked in many instances is less worrisome than what we imagined.

Some of the most useful questions to ask before taking a risk are simply, "What am I really afraid of?" "What's the worst thing that could happen to me?" "What do I stand to lose if this happens?" "What's really at stake?" "Risk what?"

And finally, "Do I care?"

The very act of posing such questions is dangerous, of course, which is why we so seldom do it. Among other things, this process involves risking the discovery that we're not the type of risk taker we imagined ourselves to be. Charles Garfield has found that some of the most painful insights come to those who realize that they aren't as interested as they thought they were in pursuing change. "They find out that they're really quite satisifed with the status quo," explains Garfield, "but they need the comforting illusion that they are on the verge of taking a risk." The graduate of one month-long life-planning workshop — a steel-company executive — discovered that daring to pursue a life's dream of becoming his company's president was not, in fact, what he really wanted. The risk he really wanted to take was both more mundane and scarier: to give up his career dream and spend more time at home with his five children.

The great, ill-appreciated value of workshops and classes of all kinds is the opportunity they offer to rehearse and think through high-stakes risks in a low-stakes setting. The real usefulness of a writing class, for example, is not for "learning how to write" (a questionable possibility), but for the opportunity it provides to practice fielding responses to our work in a relatively safe context before braving the wrath of readers, critics, and our Aunt Edna in Springfield.

Many actors take a similar approach to acting classes, using them less as an opportunity to work on their technique than to work on their daring. After years of roles on television, actress Jessica Walters resumed studying acting because, as she explained, "You can't risk failure in front of the camera. I can do things in class I'd never get hired for."

A lot of stand-up comedians get started by taking comedy courses, which they find more useful for developing nerve than routines. According to working stand-ups, the great virtue of the small showcase clubs that have become so common is the opportunity they offer to try out new material before using it in a setting with higher stakes. The creation of such "safety zones" is not limited to performers. A Seattle teacher once said of his regard for the unconventional school where he worked, "I'm not hesitant to take risks here. . . . We all feel we can fail. It's not threatening."

Even the most venturesome among us need safety zones where we can rehearse and seek support from others before taking important risks. Ideally our families, schools, and churches can serve such a purpose. But too few of them do.

In the absence of such support from existing groups, we can create new ones whose explicit task is to encourage members to take risks they've decided are worth taking. For a number of years I belonged to such a group in San Diego: the Center for Studies of the Person. In the guise of a "think tank," the Center's actual purpose was to encourage its members (largely psychologists, consultants, and a couple of writers) to be more venturesome. An observer once caught the spirit when he compared this group's office and letterhead to the hangout and insignia of a teenage gang that made everyone feel tougher. I recall in particular one Center member, a twice-widowed wife of two doctors, who used the group's support to start a successful program to help physicians become more aware of the human needs of their patients.

Such settings of support, such safety zones, can do far more to encourage actual risk taking than any exhortation to "take more risks!"

In their book *In Search of Excellence*, Thomas Peters and Robert Waterman refer to the quality of allowing employees room to experiment (including room to fail) as characterizing the best-managed American companies. Inherent in this quality, they say, is an implicit understanding of the twin needs most of us have to be both free agents and part of a team. This is like the need we also have to balance level I with Level II risk taking in our lives. Our need is not to take more risks as such, but to keep our risk taking in balance. This means making sure that some are Level I: short-term and exciting; others Level II: long-term and reassuring. And don't forget risklets.

"Taking risks" willy-nilly is not what we need to do. Nor is advising others to take more chances. Depending on who we are, when, and where, creating a balanced diet of genuine risk can mean taking more of some kinds of risks, fewer of others. And avoiding like the plague risks urged on us by others, which might be theirs but not ours.

To stay alive and lively we need a steady diet of risk. But we're the only ones who can assess what that means. The assessment of others isn't what matters, the size of a risk, or its potential to thrill. All that matters is that a risk be genuine. And no one knows but the risk taker the meaning of genuine risk.

NOTES

The purpose of these notes is to credit those whose work I've drawn upon, and to offer leads to those who might wish to read further in a particular area. Where no source is given, my own interviews are the basis for information in the book. When an interview is combined with published material as a source, this is noted. For the sake of brevity, the titles of the following publications are abbreviated: the *New York Times* (NYT), the *Philadelphia Inquirer* (PI), and the *Wall Street Journal* (WSJ). In addition, these five sources were used several times and are referred to in the notes by author's last name only:

Farberow, Norman L., editor. *The Many Faces of Suicide* (New York: McGraw-Hill, 1980).

Slovenko, Ralph, and James A. Knight, editors. *Motivations in Play, Games and Sports* (Springfield, Illinois: Charles C. Thomas, 1967).

Watson, Peter. *War on the Mind: The Military Uses and Abuses of Psychology* (New York: Basic Books, 1978).

Wilson, Ken, editor. *Games Climbers Play* (London: Diadem Books, 1978).

Zuckerman, Marvin. *Sensation Seeking* (Hillsdale, New Jersey: Lawrence Erlbaum Associates, 1979).

INTRODUCTION

3   *Getting out of bed in the morning:* Mary Cantwell, NYT, March 13, 1980.

4   *objects falling from the sky: Accident Facts* (Chicago: The National Safety Council, 1980), p. 12.

4   *"Bravado":* Edward Connery Latham, editor, *The Poetry of Robert Frost* (New York: Holt, Rinehart and Winston, 1969), p. 383.

4   *"risking linking":* Philadelphia Bulletin, September 11, 1980.

4   *Ohio gubernatorial candidate:* NYT, May 25, 1982.

5   *Air Florida pilots:* NYT, February 12, 1982.

CHAPTER 2: WHAT'S A RISK? WHO'S A RISK TAKER?

21   *a panel discussing public buildings:* NYT, April 26, 1981.

22   *smoking rates:* Surgeon General's Report, 1983 (33 percent of all Americans still smoke).

22   *seat belt use:* Gallup Poll, PI, September 12, 1982.

22   *bubonic plague, epidemiologist's response:* NYT, August 22, 1983.

23   *Paul Slovic:* Slovic et al., in R. C. Schwing and W. A. Albers, *Societal Risk Assessment* (New York: Plenum Press, 1980), p. 192. *See also* Slovic, *Journal of Safety Research* 10:58–68, Summer 1978; Slovic et al., *Journal of Experimental Psychology: Human Learning and Memory* 4:551–78, November 1978; Slovic et al., *Chemtech,* December 1979; and Slovic et al., *Psychology Today,* June 1980.

24   *"The Daredevils":* NBC-TV, November 21, 1980.

CHAPTER 3: RISK HUNGER

31   *one pharmacological researcher:* Judith Hooper, *Science Digest,* May 1981, p. 122.

32   *Peter Freuchen:* Whit Burnett, editor, *The Spirit of Adventure* (New York: Henry Holt, 1955), p. xiii.

32   *René Dubos:* quoted by W. Clarke Wescoe in *How Safe Is Safe?* (Washington, D.C.: National Academy of Sciences, 1974), p. 28.

33   *Sol Roy Rosenthal:* interview, unpublished paper, "Risk Exercise," p. 6.

34   *David Roberts: Outside,* December 1980–January 1981, p. 91.

34   *James Webb:* author, *Fields of Fire* (Englewood Cliffs, New Jersey: Prentice-Hall, 1978); p. 352 of the Bantam edition, 1979.

34   *Brooke Shields/Franco Zeffirelli: People Weekly,* August 10, 1981, p. 86.

34   *both pain and pleasure:* D. E. Redmond in William E. Fann et al., editors, *Phenomenology and Treatment of Anxiety* (Jamaica, New York: Spectrum Publications, 1979), p. 179.

34 *One school of psychological thought:* Stanley Schachter and Jerome E. Singer, *Psychological Review*, September 1962.

35 *Hans Selye: The Stress of Life* (New York: McGraw-Hill, 1956, rev. 1976) is Selye's basic work.

36 *our natural opiates [in general]:* NYT, October 2, 1977; David N. Leff, *Smithsonian*, June 1978; John Wasacz, *American Scientist*, May–June 1981; Agu Pert, *Psychology Today*, September 1981; Jean L. Marx, *Science*, November 27, 1981; WSJ, December 1, 1981; *Newsweek*, February 7, 1983; John W. Thompson, *British Medical Journal*, January 28, 1984.

36 *anesthetic property of acupuncture:* Bruce Pomeranz, *New Scientist*, January 6, 1977.

36 *euphoria . . . after giving birth:* Alan R. Gintzler, *Science*, October 10, 1980.

36 *"runner's high":* Daniel B. Carr et al., *New England Journal of Medicine*, September 3, 1981.

37 *Albert St. Gallen Heim:* Mike Quigley in Wilson, p. 529.

37 *Candace Pert:* Denise Grady, *Discover*, December 1981, p. 60; Judith Hooper, *Science Digest*, May 1981, p. 122.

37 *Solomon Snyder: Science Year* (Chicago: Field Enterprises Educational Corporation, 1977), p. 135.

37–8 *William Manchester:* author, *Goodbye Darkness* (Boston: Little, Brown, 1980), p. 372.

38 *Jane Alpert:* author, *Growing Up Underground* (New York: William Morrow, 1981), p. 213.

38 *Stephen Crane:* author, *The Red Badge of Courage*, Signet Classic edition, p. 107.

38 *"flashbulb memories":* Roger Brown and James Kulik, *Cognition* 5:73–99, 1977; Beryl Lieff Benderly, *Psychology Today*, June 1981. An earlier discussion of the same phenomenon from a neurological perspective, calling it "now print!," is by Robert Livingston in Gardner C. Quarton et al., editors, *The Neurosciences* (New York: The Rockefeller University Press, 1967).

38 *Recent evidence indicates that brain chemicals:* James L. McGaugh, *Psychology Today*, December 1980; *American Psychologist*, February 1983.

39–40 *Jimmy Doolittle:* NBC News, April 30, 1978.

40 *Harry Harlow and Stephen Suomi:* in Marvin Zuckerman and Charles D. Spielberger, editors, *Emotions and Anxiety* (Hillsdale, New Jersey: Lawrence Erlbaum Associates, 1976), p. 30.

40 *Yi-fu Tuan:* author, *Landscapes of Fear* (New York: Pantheon Books, 1979), pp. 211, 68.

44–5   *Pavlov:* Stephen M. Sales, *Journal of Personality and Social Psychology* 19:124–34, 1971.

45   Michael Balint, *Thrills and Regressions* (New York: International Universities Press, 1959).

45   *Hans Selye:* NYT, October 16, 1977.

45   *Marvin Zuckerman: Sensation Seeking* (Hillsdale, New Jersey: Lawrence Erlbaum Associates, 1979); interview.

47   *Hyperactive children: Human Behavior,* August 1976, p. 23; Joseph Hixson, *New York Times Magazine,* August 24, 1980, p. 70.

47   *the military prefers understimulated types:* Watson, p. 301.

47   *high-sensation seekers seem to produce:* Folke Johansson et al., *Psychiatry Research* 1:231–9, 1979, p. 237.

47–8   *Ervin Staub:* in Leonard Berkowitz, editor, *Advances in Experimental Social Psychology* (New York: Academic Press, 1974), p. 333; Jack Markowitz, *A Walk on the Crust of Hell* (Brattleboro, Vermont: The Stephen Greene Press), pp. 195–6.

48   *Among a wide range of psychological tests:* Gilbert Geis and Ted L. Huston in Farberow, p. 368.

48   *Perry London:* in J. Macaulay and L. Berkowitz, editors, *Altruism and Helping Behavior* (New York: Academic Press, 1970), pp. 245–6.

48   *ambulance-corps volunteer:* NYT, May 24, 1982.

49   *"reducers":* Marvin Zuckerman, *Psychology Today,* February 1978, p. 96.

49   *Bowling Green experiments:* Judith Hooper, *Science Digest,* May 1981, p. 122; Michael Liebowitz, *The Chemistry of Love* (Boston: Little, Brown, 1983), pp. 106–8.

50   *"separation anxiety":* Liebowitz, ibid., pp. 108–14.

50   *origins of war:* Paul Shepard, *The Tender Carnivore and the Sacred Game* (New York: Charles Scribner's Sons, 1973), p. 126.

LEVEL I RISK TAKING

55   *Byron:* Asenath Petrie et al., *Journal of Nervous and Mental Disease* 13: 415–421, 1962, p. 421.

55   *quiz item #1:* L. B. Taylor, Jr., *Ladies' Home Journal,* January 1982, p. 88.

55   *#2:* Zuckerman, p. 209.

56   *#3:* McKenzie Porter, *Toronto Telegram,* September 28, 1968.

56   *#4:* Lisa Davis, *Chic,* December 1977, p. 42.

57   *Goethe:* Edith Jacobson, *Depression: Comparative Studies of*

Normal, Neurotic, and Psychotic Conditions (New York: International Universities Press, 1971), p. 27.

57 *Walker Percy:* author, *The Second Coming* (New York: Farrar, Straus & Giroux, 1980), p. 16.

57 *Henry Fonda:* as told to Howard Teichmann, *Fonda: My Life* (New York: NAL Books, 1981), p. 32.

57 *woman involved with scuba diving:* Shari Steiner, *Glamour,* March 1977, p. 200.

57–8 *Dan Gerber:* author, in *Outside,* January 1981, p. 43.

58 *Lenny Bruce:* author, *How to Talk Dirty and Influence People* (Chicago: Playboy Press, 1965); pp. 28–9 of the Playboy Pocket Book edition, 1967.

59 *A. Alvarez:* author, *The Savage God* (New York: Random House, 1972); pp. 37–8 of the Bantam Books edition, 1973.

59 *survivors of wrist-slashing: Psychology Today,* April 1976, p. 20.

60 *Autopsies: Science,* June 18, 1982, pp. 1337–9.

60 *Graham Greene:* author, *A Sort of Life* (London: The Bodley Head, 1971); pp. 23, 94, and 103 of the Penguin edition, 1972. *See also* Greene, *Ways of Escape* (New York: Simon & Schuster, 1980).

60 *A reporter . . . Albert Ellis:* Mary Reinholz, *Forum,* September 1977, p. 48.

61 *Glenn Ramsey: American Journal of Psychology* 56:217–34, 1943.

61 *Aristotle:* Alfred Kinsey et al., *Sexual Behavior in the Human Female* (Philadelphia: W. B. Saunders Company, 1953), p. 706.

61 *a French psychiatrist:* René LaForgue, *International Journal of Psychoanalysis* 11:314, 1930.

61 *"risk" spelled "risque":* John Dizikes, *Sportsmen and Gamesmen* (Boston: Houghton Mifflin, 1980), wherein Andrew Jackson is quoted as saying, "You must risque to win," p. 26.

61 *William H. Masters and Philip M. Sarrel:* authors, in *Archives of Sexual Behavior* 11:117–31, 1982, p. 128.

62 *And why do psychologists:* Ellen Berscheid and Elaine Walster in Ted L. Huston, editor, *Foundations of Interpersonal Attraction* (New York: Academic Press, 1974), p. 371.

62 *P. J. O'Rourke:* author, in *Car & Driver,* June 1980, p. 149.

63 *It's also well known:* Jane Brody, NYT, March 7, 1984; Robert Schafer, *OMEGA* 7:45–50, 1976, p. 46.

63–4 *Mihaly Csikszentmihalyi:* author, *Beyond Boredom and Anxiety* (San Francisco: Jossey-Bass, 1975), pp. 45, 81.

65   *survivor of a first parachute jump:* Seymour Epstein and Wal-
       ter D. Fenz, *Journal of Abnormal and Social Psychology*
       64:97–112, 1962, p. 111.

65   *paratroopers respond to the tension:* Watson, p. 233.

66   *Antoine de Saint-Exupéry:* author, *Wind, Sand and Stars*
       (New York: Harcourt, Brace & World, 1940); pp. 27–8 of Time
       Reading Program Special Edition, 1965.

66   *Philip Caputo:* author, *A Rumor of War* (New York: Holt,
       Rinehart & Winston, 1977); p. xvii of the Ballantine edition,
       1978.

66   *Erich Maria Remarque: All Quiet on the Western Front,* Faw-
       cett Crest edition, p. 60.

66   *Caputo:* ibid., p. 6.

67   This concept of character is indebted to Erving Goffman's essay
       "Where the Action Is" in his *Interaction Ritual* (Garden City,
       New York: Anchor Press/Doubleday, 1967).

68   *Samuel Johnson:* Stanley J. Rachman, *Fear and Courage* (San
       Francisco: W. H. Freeman, 1978), p. 236.

68   *Thomas Szasz, Journal of the American Psychoanalytic As-
       sociation* 6:309–325, 1958.

68   anorexia nervosa: *New Scientist,* October 16, 1975, p. 140; Jane
       Brody, NYT, July 14, 1982.

CHAPTER 4: STIRRING THE POT

73   *Desmond Morris:* author, *The Human Zoo* (New York: Mc-
       Graw-Hill, 1969), p. 185.

74   Billy Joel: *Playboy,* May 1982, p. 83.

75   Newsweek, *feature on "The Thrill Seekers":* August 18, 1975,
       p. 52.

75   *a Federal Railroad Administration Board spokesman:* CBS
       Evening News, July 6, 1981.

75   *fatality rate for 15–24-year-olds:* PI, January 7, 1983.

75–6   *David Klein:* author, in "Adolescent Driving as Deviant Behav-
       ior," a paper given to a North Carolina Symposium on Highway
       Safety, Chapel Hill, North Carolina, Fall 1971. An abridged
       version of this paper appeared in *Journal of Safety Research,*
       September 1972.

76   *"expressive self-testing":* John Roberts, Wayne E. Thompson,
       and Brian Sutton-Smith, *Human Organization* 25:54–63, 1966.

76   *Klein:* ibid., p. 13.

76   *Klein:* ibid., p. 18.

76   *use of seat belts . . . declined:* Gallup Poll, PI, September 12, 1982; Jane Brody, NYT, December 9, 1981.

76   *53 million Americans smoke:* NYT, January 26, 1984, letter from President Edward M. Sewell of the American Lung Association.

78–9   *Dostoyevsky:* author, *The Gambler,* University of Chicago Press edition, pp. 188, 16.

79   *Vincent Coda:* NYT, December 17, 1983.

79   *Walter Matthau: Psychology Today,* February 1978, p. 43.

79   *Igor Kusyszyn:* author, in *The International Journal of the Addictions* 7:387–93, 1972. Kusyszyn's work is reviewed in *Psychology Today,* July 1979, p. 54.

79–80   *William McGlothin,* author, in *Journal of Consulting Psychology* 18:145–9, 1954, p. 147.

80   *Pennsylvania's liquor smugglers:* PI, December 2, 1979.

80   *Indian artifact diggers:* NYT, June 23, 1980.

80   *One poor Louisianan:* NYT, October 10, 1983.

81   *Lawrence Zeitlin:* author, in *Psychology Today,* June 1971, p. 24.

81   *David Downes:* author, *The Delinquent Solution* (New York: The Free Press, 1966), pp. 77–8. The study he cites and quotes (with emphasis added) is by David Matza and Gresham M. Sykes, *American Sociological Review* 26:712–19, 1961.

81   *Ray Johnson:* author, with Mona McCormick, *Too Dangerous to Be at Large* (New York: Quadrangle, 1975), p. 65.

81–2   *Merle Haggard:* Earl Blackwell's *Celebrity Register* (New York: Simon & Schuster, 1973), p. 217; Paul Hemphill, *The Atlantic Monthly,* September 1971, p. 101; John Mariani, *Saga,* November 1979, p. 46.

82   *women shoplifters:* Gini Kopecky, *Mademoiselle,* December 1980, p. 156; Michael Hennessy et al., *Criminology* 15:519–20, 1978; Lawrence A. Conner, *The Shoplifters Are Coming* (Wilmington, Delaware: Reports, Inc., 1980), p. 151.

82   *a psychiatrist who has treated women:* Sam Blum, *Redbook,* October 1970, p. 169.

82   *items most commonly taken:* NYT, October 9, 1982.

82–3   *head of security for Woodward & Lothrop: National Observer,* October 9, 1976.

83   *"I got an orgasm . . .": Time,* November 17, 1980, p. 94.

83   *"I just really liked . . .": Mademoiselle,* December 1980, p. 201.

83   *16 percent . . . used no birth control: Cosmopolitan,* September 1980, p. 264.

83   *Eugene Sandberg and Ralph Jacobs: American Journal of Obstetrics and Gynecology* 110:227–42, May 15, 1971, p. 234.

83   *"I was aware . . .":* Kristin Luker, *Taking Chances* (Berkeley: University of California Press, 1975), p. 76.

84   *Leslie Savan:* author, in *Village Voice,* February 4–10, 1981, p. 32.

84   *survey of post-abortion women:* Judith S. Wallerstein, Peter Kurtz, and Marion Bar-Din, *Archives of General Psychiatry* 27:828–832, December 1972.

85   *poll of college women: Playboy,* October 1981, p. 198.

85   *Rita Jenrette:* author, *My Capitol Secrets* (New York: Bantam Books, 1981), pp. 30–1.

86   *Pauline Kael:* author, in *New Yorker,* December 5, 1977, p. 125.

87   *Morton Hunt:* author, *The Affair* (New York: New American Library/World Publishing Company, 1969); p. 68 of the Signet edition, 1971.

87   *Herbert Gold:* author, *He/She* (New York: Arbor House, 1980), p. 23.

88   *Garson Kanin's father: Newsweek,* June 25, 1979, p. 14.

CHAPTER 6: WUFFO?

110   *Irwin Shaw:* author, *Top of the Hill* (New York: Delacorte, 1979); p. 197 of the Dell edition, 1980.

112   *"Most parachutists jump":* Dennis Farrell in Slovenko and Knight, p. 665.

113   *"Why would a parachutist . . .?":* John Delk, *The Parachutist,* May 1971, p. 12; and in Farberow, 405–6.

113   *Jack London:* quoted on a poster of Skidmore College's Adirondack Institute.

113   *Jackie Stewart: Playboy,* June 1972, p. 88.

113–4   *Michael Cooper-Evans:* author, *Risk Life, Risk Limb* (London: Pelham Books, 1968), p. 16.

114–5   *Samuel Z. Klausner:* editor, *Why Man Takes Chances* (New York: Anchor Books, 1968), p. 163. His skydivers are quoted in Klausner's reports for Washington's Bureau of Social Science Research: "Worship and the Dangerous Life: A Study of Church Attendance Among Sport Parachutists," 1965, p. 22; and "The Passion for Skydiving," 1967, pp. 4–5.

115   *Thrill seekers tend not to be gamblers:* Zuckerman, p. 211.

115   *Charles Lindbergh:* Alden Whitman, *New York Times Magazine*, May 8, 1977, p. 14.

118   *James Salter:* author, *Solo Faces* (Boston: Little, Brown, 1979), p. 84.

118   *Samuel Klausner:* with Marisal Reyes-Gavilan and Nancy Stoller, "Self-Induced Anxiety and Its Self-Control: A Prologue to a Study of Sport Parachuting" (Washington: Bureau of Social Science Research, 1963), p. 5.

118   *"You're climbing yourself . . .":* Mihaly Csikszentmihalyi: *Beyond Boredom and Anxiety* (San Francisco: Jossey-Boss, 1975), p. 93.

118   *George Mallory:* Charles Houston in Slovenko and Knight, pp. 631–2.

118   *Rob Taylor:* author, *The Breach: Kilimanjaro and the Conquest of Self* (New York: Coward, McCann & Geoghegan, 1981).

118   *David Roberts:* author, *The Mountain of My Fear* (London: Souvenir Press, 1969). Auden's poem, "Two Climbs," is excerpted on p. 6.

118   *"I've beaten that fear . . .":* Bruce Porter, *New York Times Magazine*, August 15, 1976, p. 46.

119   *"I have mastered fear":* *Newsweek*, June 8, 1981, p. 72.

119   *"Partly it's the feeling . . .":* *Esquire*, May 1976, p. 28.

119   *Edmund Hillary: People Weekly*, June 12, 1978, p. 43.

119   *Otto Fenichel:* author, in "The Counter-Phobic Attitude," *International Journal of Psychoanalysis* 20:263–74, 1939.

119   *Picasso:* Francoise Gilot and Carlton Lake, *Life with Picasso* (New York: McGraw-Hill, 1964); p. 257 of the Penguin edition, 1966. He is quoted about retaining a child's eye in *Time*, July 22, 1974, p. 78.

119   *Klausner on converting fear to enthusiasm:* in Slovenko and Knight, pp. 670–691.

120   *Salter:* author, *Solo Faces* (Boston: Little, Brown, 1979), p. 144.

120   *Karl Pfefferkorn: St. Petersburg Times*, August 2, 1982.

120   *An English rock climber:* Jim Perrin in Wilson, p. 547.

120   *Geoffrey Moorhouse:* author, *The Fearful Void* (Philadelphia: J. B. Lippincott, 1974), p. 15.

121   *a reporter who asked California skydivers:* Lisa Davis, *Chic*, December 1977, p. 42.

121   *a psychiatrist who has studied skydivers:* Dennis Farrell in Slovenko and Knight, pp. 666–7.

121   *skydivers' spouses:* Samuel Klausner, Marisal Reyes-Gavilan, and Nancy Stoller, "Self-Induced Anxiety and Its Self-Control: A Prologue to a Study of Sport Parachuting" (Washington: Bureau of Social Science Research, 1963), p. 15.

121   *Bruce Ogilvie:* author, in *Psychology Today*, October 1974.

122   *Amelia Earhart:* Paul L. Briand, Jr., *Daughter of the Sky* (New York: Duell, Sloan & Pearce, 1960); p. 75 of the Pyramid edition, 1967.

122   *Ogilvie:* author, with Keith Johnsgard and Kenneth Merritt in *Journal of Sports Medicine* 15:158–69, 1975, p. 167.

122   *a study of skydivers' friendships:* John Delk in Farberow, p. 397.

123   *"High standard mountaineers . . .":* Michael Thompson in R. C. Schwing and W. Albers, Jr., editors, *Societal Risk Assessment* (New York: Plenum Press, 1980), p. 282.

124   *James Lester:* author, in *Psychology Today*, September 1969.

124   *Drew Hyland:* at Princeton University, February 24, 1982.

125   *Theodore Blau:* in Farberow, p. 422–3.

126   *Dostoyevsky:* author, *The Gambler*, University of Chicago Press edition, p. 31.

CHAPTER 7: MAINLINING DANGER

128   *Hans Selye:* author, *The Stress of Life* (New York: McGraw-Hill, 1956, rev. 1976), p. 412.

128–34 The story of Michael Tindall is based on transcripts of his trial and to a lesser degree on interviews with Joseph Oteri, Martin Weinberg, and Sheldon Zigelbaum.

134   *Congressman Toby Moffett:* PI, December 22, 1982.

134   *an emergency-room doctor:* Stephen Seager, *Breathe, Little Boy, Breathe!* (Englewood Cliffs, New Jersey: Prentice-Hall, 1981), p. 186.

135   *Graham Greene:* author, *A Sort of Life* (London: The Bodley Head, 1971); pp. 94–5 of the Penguin edition, 1972; and *Ways of Escape* (New York: Simon & Schuster, 1980), pp. 146, 161.

136   *Richard Solomon's World War II experiences: Time*, November 10, 1980, p. 112.

136   *the "opponent-process" theory:* Richard Solomon, *American Psychologist*, 35:691–712, August 1980.

137   *Robert L. Custer:* NYT, September 6, 1983.

137   *"Boredom sickness":* Graham Greene, *A Sort of Life* (London: The Bodley Head, 1971), p. 86.

137–8   *Susan Stern:* author, *With the Weathermen* (New York: Doubleday, 1975), pp. 40–1, 134, 234, 207, 13–14, 45–6, 351–2, 179, 347.

138   *Stern's obituary:* NYT, August 2, 1976.

139   *"the trauma of eventlessness":* Robert Seidenberg, *The Psychoanalytic Review* 59:95–109, Spring 1972.

139   *"addictive personalities":* NYT, January 18 and 25, 1983, and January 27, 1981; *San Diego Evening Tribune,* February 24, 1977; Max Gunther, *Woman's Day,* May 17, 1983, pp. 56–63; Stanton Peele with Archie Brodsky, *Love and Addiction* (New York: Taplinger Publishing Company, 1975).

139   *Frank Richardson:* author, *Napoleon: Bisexual Emperor* (New York: Horizon Press, 1973), p. 52.

139   *Winston Churchill:* The CBS Evening News, March 19, 1980.

139   *Carol Bellamy:* Francis X. Clines, *New York Times Magazine,* February, 25, 1979, p. 20.

139   *Harold Lasswell:* author, *Power and Personality* (New York: Norton, 1948); p. 160 of the Viking Compass edition, 1967.

140   *Richard Nixon:* author, *Six Crises* (New York: Doubleday, 1962); pp. 181–2, 461 of the Pyramid edition, 1968.

140–1   *kibbutz managers:* Dov Eden et al. in Charles D. Spielberger and Irwin G. Sarason, editors, *Stress and Anxiety* (New York: John Wiley & Sons, 1977), p. 266.

141   *Henry Mintzberg:* author, in *Harvard Business Review,* July–August, 1976, p. 55.

141   *Jay Rohrlich:* WSJ, December 18, 1980. *See also* his book *Work and Love* (New York: Summit Books, 1980).

141–2   *Michael Maccoby:* author, *The Gamesman* (New York: Simon & Schuster, 1977).

142   *Lee Iacocca:* Gail Sheehy, *Esquire,* August 15, 1978, p. 80.

142   *controllers' sensation-seeking tendencies:* Zuckerman, p. 259.

142   *a long-term study of male controllers:* NYT, August 9, 1981.

142   *Willie Sutton:* author, with Edward Linn, *Where the Money Was* (New York: Viking Press, 1976), p. 120.

143   *armed robber:* NYT, March 4, 1982.

143   *Samuel Yochelson and Stanton Samenow:* authors, *The Criminal Personality* (New York: Jason Aronson, 1976), p. 433; Michael S. Serrill, *Psychology Today,* February 1978, p. 90.

142–3   *Ray Johnson:* author, with Mona McCormick, *Too Dangerous to Be at Large* (New York: Quadrangle, 1975), p. 65.

144   *Yochelson and Samenow:* authors, *The Criminal Personality* (New York: Jason Aronson, 1976), pp. 428–30.

146   *"When I am straight . . .":* Zuckerman, p. 293.

146   *Zuckerman:* author, p. 304.

146   *a forger:* PI, July 15, 1979.

146   *neurological disorders among delinquents:* NYT, October 11, 1983.

146   *the action addict's nervous system:* Avram Goldstein, *Science,* September 17, 1976, p. 1085.

147   *as addicting as the morphine:* Joel Gurin, *Science 80,* November–December 1979, p. 30; Judith Hooper, *Science Digest,* May 1981, p. 120.

147   *fetuses respond:* Thomas Verny and John Kelly, *The Secret Life of the Unborn Child* (New York: Summit Books, 1981), pp. 44–6, 53–6, 76, 85.

147   *the pathways of immature brains:* Candace Pert, *Omni,* February 1982, p. 110; Jack D. Barchas et al., *Science,* May 26, 1978, pp. 968–9, 971–2.

147   *a known risk factor:* NYT, September 6, 1983.

147   *Lebanese teenagers:* NYT, June 1, 1984.

148   data about Vietnam veterans: expert testimony at Michael Tindall's trial; NYT, March 23, 1981, *Time,* April 6, 1981.

148   *Some . . . have even retreated:* NYT, December 31, 1983.

149   *Caputo:* author, *A Rumor of War* (New York: Holt, Rinehart & Winston, 1977), pp. xvi–xvii.

149   *William Styron:* author, in *New York Review of Books,* June 23, 1977, p. 3.

LEVEL II RISK TAKING

153   *James Michener:* Sarah Crichton, *Redbook,* March 1981, p. 14.

154   *Grace Slick: People Weekly,* April 7, 1980, p. 63.

154   *John Higham:* in John Weiss, editor, *The Origins of Modern Consciousness* (Detroit: Wayne State University Press, 1965), p. 48.

154   *Sensory-deprivation studies:* Watson, pp. 268, 273.

155   Grace Lichtenstein: *Machisma: Women and Daring* (New York: Doubleday, 1981), p. 339.

155   *Three social scientists:* John Roberts, Wayne E. Thompson, and Brian Sutton-Smith, *Human Organization* 25:63, 1966.

156–7   *Dan Gerber: Outside,* January 1981, p. 44.

159   *50 percent of the housing:* Watson, p. 220.

159   *Kai Erikson:* author, *Everything in Its Path* (New York: Simon & Schuster, 1976), p. 196.

160   *As one woman so surveyed: Playboy,* June 1977, p. 59.

161   *One of the most consistent findings:* Zuckerman, pp. 126–7, 135.

161   *As might be expected:* Bernard Segal, *Journal of Consulting and Clinical Psychology* 41:135–8, 1973.

161–2 *Carol Gilligan:* author, *In a Different Voice* (Cambridge: Harvard University Press, 1982), excerpted in *Psychology Today,* June 1982, pp. 71, 73.

162   *Daniel Levinson:* author, with others, *The Seasons of a Man's Life* (New York: Knopf, 1978), p. 335.

162   *A typical exhortation:* NYT, January 26, 1981.

164   *An ongoing study:* Jack Botwinick, *Aging and Behavior* (New York: Springer Publishing Company, 1978), p. 73.

164   *V. S. Pritchett:* author, in *New York Times Magazine,* December 14, 1980, p. 116.

165   *Carl Rogers:* author, "Growing Old: Or Older and Growing?" reprinted in *A Way of Being* (Boston: Houghton Mifflin, 1980), p. 82.

166   *Erica Jong:* author, in *Vogue,* March 1977, p. 160.

CHAPTER 8: THE UNDERLYING RISK

167–8 *"Shooting an Elephant":* George Orwell, in Sonia Orwell and Ian Angus, editors, *An Age Like This: The Collected Essays, Journalism and Letters of George Orwell* (New York: Harcourt, Brace & World, 1968), pp. 240, 242.

169   *a woman once wrote to Ann Landers:* PI, March 9, 1979.

169   *Branch Rickey:* Ray Robinson, *TV Guide,* May 9, 1981, p. 34.

169   *Joe Namath:* NYT, June 28, 1981.

169   *Walter Cunningham:* author, *The All-American Boys* (New York: Macmillan, 1977), p. 301.

169   *[Charles] Darwin:* author, *The Expression of the Emotions in Man and Animals* (Chicago: The University of Chicago Press, 1965), p. 325. Twain's addendum is from *Pudd'nhead Wilson.*

171   *William Manchester:* author, *Goodbye Darkness* (Boston: Little, Brown, 1980), p. 375.

171   *James Jones:* Willie Morris, *James Jones: A Friendship* (Garden City, New York: Doubleday, 1978), p. 233.

172   *In a revealing study:* Thomas T. Jackson and McCauley Gray, *Perceptual and Motor Skills* 43:471–4, 1976.

172   *In another study:* Bert Brown, *Journal of Experimental Social Psychology* 6:255–7, 1970, p. 268.

172   *Andrew Tobias: Esquire,* March 1, 1978, p. 21.

172–3 *one summary of market research:* Donald Cox, *Risk Taking and Information Handling in Consumer Behavior* (Boston:

Graduate School of Business Administration, Harvard University, 1967), p. 10.

173   *R. H. Bruskin: The Bruskin Report,* July 1973; *Current Opinion,* September 1973.

173   *In Connecticut, an employee:* Andrew Tobias, *The Invisible Bankers* (New York: Linden/Simon & Schuster, 1982), p. 45.

173   *Du Pont executive:* Carl B. Kaufman, *Man Incorporated* (Garden City, New York: Doubleday, 1967); p. 123 of the Anchor Books edition, 1969.

173   *Thomas A. Murphy:* WSJ, September 16, 1980; *People Weekly,* November 24, 1980, p. 111.

173   *physicians' heart rates:* Arthur J. Moss and Bruce Wynar, *Annals of Internal Medicine* 72:255–6, 1970.

173   *normal heart rates:* Arthur Fisher, *The Healthy Heart* (Alexandria, Virginia: Time-Life Books, 1981), p. 8.

173   *A similar study:* Peter Taggart et al., *Lancet,* August 18, 1973, pp. 341–6.

174   *one extensive study of the fear of speaking:* Gordon L. Paul, *Insight vs. Desensitization in Psychotherapy* (Stanford, California: Stanford University Press, 1966), pp. 98–9.

174   *John Houseman: People Weekly,* January 17, 1983, p. 61.

174   *David Niven:* author, *The Moon's a Balloon* (New York: Putnam, 1972); pp. 198–200, 295–8, 303–4, and 320–1 of the Dell edition, 1973; and *The National Enquirer,* March 13, 1979.

174–5   *Cornelia Otis Skinner:* author, *The Ape in Me* (Boston: Houghton Mifflin, 1959), pp. 159–61.

175   *Tim Kazurinsky:* Fred Ferreti, *New York Times Magazine,* December 5, 1982, p. 144.

176   *Paul Taylor:* Robert Coe, *New York Times Magazine,* April 5, 1981, p. 43.

179   *Richard Burton says that drinking:* PI, October 3, 1980.

179   *". . . someone is going to find me out":* Barbara Gelb, *New York Times Magazine,* July 6, 1980, p. 27.

179   *Anthony Hopkins . . . "confessional":* NYT, September 9, 1979.

179   *his own drinking problem: US,* November 11, 1980, p. 41.

179   *Michael Crichton:* Barnaby Conrad, *Horizon,* December 1980, p. 33.

180   *Malcolm Cowley: Esquire,* November 1977, p. 226.

180   *W. H. Auden: Time,* February 3, 1975, p. 66.

181   *Norman Mailer's classmates: Paris Review* interview, reprinted in *Writers at Work* (New York: Viking, 1967), p. 255.

181   *"They just can't take . . .":* Scott Parkin, *Esquire,* January 1981, p. 103.

181   *Peter Drucker:* Edwin McDowell, *New York Times Book Review,* May 23, 1982, p. 38.

182   *A sociologist who interviewed:* Hershel Hearn, *The Gerontologist,* Winter 1972.

182   *John A. B. McLeish:* author, *The Ulyssean Adult* (Toronto: McGraw-Hill Ryerson Limited, 1976), p. 247.

182   *Cornelia Otis Skinner:* author, *The Ape in Me* (Boston: Houghton Mifflin, 1959), p. 163.

182   *Frank Langella:* NYT, September 4, 1980.

182–3   *Susan Sarandon:* NYT, January 14, 1983.

183   *Michael Polanyi:* John Zeisel, *Inquiry by Design* (Belmont, California: Brooks-Cole, 1980), p. 54.

CHAPTER 10: ON YOUR OWN

198–9   *Harold Gould:* Carol Lawson, NYT, December 31, 1981.

199   *Mary Ellen Pinkham:* Carol Lawson, *New York Times Book Review,* March 15, 1981, p. 34.

200   *John Naisbitt:* author, *Megatrends* (New York: Warner Books, 1982), p. 35–6.

204   *One student of the breed:* Robert Bendit, in Clifford M. Baumback and Joseph R. Mancuso, editors, *Entrepreneurship and Venture Management* (Englewood Cliffs, New Jersey: Prentice-Hall, 1975), p. 296.

206   *In 1980, 8.5 percent:* Michael Maccoby, *The Leader* (New York: Simon & Schuster, 1981), p. 34.

207   *Orvis Collins and David Moore:* authors, *The Organization Makers* (New York: Appleton-Century-Crofts, 1970), pp. 139, 112, 38.

208   *Doug Kreeger:* Lucien Rhodes, *Inc.,* December 1980, p. 34; NYT, March 13, 1979.

208   *"I could never stand . . .":* Collins and Moore, *The Organization Makers,* p. 89.

208   *"Possessions are the really . . .":* John Stickney, *Self-Made* (New York: Putnam, 1980), p. 34.

208   *one investor of "venture capital":* Burton W. Teague, *Inc.,* June 1980, p. 74.

209   *Richard Cornuelle:* author, in *Psychology Today,* November 1975, p. 88.

209   *a survey of 109 men:* Robert H. Brockhaus, Sr., *Journal of Small Business Management,* January 1980, p. 40.

209 *David McClelland:* author, *The Achieving Society,* (New York: D. Van Nostrand, 1961), pp. 233–7; *Psychology Today,* January 1971, p. 70.

209 *Ted Turner:* "Money," *Time,* August 9, 1982, p. 57.

209 *"a sense of adventure":* NYT, January 20, 1984.

209 *must have been hyperactive: Time,* August 9, 1982, p. 54.

210 *getting into the black:* NYT, August 14, 1983.

210 *an outlandish risk taker: Time,* August 9, 1982, pp. 50–7.

210 *fearless: Time,* June 9, 1980, p. 68.

210 *Julia Klein:* author, in *Philadelphia Inquirer's Today* magazine, January 3, 1982, p. 20, where his poker playing style is also discussed.

210 *Turner's nicknames: People Weekly,* September 12, 1977, p. 32.

210 *"great to win": Time,* August 9, 1982, p. 57.

210–1 *Albert Shapero:* author, in *Psychology Today,* November 1975, pp. 85–6.

211 *David McClelland:* author, *The Achieving Society* (New York: D. Van Nostrand, 1961), pp. 222–3.

211–2 *"The successful entrepreneur . . .":* Michael Palmer, *California Management Review* 13:32–38, 1971, p. 38.

213 *Steve Poses:* Carol Saline, *Philadelphia,* February 1978; PI, January 12, 1979.

213 *Nolan Bushnell:* author in *Playboy,* June 1977, p. 112.

CHAPTER 11: ULTIMATE RISK

216–7 *Leo Buscaglia:* author, *Living, Loving and Learning* (Thorofare, New Jersey: Charles B. Slack, 1982), pp. 199, 209, 261, 52, 187, 224, 152, 52, 262.

217 *of his lifelong bachelor status: People Weekly,* July 5, 1982, p. 88.

217 *intimacy does not mean exclusivity:* Peter Barry Chowka (who pointed out that Buscaglia won't reveal his age), *East West Journal,* May 1983, p. 37.

218 *Wayne Dyer:* Campbell Geeslin, *Life,* April 1983, p. 27.

219 *Bernie Zilbergeld:* the second paragraph appeared in *Psychology Today,* November 1983, p. 18; the rest was in a fuller essay on Buscaglia from which the published version was abridged.

220 *"Taking a Chance on Change":* Suzanne McNear, *Cosmopolitan,* August 1979, pp. 219, 220, 221.

220–1 *"How Taking Risks Can Enrich a Marriage":* Marcia Lasswell and Norman Lobsenz, *McCall's,* January 1980, pp. 72–3.

221 *"change-seeker" index:* Larry T. Brown et al., *Journal of Consulting and Clinical Psychology* 42:311, 1974.

221 *Grace Lichtenstein:* author, *Machisma: Women and Daring* (New York: Doubleday, 1981), pp. 294, 292.

222 *Elaine Walster and William Walster:* authors, *A New Look at Love* (Reading, Massachusetts: Addison-Wesley), 1978, p. 104.

223–4 *Sam Keen:* author, *What to Do When You're Bored and Blue* (New York: Wyden Books, 1980), pp. 187, 198.

224 *Rollo May:* author, *The Courage to Create* (New York: Norton, 1975); pp. 9–10 of the Bantam edition, 1976.

225 *In a manual for women:* Lynette Triere with Richard Peacock, *Learning to Leave* (Chicago: Contemporary Books, 1982); pp. 21, 39, 105–6 of the Warner Books edition, 1983.

226 *A marriage counselor says:* Roberta Temes, *Psychology Today*, May 1981, p. 17.

226–7 *Anatole Broyard:* author, in NYT, January 8, 1981.

228 *A Christian Youth Leaders' seminar:* offered by EMERGE Ministries in Akron, Ohio, July 27, 1981.

228 *"Lovers or Strangers":* *Creative Computing*, November 1982, p. 205; PI, December 25, 1983.

228 *One user of such visual prescreening:* Mary Alice Kellogg, *TV Guide*, June 26, 1982, p. 33.

228 *With such a sense of peril:* Harry Stein, *Esquire*, April 1981, p. 16.

229 *Arthur Egendorf: People Weekly*, May 4, 1981, p. 98.

229 *As a thirty-seven-year-old nonmother:* Nancy Eberle, *Glamour*, April 1979, p. 239.

229 *The first child: People Weekly*, March 8, 1982, p. 110.

229 *They also talk:* Dan Gerber, *Outside*, January 1981, p. 44.

229–30 *Antoine de Saint-Exupéry:* author, *Wind, Sand and Stars* (New York: Harcourt, Brace & World, 1940); p. 207 of Time Reading Program Special Edition.

230 *a more or less tongue-in-cheek portrayal:* Tom Patey in Wilson, p. 268.

231 *Richard Schickel:* author, *Singled Out*, (New York: Viking Press, 1981), p. 15.

231 *Robert Towne:* in John Brady, *The Craft of the Screenwriter* (New York: Simon & Schuster, 1981), pp. 368–9.

232 *Mario Andretti:* NYT, May 21, 1984.

232 *Congressman Jack Kemp:* Frank Gifford, ABC-TV, August 21, 1981.

232 *Senator Howard Baker:* NYT, September 9, 1982.

232–3 *A thirty-four-year-old policewoman:* NYT, February 21, 1983.

CHAPTER 13: THE AMERICAN WAY OF RISK

251   *The editor: Quest,* January/February 1978, p. 3.

251   *The publisher:* subscription offer received February 1978.

251   *Newsweek:* August 18, 1975.

251   *NYT:* May 29, 1977.

251   *U.S. News & World Report:* August 10, 1981.

252   *Altman's:* NYT, September 7, 1980.

252   *Wolverine:* PI, August 30, 1981.

253   *Levi's:* KYW radio (Philadelphia), December 4, 1982.

253   *Saab: Time,* November 1, 1982, p. 13.

253   *Volvo:* WIP radio (Philadelphia), November 5, 1982.

254   *"You learn to take . . .":* Rosabeth Moss Kanter, *Men and Women of the Corporation* (New York: Basic Books, 1977), p. 180.

254   *With 5 percent:* Tobias, *The Invisible Bankers,* pp. 21–2.

255   *Robert Coles:* author, *Walker Percy* (Boston: Little, Brown, 1978), p. 34.

255   *Rosiland Forbes:* author, *Corporate Stress* (Garden City, New York: Doubleday/Dolphin), 1979, p. 129.

256   *the National Survival Game:* PI, May 29, 1983 (in which the participant is quoted); NYT, August 15, 1982, and February 8, 1984; *Time,* July 19, 1982; and *Life,* May 1983. The ad ran in Philadelphia's *Welcomat,* August 3, 1983.

256   *Joseph Sax:* author, *Mountains Without Handrails* (Ann Arbor: The University of Michigan Press, 1980), pp. 99–101.

257   *Wagons Ho:* response dated December 6, 1980.

257   *the American Mountain Men rendezvous: Newsweek,* July 20, 1981, p. 61.

257   *wagon trains:* John D. Unruh, Jr., *The Plains Across* (Urbana, Illinois: The University of Illinois Press, 1979), pp. 408–13.

257   *One random sample:* Ray Allen Billington, *America's Frontier Heritage* (New York: Holt, Rinehart and Winston, 1966), p. 32.

257–8   *W. Eugene Hollon:* author, *Frontier Violence: Another Look* (New York: Oxford University Press, 1974), pp. 196, 211.

258   *On late nineteenth-century American culture as reflected in its literature:* David Brion Davis in Samuel Z. Klausner, editor, *Why Man Takes Chances* (New York: Anchor Books, 1968).

258   *Fanciful reenactments:* Roger Allan Hall, *The James Madison Journal* 38:105–6, 1980; Heywood Hale Broun, "The Nineties," *American Heritage,* 1967, pp. 97–105.

258   *bicycling:* Richard F. Snow, *American Heritage*, June 1975, pp. 61–72; J. C. Furnas, *The Americans* (New York: Putnam, 1969), pp. 809–12; Higham, in *The Origins of Modern Consciousness*, p. 28.

258   *"Oh, to be . . .":* T. J. Jackson Lears, *No Place of Grace* (New York: Pantheon, 1981), p. 125.

259   *economic upheaval accompanied:* Charles Hoffman, *The Depression of the Nineties* (Westport, Connecticut: Greenwood Publishing Corporation, 1970).

259   *"boredom" entered:* Sam Keen, *What to Do When You're Bored and Blue* (New York: Wyden Books, 1980), p. 28.

259   *So did "thrill":* Balint, *Thrills and Regressions* (New York: International Universities Press, 1959), p. 43.

259   *"Neurasthenia":* Lears, *No Place of Grace*, p. 50.

259   *early amusement rides:* Gary Kyriazi, *The Great American Amusement Parks* (Secaucus, New Jersey: Citadel Press, 1976).

259–60 *Daniel Beard:* Noel Perrin, *Americana*, August 1983.

260   *teenagers in the city:* Joseph Kett, *Rites of Passage* (New York: Basic Books, 1977), pp. 91–2.

260   *Tales about medieval knights:* Lears, *No Place of Grace*, p. 109.

260–1 *Kett:* author *Rites of Passage*, pp. 174, 139–40, 226.

261   *Lady Allen of Hurtwood:* NYT, May 16, 1965.

263   *"U.S. Adventure Playground Report":* Bill Vance.

265   *carnival's rides are safer:* Tobias, op. cit., p. 187.

265   *a landmark decision: Murphy* v. *Steeplechase Amusement Co., Inc.,* 250 N.Y. 479, 166 N.E. 173, Court of Appeals of New York, April 16, 1929, p. 483.

267   *"Sweaty palms . . .":* *Advertising Age*, July 12, 1982, p. 10.

267   *"You're liable . . .":* *Creative Computing*, March 1981, p. 73.

267   *Sherry Turkle:* Aaron Latham, *New York Times Magazine*, October 25, 1981, p. 108.

267   *"The armchair adventures . . .":* Bob Liddil, *BYTE*, December 1980, p. 158.

267–8 *"To be adventurous . . .":* *CompuKids*, 1982, p. 4.

268   *computer game designer:* Walter Lowe, Jr., *Playboy*, March 1982, p. 230.

269   *Robin Campbell:* author, in Wilson, p. 288.

269   *Tom Price:* author, in Wilson, p. 648.

270   *Chattooga River:* Tom Passavant, *Playboy*, April 1976, p. 34.

270–1 *After interviewing . . .":* Richard M. Schreyer et al., *Journal of Physical Education and Recreation*, April 1978.

271 *as a woman's magazine: Cosmopolitan,* May 1979, p. 244.

271 *According to a manual:* Bart Jackson, *White Water* (New York: Walker Publishing Company, 1979), p. 122.

271 *"really like a $125 . . .":* NYT, September 5, 1983.

271 *And for his part:* Colin Kirkus in Wilson, p. 672.

272 *James Finckenauer:* NYT, March 5, 1982; *Psychology Today,* August 1979, p. 10.

272 *John Hinckley:* NYT, June 12, 1982.

272 *Patty Hearst [Campbell]:* author, *Every Secret Thing* (New York: Doubleday, 1982), pp. 222–3.

272 *Susan Stern:* author, *With the Weathermen* (New York: Doubleday, 1975), p. 251.

CHAPTER 14: GENUINE RISK

273 *One British psychologist:* P. E. Vernon, *Journal of Abnormal and Social Psychology* 36:457–76, 1941. His findings and others confirming them are discussed by Watson, pp. 218–220, and Stanley J. Rachman, *Fear and Courage* (San Francisco: W. H. Freeman, 1978), pp. 27–42.

273 *Verta Taylor,* author, in *Psychology Today,* October 1977, p. 126.

275 *Luciano Pavarotti:* A. M. Sackler, *Medical News,* March 5, 1979; *Playboy,* November 1982, p. 78.

275 *Seymour Bernstein:* NYT, January 25, 1982.

276 *José Torres: Village Voice,* May 6–12, 1981, p. 22.

276 *Ski instructors:* Junior Bounous, *Ski,* Spring 1977, p. 58.

277 *Sol Roy Rosenthal:* author, in *Sport and Recreation* 12:17–20, 1971. *See also* William Barry Furlong, *Sports Illustrated,* January 27, 1969; *Outside,* December 1980–January 1981.

277 *a "late-onset phobia":* Albert G. Forgione and Frederic M. Bauer, *Fearless Flying* (Boston: Houghton Mifflin, 1980), p. 6.

277 *Even ex-stewardesses: People Weekly,* May 1, 1978, p. 37.

277 *Peter Bourne:* author, *Men, Stress, and Vietnam* (Boston: Little, Brown, 1970), p. 72.

278 *Gay Gaer Luce:* author, *Body Time* (New York: Pantheon, 1971); p. 209 of the Bantam edition, 1973.

278 *Claude Monet:* Kenneth Clark, *Moments of Vision* (New York: Harper & Row, 1982), cited by Anatole Broyard, NYT, April 14, 1982.

279 *400 Lockheed employees: USA Today,* November 30, 1983.

279 *In a rare, practical recognition:* Bill Backer, NYT advertisement, October 5, 1983.

279–80 *Robert Seidenberg:* author, in *Psychoanalytic Review* 59: 95–109, pp. 107–108.

280 *ex-prostitute:* Harry Benjamin and R. E. L. Masters, *Prostitution and Morality* (New York: The Julian Press, 1964), p. 111.

280 *call girl:* "Hooker," Home Box Office, June 3, 1983.

280 *Early surveys of such programs:* Francis J. Kelly and Daniel J. Bear, *Crime and Delinquency*, October 1971; Clark L. Thorstenson and Richard A. Heaps, *Therapeutic Recreation Journal*, First Quarter, 1973.

280 *But further research:* Joshua L. Miner and Joe Boldt, *Outward Bound USA* (New York: William Morrow, 1981), p. 265.

281 *John Berryman:* suggestion made to James Dickey, who retold it in his *Paris Review* interview, Spring 1976, p. 79.

281 *Murray Melbin:* author, in *American Sociological Review* 43:19, 1978.

282 *regular blood donors:* Jane Allyn Piliavin et al., *Journal of Personality and Social Psychology* 43:1200–13, 1982.

282 *Going further, one psychiatrist:* Paul H. Blachly, *Life-Threatening Behavior* 1:5–9, Spring 1971.

284 *A father and his son shared:* Andrew H. Malcolm, NYT, September 13, 1981.

284 *One couple went so far:* Red Smith, NYT, March 15, 1981.

285 *Bruce Ogilvie:* author, in *Journal of the American Medical Association* 205:156–62, 1968, p. 783.

285 *After being stolen blind:* Ruth Morris, *Friend's Journal*, March 1, 1981, p. 3.

285–6 *Woody Allen: People Weekly*, June 4, 1979, p. 128.

286–7 *Charles Garfield:* WSJ, January 13, 1982; Morton Hunt, *Reader's Digest*, September 1982; Richard Trubo, *Success*, April 1983, p. 33.

287 *The graduate of one month-long:* Jacqueline Thompson, *Express*, May 1982, p. 63.

287 *Jessica Walters:* Ellen Torgerson Shaw, *TV Guide*, March 21, 1981, p. 38.

288 *A Seattle teacher: Newsweek*, May 4, 1981, p. 72.